TREASURES *of the*

CZARS

from the STATE MUSEUMS *of the* MOSCOW KREMLIN

TREASURES *of the*

CZARS

from the STATE MUSEUMS *of the* MOSCOW KREMLIN

❖

Presented by

Kansas International Museum

Topeka, Kansas

❖

This catalogue is provided through the generous support of

Columbian National Bank and Trust, 701 South Kansas Avenue, Topeka, Kansas

BOOTH-CLIBBORN EDITIONS

LONDON

Design: Trickett & Webb Limited, London
Designers: Ian Butterworth, Brian Webb and
Joan Matthews
Managing Editor: Mark Sutcliffe
Editor: Ralph Hancock
Translators: Frank Althaus and Lucy Bailey,
Russian Language in London
Photographers:
L.N. Burmistrov, A.V. Sverdlov, V.N. Seregin
Front cover: Orb, Istanbul, 1662, Gold, Pecious
Stones, Enamel
Back cover: Eagle Pendant, Moscow, Kremlin
workshops, second half of 17th century, Gold, Precious
Stones, Enamel

Published in 1995 by Booth-Clibborn Editions,
12 Percy Street, London W1P 9FB

ISBN 1873968 868

Printed and bound in Hong Kong

CONTENTS

C O N T R I B U T O R S

*Scientific editors: A.V. Boldov,
kandidat of historical studies,
N.S. Vladimirskaya, kandidat of
historical studies*

*Introduction and Romanov
Dynasty: A.K. Levykin, kandidat
of historical studies*

*Articles: I.A. Bobrovnitskaya,
kandidat of art history; I.I.
Vishnevskaya, kandidat of art history; M.V. Martynova, O.B.
Melnikova, kandidat of historical
studies; T.N. Muntian, V.M.
Nikitina*

*Caption descriptions: S.A.
Amelekhina, I.A. Bobrovnitskaya,
I.I. Vishnevskaya, M.P.
Golovanova, I.V. Gorbatova, I.A.
Zagorodniaya, Z.A. Kodrikova,
I.A. Komarov, I.D. Kostina, A.K.
Levykin, M.V. Martynova, N.D.
Markina, O.B. Melnikova,
O.I.Mironova, E.A. Morshakova,
T.N. Muntian, V.M. Nikitina, A.I.
Romanenko, N.N. Smirnova, V.G.
Chubinskaya, E.V. Shakurova,
E.A. Iablonskaya*

*Biographies of historical figures
compiled by A.K. Levykin*

*Restorers, State Museums of the
Moscow Kremlin: A.I. Iakovleva,
N.P. Sinitsina, M.N. Kruzhalin,
V.A. Vynuzhanin, V.M. Roslavskii,
Iu. A. Osipov, S.E. Gorbunov, T.N.
Kashliakova
Restorer, I. E. Grabar Institute of
Restoration: T.B. Rogozina
Restorers, share company
"Kupina": led by A.A.Koszmina
and A.V. Neretina
Restorers, Special Scientific
Restoration Centre: V.V.
Romanova, N.I. Chernushevich,
V.I. Alisov, M.A. Vasilieva, V.P.
Smirnov, P.G. Iudakov*

FOREWORD

There is nothing which draws nations together so much as a mutual knowledge of their history and culture. It is therefore difficult to overestimate the role played in today's world by an international exchange of such academic and cultural significance as this exhibition. *Treasures of the Czars from the State Museums of the Moscow Kremlin*, presented by Kansas International Museum, Topeka, is an unexpected, but natural event in the life of our two nations - Russia and the United States - above all in this, the year of the 50th anniversary of the defeat of fascism in the Second World War.

It is the first time that an exhibition of this scale has left the walls of the ancient Moscow Kremlin. Many of the 250 or so exhibits have never before been on show. But the significance of the exhibition is not confined to statistics. Of fundamental importance is its central aim - to show, by means of treasures taken from the richest collections of the historic museum, the Moscow Kremlin, the life of the Russian court. Everything that the American visitor sees here - the royal regalia, the priceless equipment, court and ecclesiastical vest-

ments, icons, ceremonial equipage, arms and orders - all this was acquired and made over the more than 300 years of the rule of the House of Romanov. These objects surrounded the Russian czars from the moment of their birth until their death. They served as symbols of state power, used for solemn ceremonies as well as for everyday purposes. Each exhibit is not simply a magnificent work of Russian, or world, art; behind it lie real names and events in Russian history. The exhibition visitor can witness the wonderfully beautiful ceremony of the consecration of the czar, be present at royal weddings and court balls, and take part in the reception of foreign ambassadors.

Ten years ago such an exhibition would have been out of the question. It has only been possible as a result of the changes that occurred in Russia at the end of the eighties and the beginning of the nineties. Before then the Moscow Kremlin was perceived as the political citadel of communism; its thousand-year history was all but forgotten. The idea for this exhibition arose from the great wave of public interest in Russia's history in general, and in the Romanov dynasty - the rulers of Russia for 300 years -

in particular. It can be seen as a symbol of a new approach to the study of Russian history and culture.

The State Historical and Cultural Museum "The Moscow Kremlin" is one of the most ancient museums in the country. It is truly the heart of Russia. Its architectural masterpieces of the fifteenth to nineteenth centuries, and its collections of artistic treasures of the tenth to twentieth centuries can be seen as a precious jewel or a standard of aesthetic ideal, spanning the centuries and preserved even today. It is natural, therefore, that Moscow's Kremlin and Red Square should be designated a World Heritage Site by UNESCO.

This new exhibition, which we believe will enjoy great success, presents the American visitor with a rare fusion of history and art, beauty and craftsmanship, work and inspiration, and it will surely further enhance the ever-increasing bonds of friendship uniting the Russian and American peoples.

I.A. Rodimzeva
Director
The State Museums of the Moscow Kremlin

STATE OF KANSAS

BILL GRAVES, *Governor*
State Capitol, 2nd Floor
Topeka, Kansas 66612-1590

(913) 296-3232
1-800-432-2487
TDD: 1-800-992-0152
FAX: (913) 296-7973

OFFICE OF THE GOVERNOR

Dear Friends:

On behalf of the people of Kansas, I cordially invite you to share in the grandeur of an era long since passed. A time when the trappings of power and influence for one of the world's richest and most powerful ruling families, the Romanovs, were exceeded only by the most opulent artistic creations.

Magnificent art treasures sprang from the imaginations of artisans and craftsmen to celebrate Russia's rich heritage and to honor their participation in the Russian Orthodox Church. These treasures form the breathtaking collection that awaits you.

This collection is also an opportunity to celebrate the cultural heritage of many Kansans, descendants of 19th century Russian immigrants. As you marvel at the beauty of this collection of magnificent art treasures, remember the hardships and sacrifices of Russian peasants, which made it possible.

We are honored that Kansas' capital city is host to this remarkable exhibit.

Sincerely,

BILL GRAVES
Governor

Mayor Felker welcomes you to the Golden City

n behalf of the citizens of Topeka, welcome to our community and to the magnificent *Treasures of the Czars* exhibit. Topeka was called the Golden City by early visitors who marveled at the beauty of its rolling hills and autumn elms. Now, as host to some of the world's most beautiful works of art, Topeka is literally living up to its early reputation.

Treasures of the Czars is a landmark cultural event for our community and for the entire Midwest. Thanks to the support of our citizens and business leaders, we were able to bring this once-in-a-lifetime exhibit to the Heartland. It shows the value our people place on great art and craftsmanship— the inspired expressions of the human spirit. We feel that the *Treasures of the Czars* will help us attract many more major cultural exhibits to Topeka.

Whether you have come from near or far, I hope you enjoy your visit to the Golden City and the *Treasures of the Czars.*

Yours truly,

Butch Felker
Mayor of Topeka

PREFACE

The innocent face of nine-year old Dimitri staring from his golden casket lid sets the tone for this magnificent Treasures of the Czars Exhibition, for it portrays the sense of mystery, the opulence of the era and the craftsmanship of the Russian artisans.

The historical, educational and cultural significance of the Treasures of the Czars Exhibition allows our two countries a marvelous opportunity to forge a bond with our people. Through this Exhibition, the children of both countries will perhaps find a bridge to a better understanding of the two cultures and in the process realize a better appreciation of one another's heritage.

Our deep appreciation to Madame Irina Rodimzeva, the Director of the State Museums of the Moscow Kremlin, for allowing the Kansas International Museum to be one of two venues for the Treasures of the Czars Exhibition. Our appreciation is also extended to Madame Elizabeth Shakurova, the Curator of the Exhibition, and to the staff of the Kremlin Museums, for their many months of dedicated work devoted to making this wonderful collection come together in this outstanding Exhibition.

The Board of Directors of the Kansas International Museum also wants to acknowledge His Excellency, Evgeny Sidorov, Russian Minister of Culture, and His Excellency Yuly Vorontsov, Russian Ambassador to the United States, for their invaluable assistance in making this Exhibition possible. A special thanks to Edward R. Malayan, Senior Counselor, Embassy of the Russian Federation; Gregory Guroff and Vladimir Litvinov for all of their efforts over the past few months.

To Governor Bill Graves, Secretary of Commerce Gary Sherrer; Mayor Butch Felker and the City of Topeka; Shawnee County, and the Topeka Convention and Visitors Bureau, thank you on behalf of the Kansas International Museum Board of Directors, for these efforts have truly made the Treasures of the Czars Exhibition a reality in Topeka, Kansas.

Our many sponsors have shown this country what Kansas and the Heartland of America is all about with their generous contributions of money, time and expertise. They are honored in the lobby of the exhibition; to each, our heartfelt thanks.

The dedication and expertise of the professional staff and all of the many, many wonderful volunteers has been a delight to witness and we thank each and every one of you from the bottom of our hearts.

A final thank you to Vera Espinola, technical director of the Exhibition; Randy Austin, for his assistance with the catalogue; and as enormous thanks to John Glassman, CEO for the Treasures of the Czars Exhibition and to everyone of the Kansas International Museum Board of Directors – thanks! It would not have happened without you!

Betty J. Simecka, President
Kansas International Museum
Board of Directors

THE KANSAS INTERNATIONAL MUSEUM
BOARD OF DIRECTORS

Betty J. Simecka, President
John Glassman, Vice-President/Chief Executive Officer

Ken Alexander, Secretary
Gary Fleenor, Treasurer
Senator Paul Feleciano
Mayor Harry "Butch" Felker
John Petersen
Ruth Stauffer

Ex Officio
Jim Kelley

General Counsel
Goodell, Stratton, Edwards & Palmer, L.L.P.

INTRODUCTION

❖

The Armory is Russia's oldest museum. It is one of the State Museums of the Moscow Kremlin, and contains one of the most significant collections of decorative art in the world, including some of the rarest works of Russian and foreign craftsmen of the fourth to the twentieth century, all closely connected with the history of Russia. The Kremlin itself was the home of the Great Muscovy Princes and of the Russian Czars. This unique architectural ensemble consists of fortifications designed by Italian and Russian architects at the beginning of the sixteenth century, royal palaces and chambers, cathedrals and monasteries, departments of state and government, treasuries and artistic workshops.

Over the course of several centuries the architectural complex known as the Treasury of the Great Princes and the Czars came to include many different buildings: the Treasury House (Kazennyi Dvor), the Arsenal (known today as the Armory), the Stables Office (Koniushennaya Kazna), the Bedchamber and others. The earliest references to these buildings date from the time of the first Muscovy Princes. Thereafter, year by year, the scope of the Treasury broadened and the number of its buildings multiplied. Many works of art became part of the Treasury collections: the works of the finest Russian craftsmen, made in the Kremlin workshops; valuable ambassadorial gifts from other lands; and the

The Armory's Hall of W. European Silver

property of Russian nobles acquired after their deaths. Writers of the time described the treasuries of the Kremlin with undisguised admiration and wonder. Priceless church plate, jeweled decorations, tableware, opulent clothing, weapons, parade horse-trappings – all formed the material foundation of the power of the state. They were part of daily life at the royal court, used as the regalia of state in solemn ceremonies.

At the same time the Russian royal court began to establish its ceremonial tradition. It was at this time that a centralized Russian State replaced the Great Muscovy Principality and the disparate lands of Rus´. The court of the Great Princes was replaced by that of the Czar, more numerous and more splendid. New structures of state and court government were established; the Treasury increased its wealth, and many of its possessions became part of the state regalia; new ceremonies were adopted, combining the traditional ritual of Old Rus´ with new elements from East and West. Foreigners were amazed at the pomp and the refinement of court etiquette. These changes culminated with the accession in the seventeenth century of the new dynasty of the Romanovs.

The splintered state which was so much part of the feudal period under the Muscovy Princes meant that government at

The Armory of the Moscow Kremlin

court was patriarchal and militaristic. With the accession of the Romanovs, this gave way to a new system, where every action of the sovereign was viewed as essential to the welfare of the nation, perpetually underlining the difference between the position of the "Sovereign of All Rus'" and that of his subjects.

Every aspect of the life of the Moscow Czars was subject to the court ceremonial. It was worked out in great detail, and remained largely unchanged until the reforms of Peter the Great at the beginning of the eighteenth century. The reforms of Peter the Great created a new and mighty Russian Empire. The whole court was changed: its manners, customs, ceremonies. It became more European in its clothes and fashions, and in its artistic taste. Most important of all, the court moved to a new capital.

In 1711 St. Petersburg was declared the new capital of Russia, and thus the new residence of the Russian Emperors. Court and state structures were moved to St. Petersburg, along with the finest court artists, jewelers, sword and gunsmiths, engravers and carvers. At the same time the life of the Moscow Kremlin entered a new phase. Moscow, having lost its status as capital, became a kind of guardian of the Russian national identity, of the traditions and customs of the nation. Here the treasury and regalia of the state remained, and the center of Russian Orthodoxy was retained in the Kremlin. Here it was, in the Dormition Cathedral, that most ancient of sacred places, that the ceremony of the consecration took place. Here, too, the descendants of the first Romanovs established the first museum of Russian history and culture: the Imperial Museum of Antiquities, or the Armory, which was based on the ancient treasure houses of the Moscow Kremlin.

The *Treasures of the Czars* exhibition is thus given a unique character by the nature of the museum itself. Its aim is twofold: first, to present to a foreign audience masterpieces of jewelry, decorative art and arms from Russia, the Orient and Western Europe – fields in which the collection is unique in variety and artistic merit. Secondly, the exhibition aims to illustrate the life of the Russian court, its traditions and ceremonials, stretching over three centuries, from 1613 to 1913. The background to the exhibition is the history of the Romanov dynasty. The rule of the Romanovs saw the culmination of Russian traditional culture in the seventeenth century, then, following the reforms of Peter the Great, the adoption in Russia of European values. This whole process is reflected in the relics which are preserved in the Armory and which make up this exhibition. Many of the exhibits on display here are rightly considered masterpieces of world art. Some of them have never been displayed before, not even in Russia.

A.K. Levykin

THE ROMANOV DYNASTY

✣

The royal dynasty of the Romanovs ruled Russia from the seventeenth to the twentieth century. Its founder was Andrei Kobyl, a landowner who served at the court of the Muscovy Princes in the mid-fourteenth century. His descendants included not only the Romanovs, but many of the most eminent Russian noble families. The direct line to the Romanovs was through Feodor Koshkin, Kobyl's youngest son, who had four sons, Ivan, Feodor Goltiaia, Alexander Bezzubets, and the childless Mikhail Durnyi. Ivan Feodorovich, the eldest, had four sons of his own, but the line continued only through the last son, Zakharii, although his brothers helped to strengthen the position of the Koshkin family at court through marriages into the families of princes and boyars (nobles). Zakharii had three sons, Iakov, Iurii, and Vasilii Liatskii. Iurii was in charge of several *volosti* (rural districts), and in 1479 was awarded the title of "First of the Boyars' Sons." From 1487 to 1489 he acted as vicegerent in the political centre of Rus′ Novgorod, and played a leading role in affairs of state. His children were to become leading members of the royal Duma (council). The Romanovs were direct descendants of Iurii's second son, Roman Iur′evich. Roman's elder brother, Mikhail Iur′evich

Zakharin, was a boyar, and held the second most important post in the Duma of the Great Prince Vasilii III; he therefore had strong connections with several noble princes. As one of Great Prince Vasilii's closest friends, Mikhail Iur′evich was in attendance at his deathbed. It seems likely that Mikhail's closeness to the Prince led to the choice of his niece Anastasia Romanova, the daughter of Roman, as bride for Vasilii's son Ivan IV (the Terrible).

The Romanovs therefore came from an ancient and noble line; yet this did not make them heirs to the Russian throne, since they were originally boyars and servants to the sovereign. At the turn of the seventeenth century, however, events took place which radically affected the history of the Russian state.

In 1584 Ivan the Terrible died. He had three sons from his first marriage (he was married seven times). Dmitrii, the eldest, died young, and the second son, Ivan, was pronounced heir to the throne. But he was mortally wounded in a quarrel with his father, whose death was also hastened by the fight. As a result, Feodor Ivanovich, Ivan the Terrible's youngest son from his first marriage, was crowned Czar.

Feodor's reign was short: he died on January 7 1598. His death also marked the

end of the ruling Riurik dynasty, who were descended from the first Muscovy Prince, the youngest son of Alexander Nevsky Daniil. The country was now faced with the problem of electing a new Czar.

From the second half of the sixteenth century, there were several families who had genuine claims to the Russian throne. Although the Moscow branch of the Riurik dynasty was now extinct, the southern and northern descendants of Prince Riurik (the Suzdal and Chernigov branches of the family) survived; but they had lost all influence through unsuccessful struggles with the Muscovy Princes. At the beginning of the seventeenth century the most important descendants of this family were the Shuiskii Princes.

The second group of pretenders to the Russian throne were the descendants of the Lithuanian Great Prince Gedemin, the so-called "Gedeminovichi," who had come to Moscow in the service of the sovereign. Of these, the Mstislavskii and Golitsyn families enjoyed high esteem, the most influential member being Ivan Feodorovich Mstislavskii.

In addition to the descendants of Riurik and the Gedeminovichi, there were two families of Muscovy boyars who could also lay claim to the throne: the Godunovs and the

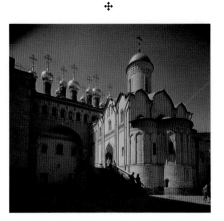

Church of the Placement of the Vestments of the Virgin

Romanovs. These families had greatly increased their influence at court during the reign of Ivan the Terrible, in the wake of the *oprochnina* (when the Czar assigned large areas of the country as his personal property, effectively destroying many noble families). Both the Godunovs and the Romanovs were popular in the country, and both were directly linked to the late Czar through the female line. Ivan's first wife had been Anastasia Romanova, the daughter of Roman Iur´evich Zakharin. At the age of sixteen Ivan, who had come to the throne when only three, expressed the desire to be consecrated as Czar, in other words to assume the title of Czar. The consecration took place on January 16 1547, shortly followed by the royal marriage on February 3rd Opponents of Ivan the Terrible looked upon Anastasia and her family as enemies of Russia and compared her to Eudoxia, wife of the Byzantine emperor Arcadius, who had persecuted St John Chrysostom. Others, however, thought that she had a beneficial effect on the Czar. They believed she directly influenced the early successes of his reign, and that her death led to the most savage of his repressions.

The influence of the Romanovs was thus increased by the fact that it was their sister Anastasia who had borne Ivan his three eldest sons. They were therefore the closest relatives of the Czareviches. Even while Ivan the Terrible was alive, the Romanovs were amassing state power. After Ivan's second marriage, when he alienated his sons, the Romanovs controlled the Duma.

During the reigns of Ivan and Feodor the Romanovs became powerful landowners. Most influential among them was Nikita Romanovich Iur´ev-Zakharin, the "favorite brother-in-law" of Ivan the Terrible. He was appointed guardian to Feodor and held the most important position in his court. Nikita is often referred to in Russian legend as intercessor between the Czarevich Feodor and his brutal father.

When Nikita Romanovich died Boris Godunov became the most most influential figure in the state. He had been one of Ivan the Terrible's most loyal allies, and occupied the high rank at court of Cavalier. His sister Irina was Feodor's wife. Godunov's influence at court was enormous. He was commander-in-chief of the armed forces, he received diplomatic missions and conducted negotiations, and was in charge of both internal and foreign policy: in effect, he was ruler of the country.

When Feodor died and the Riurik dynasty came to an end, a bitter power struggle ensued between the Romanovs and the Godunovs, in which Boris was the victor. In an account of Feodor's death, written by a foreigner, Bussov, "The Czarina Irina tried to persuade her dying husband to present the sceptre to her brother, Boris Godunov, but the Czar offered the crown to the elder of his two cousins, Feodor Nikitich Romanov [the nephew of the Czarina Anastasia, and son of Nikita Romanovich]. Feodor in his turn passed the crown on to his brother Alexander, who gave it to Ivan. Ivan passed it on to Mikhail, who presented it to one of the noble princes present, with the result that no one took the sceptre, although everyone wanted it. The Czar, seeing the staff passed from hand to hand, eventually lost his patience and cried: "Whoever wants it can have it!" At this point Godunov stretched his arm through the crowd and seized the sceptre."

Irina was declared the official heir to the throne, but she declined: instead she entered the Novodevichii Convent. A council was then convened of 474 representatives of the clergy, the boyars, the gentry, people in service at court, and foreign tradesmen; they solemnly declared Boris Godunov Czar.

Boris Godunov and his actions are often described in Russian history in flattering terms: "He was a wonderful, soft-spoken man; under his rule many beneficial state structures continued to be established in Russia. He abhorred bribery, and tried to eradicate thieving and robbery; he was pure-spirited, gracious and humble. Boris introduced a number of reforms directed at the common good, and was consequently loved by all in the early years of his reign. Russia was blessed and the nation flourished."

However, the shortcomings which had been forgiven when Godunov was merely a ruler were not permitted in a Czar. He took harsh measures against his enemies, expelling the Romanovs from Moscow. Feodor Nikitich Romanov, the most influential among them, was forced to enter the Antoniev-Siiskii monastery, while his wife and children, including the future Czar Mikhail, were banished to Beloozero. Godunov was also accused of the murder of the Czarevich Dmitrii.

In 1601 Russia was struck by disaster. It rained throughout the summer, and a heavy frost in early autumn detroyed the harvest. The same thing happened the following year. Famine set in, followed by epidemics. This was only the start of a decade known as the "Time of Troubles."

Meanwhile rumors were spreading

across Russia that Dmitrii, son of Ivan the Terrible, was not dead after all. Soon someone appeared claiming to be the Czarevich himself, "saved by a miracle." In fact this was a monk called Grigorii Otrep´ev, from a family of minor landowners from the town of Galich. Forced to flee to Poland, the "False Dmitrii" gained the support of the Polish king and his court, and claimed the Russian throne. In 1604 his supporters crossed the river Dnieper into the Russian state. Boris died in 1605, and although the Muscovites had sworn allegiance to his son Feodor, he was overthrown and killed by the False Dmitrii's men. On June 20 1605 the pretender entered Moscow, and within a month was consecrated as Czar Dmitrii Ivanovich.

Within the year rebellion broke out in Moscow, organised by the Shuiskii Princes. The False Dmitrii was killed; his body was burned and his ashes, mixed with gunpowder, were fired from a cannon in the direction from which he had come. On May 19 1606 a new ruler was elected, and Prince Vasilii Ivanovich Shuiskii became Czar of Russia. He was to be the last of the Riurik dynasty to ascend the Russian throne.

The civil war, which had broken out the previous year, continued. A new pretender

appeared who also announced that he was the Czar Dmitrii Ivanovich. His identity, however, was no secret: he was a landowner named Mikhail Molchanov, a former supporter of the first False Dmitrii. At the same time forces from Poland and Sweden entered the war. All these factors led to a popular uprising, and Vasilii was overthrown and deported to Poland in 1610. Power now rested in the hands of a group of boyars headed by the Gedeminovich Prince Feodor Ivanovich Mstislavskii. Seeing the need for a strong central power base, they entered negotiations with the Polish king Sigismund, with the aim of appointing his son Prince Vladislav the new Czar of Russia. The Patriarch Filaret headed the delegation; in fact this was none other than Feodor Nikitich Romanov, once himself a pretender to the Russian throne but banished to a monastery by Boris Godunov. It was his son, Mikhail Feodorovich, who was to become the first Czar of the Romanov dynasty.

At this point, the struggle in Russia ceased to be a civil war and became a war of national liberation. Moscow was in the hands of the Poles, who also seized the fortress town of Smolensk. After a siege lasting twenty months their king Sigismund declared himself Czar. In the north, Novgorod and the sur-

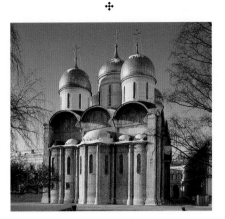

Dormition Cathedral

rounding land fell to the Swedes, who were allies of Vasilii Shuiskii. With Russia threatened with the loss of national independence, resistance to the invaders grew and in the spring of 1611 the first militia was organized in towns across Russia. It was initially successful but petered out in disagreements among its leaders. Shortly afterwards, however, new resistance arose along the river Volga, based in the rich trading towns of Nizhnii Novgorod, Yaroslavl´, Kostroma and others. It was headed by two men who were destined to become part of Russian folklore: Kuz´ma Minin, known as "The Merchant," and the *voevoda* (provincial governor) Dmitrii Pozharskii. In August 1612 forces under their command reached Moscow, and after a long siege seized control of the town and the Kremlin.

This did not end the war. It was essential to unite all the forces opposed to the Poles, which could be achieved only by the election of a legitimate monarch. Representatives of local powers were summoned from all over the country to Moscow. These included boyars, clergy, landowners, merchants, and local officials. The first and unanimous decision of this council in 1613 was that the Russian throne would never pass to a Polish or Swedish king, any of their descen-

dants, or any representative of another state – even of a practising Orthodox state. Disagreements, however, quickly ensued as to a suitable candidate for the Russian throne. Many historians believe that the name of Mikhail Feodorovich Romanov was put forward only by chance:

" A landowner from Galich brought a letter to the Council stating that Mikhail Feodorovich Romanov should be elected Czar because he was the most direct descendant of the former Czars. Voices cried out in disagreement: "Who brings this letter? Where is it from?" At that moment a chieftain from the Don region appeared and also presented a letter. Prince Dmitrii Ivanovich Pozharskii asked him: "Whom does your letter concern, Chieftain?" "The natural Czar Mikhail Feodorovich," replied the chieftain. The identical opinion, expressed by both the landowner and the Don chieftain, decided the matter. Mikhail Feodorovich was proclaimed Czar."

This account actually reveals how well the so-called "identical opinion" was prepared. Mikhail Romanov was a member of one of the most powerful families of boyars; he had support from many different levels of Russian society. His father, Patriarch Filaret, was now head of the Russian Orthodox Church. In addi-

tion, the Romanovs had married into the families of some of the most noble Russian boyars and princes and could count on their support.

There is, however, another explanation for the election of Mikhail Feodorovich. By electing a sixteen-year-old boy, the boyar leadership intended to limit his power and keep the control of the state in their own hands, particularly since his father was in a Polish prison and could not help his son. This may explain the dismay with which Mikhail and his mother greeted the news of his election, although traditionally his initial refusal was thought to have been due to the history of treachery shown by the boyars to previous rulers, from Boris Godunov to Vasilii Shuiskii. He agreed only after long persuasion. Three months after the decision of the council, Mikhail was brought from the Ipatievskii monastery in Kostroma, where he had been living with his mother, entered Moscow in great ceremony, and was consecrated as the first Czar of the Romanov dynasty.

The election of Mikhail as Czar stabilized the country, and within a short time internal strife came to an end. Later, external problems also began to be resolved. Although Russia had had to give up a number of its territories and towns, Polish and Swedish expan-

Cathedral Square showing the Archangel and Annunciation Cathedrals

sion halted. Old state structures were resurrected and new ones established. The court of the Sovereign was set up once more. Particular attention was paid to the re-introduction of the Royal Treasury and the Royal Regalia, which had fallen into disrepair during the Time of Troubles. Work began again in the workshops of the Kremlin: the Armory, the Gold and Silver Chambers, and the workshops of the Stables Office.

The early stages of the Romanov dynasty in the seventeenth century were a time of struggle between old and new, when a new culture began to emerge within the old culture of the Middle Ages. Reforms begun in the reign of Mikhail Feodorovich continued under his son Alexei Mikhailovich and his grandchildren Feodor, Czarina Sofia, and especially Peter – Peter the Great.

Peter the Great was born in 1672 to Czar Alexei and his second wife Natalia Kirillovna Naryshkina. In 1682, after the deaths of his father and of the next Czar, his brother Feodor, Peter was crowned jointly with his other brother Ivan. At once he was embroiled in a bitter seven-year struggle with his sister, the Czarina Sofia, who held all the reins of government. But Peter was quite

unlike any of his ancestors. Here was a working Czar who had been a shipwright; a fighting Czar, in the thick of the Battle of Poltava or leaping aboard Swedish galleys. He established new institutions, dividing the country into new administrative regions, reforming the armed forces, and transforming economic and cultural life. Through its victory over Sweden, Russia gained access to the Baltic, on whose shore a new capital of Russia was founded: the city of St. Petersburg. In place of the Muscovy Czardom a new empire was established, and in 1721 Peter became the first Emperor of Russia.

Under Peter's rule the country began to resemble a European state. Yet he left a legacy of insecurity which greatly influenced the course of Russian history throughout the eighteenth century. As had happened before at the end of the sixteenth century, Peter's death led to a break in the line of succession. His eldest son, the Czarevich Alexei, had been executed by his father as a traitor. His sons from his second marriage, Peter and Paul, died in childhood. In accordance with the law of royal succession drawn up by Peter the Great himself, the heir to the throne was to be nominated at the personal discretion of the Emperor;

before his death, however, Peter the Great managed only to write down the words: " I leave everything to ..."

In the years that followed Peter's death the line of succession was in some sense preserved. The throne passed to his widow, Catherine I, and from her to his grandson, Peter II, son of the executed Czarevich Alexei. Thereafter, however, the single line of the Romanov dynasty divided into several branches. After Peter II's death in 1730, there were no living male heirs. Anna Ivanovna, daughter of Peter the Great's brother, Ivan Alexeevich, became Empress. After Anna Ivanovna's death the throne passed to the child Ivan Antonovich, whose mother was Anna Ivanovna's niece, Anna Leopoldovna of Brunswick. Anna's mother was Ekaterina Ivanovna, another niece of Peter the Great. Thereafter, power returned once more to Peter's direct descendants – to his daughter Elizaveta Petrovna and then to her nephew, who became Peter III but was eventually deposed by his wife Catherine II – Catherine the Great.

This fragmented line of succession, disrupted by plots and coups, has no parallel in any other country. The thirty-seven years from the death of Peter the Great to the coronation of Catherine is known in Russian history as the "Era of Court Intrigues."

Catherine's long and successful reign stabilized both the country and ruler's position. After her death the throne passed to her son and legitimate heir, Paul I. Although the beginning of the nineteenth century saw a new court coup, this was of a political rather than a dynastic nature. Dissatisfaction with his internal and foreign policy led to a plot against Paul I, and his murder. His successor was Alexander I, eldest son of his second marriage to Maria Feodorovna of Württemberg.

In accordance with the law of succession adopted by Paul on April 5 1797, the throne now passed from the father to the eldest son, the only exception being Emperor Nicholas I. In 1825, Alexander I travelled to southern Russia and on November 19 died of typhoid in Taganrog. He had no children and the throne should have passed to his brother Constantine. However, Constantine's second wife was Polish and his children therefore had no rights of succession. Alexander had consequently nominated his younger brother Nicholas as his heir, although the edict was not published and was not even witnessed by the chosen heir himself. When Alexander died the

Grand Duke Nicholas went to Constantine to swear an oath of allegiance, but it was Constantine who in fact swore allegiance to Nicholas. Thereafter the line of succession followed its normal course. Nicholas was succeeded by his eldest son, Alexander II. After Alexander II was murdered by a terrorist in 1881, the throne passed to his son Alexander III, father of the last Russian Emperor, Nicholas II.

In contrast to the orderliness of the succession, the nineteenth century began with a long and bloody war with France. In 1812 Napoleon's army invaded Russia; Moscow was captured and set ablaze. But Russian tactics and the Russian winter defeated Napoleon, whose campaign never recovered from this failure.

The nineteenth century also saw the beginning of a revolutionary movement directed against autocratic rule. Its first attempt to overthrow the Emperor came in 1825. The revolutionaries were mainly officers who were members of various secret societies. Taking advantage of the confusion after the death of Alexander I, on December 14 1825 they led a group of soldiers on to the Senate Square in St Petersburg. The Decembrist Uprising was bru-

tally crushed: the leaders were executed and the rest sentenced to hard labour. This, however, was only the beginning of a bitter struggle by various movements against the rule of the Czar, leading to the tragic events of the beginning of the twentieth century.

In 1861 Czar Alexander II issued an edict abolishing serfdom. The peasants, who until this time had been the personal property of landowners, were liberated.

In 1913 the Russian Empire celebrated the tercentenary of the ruling Romanov dynasty. Celebrations across the country included church services, processions, and the building of new monuments. Yet within four years the monarchy was overthrown. The final and successful revolution began in February 1917. The Emperor Nicholas II was forced to abdicate in favour of his brother Mikhail. Mikhail, in turn, also abdicated the throne. The Romanov family was arrested, and within a year they were shot in Ekaterinburg.

A. K. Levykin

OKLAD (FRAME) FOR THE ICON: HODEGETRIA
MOTHER OF GOD

✛

MOSCOW, KREMLIN WORKSHOPS, 1557–60

GOLD, PRECIOUS STONES, PEARLS, WOOD,

VELVET, ENAMEL, FILIGREE, NIELLO

47.5 x 38.5 CM

INV. NO. MR-1148

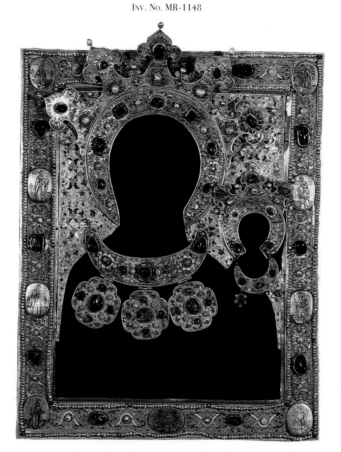

Hodegetria means "indicator of the way". The icon was kept in the Archangel Cathedral, the burial place of the Great Princes and Czars. It celebrates two epochs in Russian history, and two royal dynasties, the Riurik and Romanov. Around the *oklad* are gold miniatures containing niello portraits of the patron saints of the Czar Ivan the Terrible and of members of his family. Most interesting among these are the portraits of St Theodore the Recruit and St Anastasia. The Czar's third son, Feodor, born in 1557,

was named after the former; the latter was the patron saint of the Czar's first wife, Anastasia Romanova, who died in 1560. Feodor, who became Czar after Ivan the Terrible's death, was the last member of the first Russian royal dynasty. At the same time, Mikhail Feodorovich, the first member of the new Romanov dynasty, was indirectly descended from Feodor through Anastasia Romanova.

The *oklad* is one of the finest examples of the Russian jeweler's art of the second half of the sixteenth century. Its elegant filigree

ornament consists of trefoils and flowers with undulating stems, filled with delicately colored enamel. The deep red which is introduced into the range of blues, whites and greens makes the design particularly striking; the effect is further enhanced by drops of gold interspersed among the enamel. In the middle of the filigree design, echoing the colors of the enamel, are pearls and other precious stones: sapphires, rubies and splendidly natural round, uncut diamonds.

SHRINE LID OF THE CZAREVICH DMITRII

✥

MOSCOW, KREMLIN WORKSHOPS, 1630

A GROUP OF CRAFTSMEN LED BY

GAVRILA OVDOKIMOV

GOLD, SILVER, PRECIOUS STONES, PEARLS

157 X 60 X 4 CM

INV. NO MR-9989

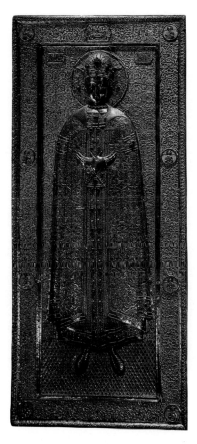

The Czarevich Dmitrii was the youngest son of Ivan the Terrible; Boris Godunov was accused of his murder. He was canonised in 1606. A quarter of a century later, Czar Mikhail Feodorovich ordered a silver-gilt shrine to be made for his remains, which were in the Archangel Cathedral of the Moscow Kremlin. The work was undertaken by a large group of Kremlin craftsmen, under the leadership of Gavrila Ovdokimov. The lid of the shrine shows the figure of the young Czarevich stamped in high relief; he is dressed in parade garments, and the whole is almost a complete sculpture. Similar portraits of saints, made from precious metals, were known in Rus´ from the second half of the fifteenth century. In the first half of the seventeenth century, several silver shrines were made in the Kremlin workshops. The portrayals of the saints on them always corresponded to a specific canon. In this example, however, the softly modeled face of the child Czarevich, with his lower lip lightly protruding, and his eyes wide open, gives the impression of a portrait. The rhythmic stamped design which covers the clothing of Dmitrii and the background reveals the influence of Eastern arabesques. Medallions are positioned along the edge of the lid, containing half figures of the patron saints of Czar Mikhail Feodorovich and members of his family.

During the capture of the Kremlin by Napoleon's forces in 1812, the shrine disappeared, but not before the lid had been hidden as the enemy approached, and hence it has survived to this day.

✛

VIEW ONTO IVANOV SQUARE
IN THE KREMLIN

✛

RUSSIA, BEGINNING OF 19TH CENTURY

F.IA. ALEXEEV

OIL ON CANVAS; 81.5 X 111.5 CM

INV. NO. ZH-1940

The Moscow Kremlin was one of the principal themes of the founder of Russian townscape painting, F.Ia. Alexeev. His many portrayals of it are notable for their delicate poetic feeling; they are also of great historic and documentary value for their faithful reproduction of landscape and architecture.

In deep perspective and gentle rhythms the picture portrays the second of the Kremlin's squares, Ivanov Square. In contrast to the ceremonial nature of Cathedral Square, this was the civil center of the ancient capital. It was here in the seventeenth and eighteenth centuries that royal decrees were read out; in the centuries that followed it was used for military parades.

The enclosed architectural ensemble of Ivanov Square includes the following buildings. On the left is the 80 m tall Ivan the Great Bell Tower, the heart of the Kremlin (architect Bon Friazin, built 1505-08; the third tier was added under Boris Godunov in 1599-1600). The first floor of the tower contains the church of St John Climacus (who gave his name to the whole square). The original Ivan the Great Bell Tower had later additions: a four-storeyed belfry was added on the north side (by Petrok Malyi, 1532-43), along with the Filaret extension (by Bazhen Ogurtsov, 1624). The left of the composition shows the Cathedral of the Twelve Apostles (by Alexei Korol'kov and Ivan Semeonov, 1653-56), part of the palace complex of the Patriarch Nikon. In the background is the façade of one of the buildings of the Chudov monastery with the Gothic Portico, added in 1780 by M.F. Kazakov. Behind this can be seen the five-domed monastery church of St Alexei (1680). The right side of the square is enclosed by the palace of the Metropolitan Platon, crowned by a belvedere with his monogram, and built in 1776, also by Kazakov.

✤

VIEW OF THE KREMLIN FROM THE BANK
OF THE MOSCOW RIVER

✤

RUSSIA, MID-19TH CENTURY

N.I. PODKLIUCHNIKOV

OIL ON CANVAS

104 X 161.5 CM

INV. NO. ZH-1988

This painting portrays the imposing prospect of Russia's most sacred place – the Moscow Kremlin. The artist has chosen one of the most effective viewpoints, the south bank of the Moscow River. This has allowed him to show the main façade of the Kremlin, and to create a panorama of its architectural wonders

The work shows the Kremlin looming along the brow of the Borovitskii hill, above the steep banks of the river, behind its mighty walls and towers (the First and Second Unnamed Towers and the Secret Tower). The panorama includes the Armory (1844-51, architect K.A. Ton); the Great Kremlin Palace (1838-50, chief architect K.A. Ton), the Moscow residence of the Emperors; the Annunciation Cathedral (1484-89, by the Pskov school of architects), the private church of the Moscow Great Princes and Czars; the Archangel Cathedral (1505-08, by Alovisio Novo), the principal church of the Great Princes and Czars, and the burial place of the Riurik and Romanov dynasties; the Dormition Cathedral (1475-79, by Aristotele Fioravanti), the original church of the Kremlin; and the Ivan the Great Bell Tower and belfry.

✤

THE BOYARS' SQUARE IN THE KREMLIN

✛

RUSSIA, BEGINNING OF 19TH CENTURY

F.IA. ALEXEEV

OIL ON CANVAS; 87 X118 CM

INV. NO. ZH-1930

This picture recalls a part of the Kremlin which no longer exists. The Russian architectural forms on display here were never to be repeated: the many-tiered gallery with its tall roofs, the wonderful perrons, crowned with pointed hipped roofs, the open terraces and promenades, and the sheer intricacy of the churches. The combined effect is overwhelming. This is conveyed with great success by the artist through the asymmetry of the composition, and he has clearly enjoyed the unexpected contrast between the scale of the façades and the polychrome pattern of their tiles, the abundance of carved stonework, and the bright gilding of the cupolas.

The Boyars' Square was the internal courtyard of the royal palace, where high-ranking officials of various departments awaited reception or the issue of decrees. The square was surrounded by a group of ancient buildings. On the left of the picture is the Terem Palace (1635-36, by the architects Bazhen Ogurtsov, Antip Konstantinov, Trefil Sharutin, and Larion Ushakov). On the second tier of the palace are the living quarters and the Upper Cathedral of Our Saviour. These were entered through the Bedchamber Porch, with its semi-circular spiral stairway, and the Gold Front Porch, closed by a gilded gate installed in 1670. On the right of the stairway are the four private palace churches: the Church of the Saviour Not Made with Hands, the Church of St Catherine, the Church of the Resurrection of the Prophet, and the Church of the Crucifixion. All four churches are united under one roof with eleven gold cupolas. In the background, on the right, the composition ends with the vestibule of the ceremonial throne hall of the Russian Czars in the Granovitaya Palace (1487-91, by the architects Marco Friazin and Pietro Antonio Solari). The domes of the Dormition Cathedral, and the cupola of the Ivan the Great Bell Tower are visible behind it.

KEY TO THE GATES OF THE SAVIOUR TOWER OF
THE MOSCOW KREMLIN

✜

MOSCOW, 1833
MASTER LEBEDEV, FROM A DESIGN
BY LT-COL RYNDIN
STEEL
L. 37.5 CM
INV. NO. MR-7591

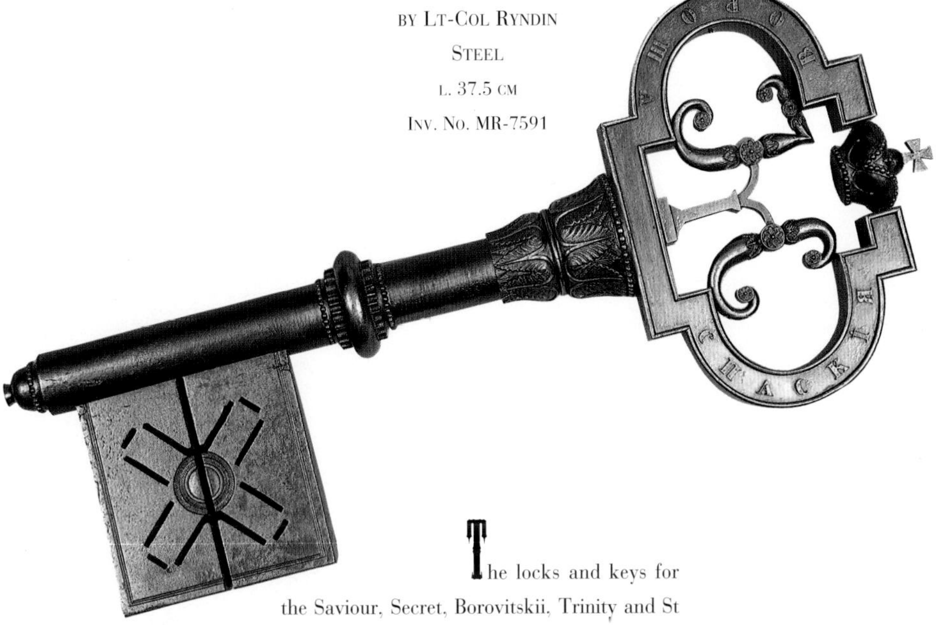

The locks and keys for the Saviour, Secret, Borovitskii, Trinity and St Nicholas Gates of the Moscow Kremlin were made between 1831 and 1833 by the well known Moscow mechanic Lebedev, from designs by Lieutenant-Colonel Ryndin of the Guards. Masters from Tula were employed for the carved work. When he saw the finished pieces, Ryndin noted that "the combined refinement and solidity of the work has exceeded all my expectations," and that "it would be impossible – indeed wrong – to ask for anything better."

In 1834 the locks were installed in the gates, and the keys were transferred from the Moscow Palace Office to the Moscow Commandant. They were kept on cushions of crimson velvet, attached to ribbons of the Order of St George. Later, leather cases were woven for the keys, with carrying straps.

In 1877, when the Kremlin had ceased to be considered a military fortress, the keys and cases were transferred to the Armory.

**MEDAL FOR THE THREE HUNDREDTH
ANNIVERSARY OF THE RULE OF THE ROMANOVS**

✣

RUSSIA, ST. PETERSBURG, 1913

MASTER A. ZHAKAR

DIAM. 7.5 CM

INV. NO. OM-309

On February 21 1913 Russia celebrated three hundred years of rule by the House of Romanov. The event was marked by the issue of a whole range of commemorative medals, medallions and badges. In addition to the Royal Mint, a large number of private firms and workshops in St. Petersburg and Moscow took part in their production.

Official commemorative medals, struck at the St. Petersburg Mint, were to be distributed by the Ceremonial office of the Ministry of the Imperial Court during the celebrations. They were intended for participants and guests at the ceremonies, as well as for other officials and bodies taking part in the event. Members of the royal family were given a set of three copies of this medal, in gold, silver and bronze. All three were of the same size, and were enclosed in a specially made leather case stamped with the date.

The obverse shows half-length portraits of Czar Mikhail Romanov wearing the Cap of Monomach in the background, and the Emperor Nicholas II in the foreground (the first and last Czars of the Romanov dynasty). Beneath are the dates 1613-1913.

On the reverse of the medal is a portrait of the scene of Mikhail Feodorovich Romanov's election to the Czardom. The young Czar stands on a platform in the center, with a staff in his hand. On his right are his mother Martha the Nun and the Archbishop Feodorit; on his left, representatives of the people and the clergy. A kneeling boyar kisses his hand. Beneath the portrait is the inscription "IN THE YEAR 1613 IN THE MONTH OF MARCH ON THE FIRST DAY"; to the right of the portrait the name of the engraver, A. Zhakar, runs along the rim of the medal.

Avgust Zhakar was a medal engraver who ran his own workshop. Several medallists from the Royal Mint worked there, and he himself sometimes undertook commissions from the Royal Mint.

OKLAD (FRAME) FOR THE ICON: ST NICHOLAS OF
ZARAISK WITH THE LIVES OF THE SAINTS

✢

MOSCOW, 1608

SOME DETAILS: MOSCOW, 1831,

MASTER ALEXEI POSTNIKOV

PECTORAL CROSS: ATHOS, 16TH CENTURY

SILVER, GOLD, PRECIOUS STONES, PEARLS

112.5 X 90.5 CM

INV. No. MR-10094

This precious *oklad* was given to the St Nicholas Cathedral in the ancient Russian town of Zaraisk by Czar Vasilii Shuiskii in 1608. It is a magnificent example of the Russian jeweler's art.

This work is closely linked to the history of the Russian state, and dates from the complex epoch of the Time of Troubles. At the beginning of the seventeenth century many Russian towns, including Moscow, were sacked and razed to the ground by invading enemies. Most of the gold and silver kept in the Royal Treasury and in the vestries of the largest cathedrals was stolen. The creation of this *oklad* at that time, for which almost more than 4.5 kg of gold were used, was therefore a unique event. Clearly the unstable position of the new Moscow sovereign made it imperative to create a monument which would immortalize his name in history, as well as pay tribute to St Nicholas. The saint had been revered as the defender of Russian towns from the time of the Mongol Tartar invasion, and was given the title of "Principal Protector of the Russian Lands."

In the nineteenth century the *oklad* underwent some changes. In 1831 the stamped medallions on the central strip of the icon were remade, along with the vestment of the saint and the hagiographic badges.

The icon itself dates from the first half of the sixteenth century. It is now kept in the Andrei Rublev Museum of Ancient Russian Art in Moscow. The iconography of the icon became canonical, and can be found in later Russian icons, wooden sculptures and other works of the plastic arts, and in embroideries.

EASTER EGG WITH GLOBE: THREE HUNDRED YEARS OF THE HOUSE OF ROMANOV

✤

RUSSIA, ST. PETERSBURG, 1913,
WORKSHOP OF CARL FABERGÉ
MASTER H. WIGSTROM
GOLD, SILVER, STEEL, DIAMONDS, ENAMEL,
WATERCOLOR ON IVORY
H. 19 CM, DIAM. 7.8 CM
INV. NO. MR-651/1-2

Easter is the most important and festive of Christian holidays in the Orthodox Church as in others. In Russia it is customary to mark this day with the exchange of painted eggs. They commemorate the suffering of Christ, and are a symbol of his miraculous resurrection from the dead and his redemption of the sins of man. The egg was also seen as a symbol of the world reborn in Christ.

The Easter eggs which members of the royal family and the noble and wealthy gave to each other differed greatly from the traditional painted eggs of the people. They were made of gold and silver, and decorated with enamel, precious stones, and miniature paintings. Particularly splendid were the Easter eggs commissioned by the Czar from Fabergé, the leading firm of Russian jewelers; at the turn of the twentieth century they were renowned throughout the world.

Alexander III started the tradition in 1885. Every year he commissioned an egg from his court jeweler, Peter Carl Fabergé, as a gift to his wife, the Empress Maria Feodorovna. After Alexander's death his son Nicholas II continued the tradition, commissioning two eggs from the firm. At Easter Fabergé himself would present one egg to the Dowager Empress Maria Feodorovna, while his assistant would present the second to Alexandra Feodorovna, Nicholas's wife. In all fifty-six of these masterpieces were produced

between 1885 and 1917; however, only ten of these have remained in Russia. Masters from the Fabergé firm worked on each Easter egg for nearly a year. Designers, gold- and silver-smiths, jewelers, stone carvers, enamelers and sculptors all took part in its preparation, from the initial sketches to the finishing touches. The final word, however, was always had by Fabergé, "a great, incomparable genius," in the words of Maria Feodorovna.

These astounding creations often included delicate mechanisms. They were equally remarkable for their unusual design, the extraordinary precision of their execution, their magnificent detail, and the wonderful selection of the most precious materials. The subject and form of each Imperial Easter egg were unique. Some celebrated intimate family themes, while others honored notable events in the life of the Russian state and the Imperial family.

During the reign of Nicholas II the three hundredth anniversary of the rule of the Romanov dynasty was celebrated with great ceremony and opulence. This Easter egg, presented to Empress Alexandra Feodorovna in 1913, commemorates this event. It was made under the direction of Master Henrik Wigstrom, in whose workshop nearly all the Easter eggs produced after 1903 were made.

The decoration shows a rich use of elements of state symbolism. The gold egg, faced with white enamel, is decorated with

applied stamped two-headed eagles, royal crowns and wreaths, and eighteen miniature portraits of all the representatives of the House of Romanov. These are in diamond frames, painted in watercolor on ivory by the artist V.I. Zuev. The egg rests upon a threefold heraldic eagle, which in turn stands on a circular base of purple, imitating a state shield.

Traditionally the egg held a surprise which would become visible when the hinged lid was opened. Here, the interior of the lid is decorated with a delightful illustration in white opaline enamel on a ground carved with guilloche ornament. A rotating globe is attached to the inside of the egg; it is made of blued steel, imitating the sea. The land on the globe is executed in gold of several colors. The globe consists of two northern hemispheres. One half shows the territory of Russia at the end of 1613, the date of accession to the throne of the first Romanov Czar, Mikhail Feodorovich. The other shows the territory of the Russian Empire in 1913, under Nicholas II.

The creative fantasy of the artists of the Fabergé firm was unparalleled. In this example a significant historical theme has been given splendid artistic expression. One of the most important events in the history of the royal family and in Russian life of the beginning of the twentieth century has been preserved in the form of a jeweled souvenir; yet the work's historical significance has not diminished its artistic expressiveness.

PORTRAIT OF EMPEROR NICHOLAS II
⁜

RUSSIA, 1896

N.F. IASH

OIL ON CANVAS

175 x 240 CM

INV. NO. 68257/11-4991

GIM

This portrait was painted in the year of Nicholas II's coronation, and is one of the earliest pictures of the last Russian emperor. Nicholas's portrait was later painted by such eminent Russian artists as I.E. Repin, V.A. Serov, and L.S. Bakst. They developed the tradition of the grand royal portrait, and enriched it with the bold aesthetic innovations so characteristic of Russian art at the turn of the twentieth century. This portrait by N.F. Iash was not, however, in the mainstream of artistic developments of this time; indeed, against a background of the creative achievements of Russia's leading masters, it could be said to be quite archaic. Nevertheless, this little known artist has shown a keen awareness of the demands of his contemporaries, and in his portrait of Nicholas II he has embodied the national ideal of a Russian "Czar-batiushka", or paternalistic Czar.

In his treatment of the interior the artist has taken account of traditional royal portraits but has, however, introduced significant changes. The traditional luxury of the surroundings is here replaced by the strength and simplicity of the Emperor's study in the Great Kremlin Palace, underlining the modesty of the young Czar's lifestyle. Nicholas wears the uniform of a Life Guard of the Preobrazhenskii Regiment, with a ribbon and star of the Order of St Andrew the First Called, along with other medals. He is portrayed more as just a good-looking man than as a magnificent and powerful figure. He stands alongside a table on which, instead of the traditional royal regalia, are what seem to be everyday objects: writing implements and a pile of books. On closer inspection, however, the titles on the spines of the books show that these are works of Russian history. The Emperor's hand rests on the books, accentuating their symbolic significance in the ideological design of the portrait.

Through the window can be seen the ancient Borovitskii Tower of the Kremlin and the Cathedral of Christ the Saviour. These, too, are a clear demonstration of the new Czar's devotion to antiquities and national traditions. The Cathedral of Christ the Saviour was built by the architect K.A. Ton between 1837 and 1883 (the date of its final dedication) in the Russian-Byzantine style. Erected to celebrate victory in the Great Patriotic War of 1812, the cathedral was an important national, as well as religious, symbol.

The programmatic content and artistic style of the portrait are intended to appeal to all strata of society. The bright coloring, the naive illusionism, the careful depiction of detail, and the photographic quality of the Emperor's face all reflect popular taste of the time. The portrait is, in fact, an example of popular culture which, at the turn of the twentieth century, had assimilated the more prestigious convention of the royal portrait. It may be said that royal portraiture completed its evolution at the same time as the Romanov dynasty.

POCKET WATCH
⁜

SWITZERLAND, BEGINNING OF 20TH CENTURY

THE FIRM OF PAUL BOURET

DONATED TO THE ARMORY BY THE SON OF

F. I. CHALIAPIN IN 1994

GOLD, SILVER, METAL, DIAMONDS, ENAMEL

INV. NO. VKH-5373

The Swiss firm of Paul Bouret was the most important supplier of clocks and watches to the Russian market, and the head of the firm had the title of Purveyor to the Court of His Imperial Highness. One of the firm's specialities was the production of pocket watches with smooth lids, which after decoration with an appropriate inscription, would be presented by the Emperor to civil servants, military leaders or leading figures from the world of the arts.

The most important event of court life in 1903 was a vast masked ball, accompanied by concerts given by leading artists. Among them was the gifted singer F. I. Chaliapin, who, it is known, sang at one of the concerts in St. Petersburg. On March 14 he was presented by the Directors of the Imperial Theaters with a gold watch decorated with the emblem of the Russian Empire made of brilliant cut diamonds in silver. Chaliapin wore the watch throughout his life, and after his death it was kept in the family by his descendants.

MIKHAIL FEODOROVICH

✛

1596-1645

CZAR 1613-1645

Founder of the royal dynasty of Romanovs, Mikhail Feodorovich was born on July 18 1596 to the boyar Feodor Nikitich Romanov (subsequently known by the ecclesiastical name Filaret) and Ksenia Ivanovna Shestovaya (ecclesiastical name Grand Old Martha). He was elected Sovereign of All Russia in Moscow's Red Square by the Assembly of the Land (*Zemskii Sobor*) on February 21 1613 at the age of sixteen, and consecrated Czar on July 11 1613 in the Dormition Cathedral of the Moscow Kremlin.

Before his accession to the throne he lived with his mother in the village of Domnina, the family estate of the Romanovs, not far from Kostroma.

During his reign he established a unified Russian state, ended internal conflicts, and resumed relations with foreign states. He also made various early reforms, particularly in the Russian army. He was married twice: to Maria Vladimirovna Dolgorukaya (d. January 7 1626) and to Evdokia Lukianovna Streshneva (c.1608-August 18 1645). There were ten children from the second marriage.

He died on July 13 1645 from dropsy, and was buried in the Archangel Cathedral of the Kremlin

ALEXEI MIKHAILOVICH

✛

1629-1676

CZAR 1645-1676

Born on March 19 1629, Alexei Mikhailovich was consecrated Czar on July 16 1645 after the death of his father. One of the most educated men of his time, he wrote and edited many important decrees and documents. He was known as "Tishaishii" (most quiet one) because of his meek, devout nature. His rule, however, was characterized by active internal and external policies. A collection of laws, The Code of the Assembly, was passed on his personal authority in 1649. He supported Nikon, Patriarch of the Russian Orthodox Church, in ecclesiastical reforms. His greatest foreign policy achievements were the unification of Russia and Ukraine, and preventing an incursion by Crimean Tartars into central regions of the country.

He was married twice: from 1648 to 1669 to Maria Il'inishna Miloslavskaya (1626-69) and from 1671 to 1676 to Natalia Kirillovna Naryshkina (1651-94). He had twenty-one children from both marriages.

He died on January 30 1676 and was buried in the Archangel Cathedral of the Kremlin.

FEODOR ALEXEEVICH

✛

1661-1682

CZAR 1676-1682

Son of Czar Alexei Mikhailovich, Feodor Alexeevich was born on April 30 1661. Officially declared heir to the throne on September 1 1674 at age of twelve, he was consecrated Czar in the Dormition Cathedral of the Kremlin, after the death of his father, on June 18 1676.

He received an excellent education for his time, knowing Latin well, reading and speaking Polish fluently, and writing poetry. Physically unhealthy, he also had a weak character. During the six years of his reign he was unable to rule with any independence. Power was concentrated in the hands of his maternal relatives, the Miloslavskii boyars. However, reforms in the organization of the army and the state, begun under his grandfather and father, continued during his reign. A national consensus conducted in 1678 and in 1682 ended *mestnichestvo*, a practise whereby boyars and gentry were appointed to particular posts on the basis of their ancestors' services. The major foreign policy success of his reign was halting Ottoman expansion into the Ukraine.

Feodor Alexeevich married twice and had one child which died in infancy. He died on April 27 1682 without leaving arrangements for the succession, and was buried in the Archangel Cathedral of the Kremlin.

IVAN V (IVAN ALEXEEVICH)

✢

1666-1696

CZAR 1682-1696

Son of Alexei
Mikhailovich, Ivan was born on August 27
1666 from his father's marriage with Maria
Miloslavskaya. Although not an official heir to
the throne, after the death of Feodor
Alexeevich, as eldest remaining son he should
have succeeded. However, because of Ivan's ill
health, the Boyars' Duma voted the ten-year-
old Peter Alexeevich (the future Peter the
Great) Czar, on the suggestion of the Patriarch
Ioakim. But following an insurrection of the
Moscow *strel'tsy*, Ivan's relatives, the
Miloslavskii boyars, led by Czarevna Sofia,
opposed the election of Peter. The Boyars'
Duma gave way to these demands and
declared Ivan First Czar, Peter Second Czar,
and Sofia Alexeevna Regent. Both Ivan and
Peter were consecrated Czars on June 25 1682.

Because of ill health, Ivan V played
no role in political affairs of state. He married
Praskovia Feodorovna Saltykova and had five
children, including the future Empress Anna
Ivanovna.

He died on January 29 1696 and
was buried in the Archangel Cathedral of
the Kremlin.

SOFIA ALEXEEVNA

✢

1657-1704

RULER OF RUSSIA 1682-1689

Born on September 5
1657, Sofia Alexeevna was well educated and
noted for her intelligence, energy, and ambi-
tion. After the death of Feodor Alexeevich she
led a group of Miloslavskii boyars in a struggle
for power. On May 29 1682 she became
Regent to Ivan and Peter, and thus effectively
the ruler of Russia.

She was extremely active in internal
and foreign policy. Russia concluded "The
Eternal Peace" with Poland in 1686, and the
Nerchinskii Treaty with China in 1689; there
were also two military expeditions to the
Crimea. In 1687 the first educational establish-
ment opened in Russia: the Academy of Slavic,
Greek, and Latin Studies.

In 1689 Sofia was overthrown by
supporters of Peter the Great and exiled to the
Novodevichii Monastery. In 1698 she was
forced to take the veil under the name of
Susanna.

PETER THE GREAT

(PETER ALEXEEVICH)

✢

1672-1725

CZAR 1682-1721;

EMPEROR OF ALL RUSSIA 1721-1725

Peter the Great was the
fourteenth child of Alexei Mikhailovich, born
on May 30 1672 from his second marriage to
Natalia Kirillovna Naryshkina. Having ruled
jointly with his brother Ivan V from 1682, with
Ivan's death in 1696 Peter was officially
declared Sovereign of all Russia.

During his reign Peter undertook
extensive reforms: he created a regular army
and navy, subjugated the Church to the state,
and introduced new administrative and territo-
rial divisions of the country. He paid particular
attention to the development of science. He
was a far-sighted and skillful diplomat and a
talented military leader.

Under Peter's rule Russia became a
great European nation. In 1721 he proclaimed
Russia an Empire and was accorded the title of
Emperor of All Russia, Great Father of the
Fatherland and "the Great".

He married twice and had eleven
children, many of whom died in infancy. The
eldest son from his first marriage, Czarevich
Alexei, was convicted of high treason by his
father and secretly executed in 1718.

Peter died from a chill on January
28 1725 without nominating an heir. He was
buried in the Cathedral of the St Peter and
St Paul Fortress in St. Petersburg.

CATHERINE I (EKATERINA ALEXEEVNA)

✛

1684-1727

EMPRESS OF ALL RUSSIA 1725-1727

The first Empress of All Russia was the second wife of Peter the Great. Before converting to the Orthodox faith she was called Marta Skavronskaya, and was the daughter of a Lithuanian peasant named Samuil. Employed as a servant by the minister Gluck of Marienburg, at seventeen she married a Swedish dragoon. When Marienburg fell to Russian forces, Marta was captured by Count B. P. Sheremetev and put to work in the regimental laundry. From Sheremetev she was passed on to Prince A.D. Menshikov, a favorite of Peter the Great. In 1703 Peter saw Marta at Menshikov's home and took her as his mistress. In 1705 she converted to the Orthodox faith, and on February 19 1712 married Peter.

After the death of Peter, Catherine was placed on the throne by guards regiments. Real power, however, remained in the hands of Menshikov and the Supreme Privy Council.

She died on May 6 1727 and was buried in the Cathedral of the St Peter and St Paul Fortress in St. Petersburg.

PETER II (PETER ALEXEEVICH)

✛

1715-1730

EMPEROR OF ALL RUSSIA 1727-1730

Grandson of Peter the Great and son of Czarevich Alexei Petrovich from his marriage to Crown Princess Sofia Charlotta of Braunschweig-Wolfenbüttel, Peter II was born on October 12 1715. His mother died three days after his birth, his father when he was three years old. After the death of Catherine I he ascended the throne at the age of twelve. By order of Catherine, until he reached his majority the state was to be ruled by the Supreme Privy Council with the participation of Czarevnas Anna Petrovna and Elizaveta Petrovna. During the first year of Peter's reign, actual power was in the hands of the former favorite of Peter the Great, Prince A.D. Menshikov, the young sovereign's guardian.

On January 9 1728 Peter II moved to Moscow with his court and the Supreme Privy Council. Here his coronation took place on February 25 1728 in the Dormition Cathedral of the Kremlin.

On November 30 1729 he was engaged to the eighteen-year old beauty Ekaterina Alexeevna Dolgorukova. But on January 6 1730 he caught a chill during a military review and subsequently contracted smallpox, dying on January 19 1730. He was buried in the Archangel Cathedral of the Kremlin. The male line of the Romanov dynasty ended with Peter II.

ANNA IVANOVNA

✛

1693-1740

EMPRESS OF ALL RUSSIA 1730-1740

Born on January 28 1693, Anna Ivanovna was the daughter of Peter the Great's co-ruler, Ivan V, and Praskovia Feodorovna Saltykova. Up to the age of seventeen she spent most of her time in the village of Ismailovo, near Moscow, where her mother lived.

After the death of Emperor Peter II she was elected to the Russian throne by the Supreme Privy Council which, however, set limits to her power. On March 4 1730 Anna Ivanovna rejected their conditions and dissolved the council; then on April 28 1730 she crowned herself in the Dormition Cathedral of the Moscow Kremlin.

Historians have different opinions of her reign. On the one hand, the Empress herself spent little time on affairs of state, surrounding herself with German grandees. Power lay in the hands of her favorite, Count Biron. On the other hand, her rule was a period of internal stability and successful foreign policy.

Anna Ivanovna died of kidney disease at the age of 47, leaving no heirs, and was buried in the Cathedral of the St Peter and St Paul Fortress in St. Petersburg.

IVAN VI (IVAN ANTONOVICH)

1740-1764

EMPEROR OF ALL RUSSIA 1740-1741

Ivan VI was the son of the niece of Empress Anna Ivanovna, Princess Anna Leopoldovna of Mecklenburg, and Anton Ulrich, Duke of Braunschweig. He was born on August 12 1740, and officially declared heir to the throne by Anna Ivanovna on October 5. After her death he became Emperor of Russia at the age of two months. Count Biron, favorite of the late Empress, remained Regent. However, on November 9 Biron was arrested and sent to Siberia. The child Emperor's mother was declared Regent.

The reign of Ivan VI and Anna Leopoldovna was extremely short. On November 25 1741 the Emperor was overthrown by the Imperial Guard led by Elizaveta Petrovna, daughter of Peter the Great. The child and his family were exiled first to Riga, then to Rannenborg Castle, and finally in 1744 to Kholmogory where, on March 7 1746, Anna Leopoldovna died. At the beginning of 1756 Ivan Antonovich was taken to the Schlisselborg Fortress, where he was kept in extreme secrecy and under strict guard. On the night of July 5 1764, the twenty-four-year-old Ivan was killed by his guards when his lieutenant, V. I. Mirovich, attempted to free him. He was secretly buried in a hidden place near the walls of the fortress; the grave was later destroyed.

ELIZAVETA PETROVNA

1709-1761

EMPRESS OF ALL RUSSIA 1741-1761

Daughter of Emperor Peter the Great, Elizaveta Petrovna was born on December 18 1709 before her father's official marriage to Catherine I. As soon as Catherine died the position of the Czarevna became most precarious, particularly during the reign of Anna Ivanovna and the Regency of Anna Leopoldovna; both feared the Imperial Guard's loyalty to Peter's daughter. Elizaveta was saved from taking the veil by the existence abroad of her nephew, the Prince of Holstein (the future Emperor Peter III); during his lifetime any measures taken against her would have been pointless cruelty.

On the night of November 25 1741 Elizaveta went to the barracks of the Preobrazhenskii regiment and persuaded the soldiers to follow her. The Braunschweig clan and a number of senior officials were arrested, and the thirty-two-year-old Elizaveta proclaimed Empress. On April 25 1742 Elizaveta was crowned in the Dormition Cathedral of the Moscow Kremlin.

During her reign significant advances were made economically and culturally. In foreign policy, Russia became so important that all states were eager to make treaties. One of Elizaveta's most important decrees was made on May 7 1744: the abolition of capital punishment. During her reign not a single person was executed.

She died on December 25 1761 at fifty-three, leaving no heir, and was buried in the Cathedral of the St Peter and St Paul Fortress in St. Petersburg.

PETER III (PETER FEODOROVICH)

1728-1762

EMPEROR OF ALL RUSSIA 1761-1762

Son of Karl Friedrich, Duke of Holstein-Gotorb and Anna Petrovna, Peter the Great's daughter, Peter III was born on February 10 1728 in Kila and christened Karl Peter Ulrich. Up to the age of fourteen he lived and was educated at the court of Holstein. He was proclaimed official heir to the Russian throne on November 7 1742 by his aunt Elizaveta Petrovna.

On August 21 1745 Peter Feodorovich married Princess Sophia Augusta Frederica of Anhalt-Zerbst, who was christened into the Orthodox faith as Ekaterina Alexeevna (the future Catherine the Great).

Peter ascended the Russian throne on December 25 1761, the day Empress Elizaveta Petrovna died. His first action was an amnesty for and return from exile of state figures arrested by Elizaveta after her accession. During his short reign he introduced various reforms, banned the persecution of dissenters, dissolved the Privy Council, and by special decree released the gentry from compulsory state service.

On June 28 1762 he was over-thrown by a court coup led by his wife. After his deposition he was imprisoned in Ropshinskii Castle, where on July 7 1762 he was killed by Count Alexei Orlov, Catherine's favorite and one of the organizers of the coup.

He had two children from his marriage with Catherine: a son, later Emperor Paul I, and a daughter who died in infancy.

Peter III was buried in the Annunciation Church of the Alexander Nevsky Monastery but in December 1796, by order of his son Paul I, his remains were reburied with full honors in the Cathedral of the St Peter and St Paul Fortress in St. Petersburg.

CATHERINE THE GREAT
(EKATERINA ALEXEEVNA)

⁑

1729-1796
EMPRESS OF ALL RUSSIA 1762-1796

Born on April 21 1729 in Stettin (now Szczecin), Poland, into the family of Prince Christian August of Anhalt-Zerbst, Catherine was christened Sophia Augusta Frederica. On February 9 1744, aged fifteen, she came to Russia at the invitation of Empress Elizaveta Petrovna as the bride of the heir to the throne, Peter Feodorovich. The marriage took place in St. Petersburg on August 21 1745, and she was christened into the Orthodox Church as Ekaterina Alexeevna. Industrious, highly intelligent and strong-willed, she quickly

mastered the Russian language. A reader of historical and philosophical works, she entered into correspondence with some of the greatest minds in Europe, including Voltaire.

On June 28 1762, with the support of the Imperial Guard, she overthrew her husband Peter III. She was crowned Empress of All Russia on September 22 1762 in the Dormition Cathedral of the Moscow Kremlin. Her rule was one of the most prosperous periods of the Russian Empire. She undertook a wide range of internal political reforms, waged two successful wars against the Ottoman Empire, and occupied vast territories on Russia's southern boundaries, eventually advancing the country's border to the Black Sea.

She died on November 6 1796 and was buried in the Cathedral of the St Peter and St Paul Fortress in St. Petersburg.

PAUL I (PAVEL PETROVICH)

⁑

1754-1801
EMPEROR OF ALL RUSSIA 1796-1801

Son of Peter III and Catherine the Great, Paul was born on September 20 1754 and brought up at the court of his grandmother, Empress Elizaveta Petrovna, who intended to appoint him her heir instead of Peter Feodorovich (Peter III). After the overthrow of Peter III he lived with his family in Gatchina Palace, given him by his mother, where he had his own court and a small army. The violent events of his childhood, and his estrangement from his mother, made him irritable and suspicious of those around him.

On the day of Catherine the Great's death the forty-two-year-old Paul declared himself Emperor.

Historians are equivocal about his short reign. He was unpopular at court and extremely hostile towards his mother. His coronation signalled a break with the stability of

Catherine's reign. Paul I freed those imprisoned by the Privy Council, liberated the Poles, abolished conscription, and limited the power of landowners over the serfs. On April 5 1797 he issued a decree on rights of succession which established procedures for the transfer of power from one monarch to the next. In foreign policy he performed an abrupt reversal, changing from war with France to union with her. This was probably one of the main reasons for his murder.

Paul I was married twice; secondly in 1776 to Princess Sophia Dorothea of Württemberg (Maria Feodorovna). He had ten children from the second marriage.

On the night of March 12 1801 he was suffocated by conspirators. He was buried in the Cathedral of the St Peter and St Paul Fortress in St. Petersburg.

ALEXANDER I
(ALEXANDER PAVLOVICH)

⁑

1777-1825
EMPEROR OF ALL RUSSIA 1801-1825

Eldest son of Emperor Paul I, Alexander was born in St. Petersburg on December 12 1777. From childhood he was greatly influenced by Catherine the Great, who brought him up and considered him her successor.

He came to the throne after the murder of his father Paul I on March 12 1801, and was crowned in the Dormition Cathedral of the Moscow Kremlin on September 15. The

young Emperor was extremely popular among all levels of society. The first half of his reign was marked by a liberal internal policy; his various reforms included a restructuring of the country and an attempt to codify Russian legislation. Later, however, he reversed many of these changes.

Alexander died on November 19 1825 in Taganrog and was buried in the Cathedral of the St Peter and St Paul Fortress in St. Petersburg. There is a story that he secretly abdicated and lived under the name of Feodor Kuz´mich the Monk.

NICHOLAS I (NIKOLAI PAVLOVICH)
✣
1796-1855
EMPEROR OF ALL RUSSIA 1825-1855

Nicholas I was born on May 25 1796 in Gatchina near St. Petersburg, the third son of Emperor Paul I. Not considered likely to succeed to the throne, he received an education in military engineering. In the 1820s he held the post of Inspector-General of the army's engineers. He also became Commander of the First Guards Division.

Nicholas I came to throne after the death of his elder brother Alexander I and the refusal of the second brother, Grand Duke Constantine, to accept sovereignty. His first measure as Emperor was the execution of the participants in the uprising of December 14 1825. He was crowned on August 22 1826 in the Dormition Cathedral of the Moscow Kremlin.

His reign saw the flourishing of absolute monarchy in both military and civil areas. He strengthened and centralized bureaucratic structures to an unprecedented degree. Harsh and despotic by nature, he had little time for abstract ideas. Any sign of liberalism in Russia was brutally suppressed.

The principal issue in foreign policy was the "Eastern Question" – maintaining pro-Russian regimes in the Black Sea Straits. Nicholas attempted to resolve this by the partition of the Ottoman Empire. The result was the Crimean War of 1853-56, in which Russia suffered a bitter defeat at the hands of a coalition of Western European states and Turkey.

He married Frederica Louisa Charlotta Wilhelmina (Alexandra Feodorovna), daughter of King Friedrich Wilhelm III of Prussia, and had seven children.

Nicholas died on February 18 1855. Many researchers believe that he poisoned himself after receiving news of the defeat of Russian forces at Evpatoria. He was buried in the Cathedral of the St Peter and St Paul Fortress in St. Petersburg.

ALEXANDER II (ALEXANDER NIKOLAEVICH)
✣
1818-1881
EMPEROR OF ALL RUSSIA 1855-1881

Eldest son of Emperor Nicholas I, Alexander was born in Moscow on April 17 1818 and came to the throne on February 19 1855 after the death of his father. He was crowned in the Dormition Cathedral of the Moscow Kremlin on August 26 1856.

After his accession to the throne Alexander II implemented important reforms, notably the abolition of serfdom, as well as changes in national, military, and municipal organization. He also rethought foreign policy: Russia now refrained from overseas expansion and concentrated on strengthening its borders. In 1867 he sold Alaska and the Aleutian Islands to the USA. His greatest foreign policy achievement was the successful war of 1877-8 against the Ottoman Empire, resulting in the liberation of Bulgaria and annulment of the conditions of the Treaty of Paris of 1856, imposed after Russia's defeat in the Crimean War.

In 1841 Alexander II married Maria of Hessen-Darmstadt (Maria Alexandrovna). The marriage produced seven children.

On March 1 1881 in St. Petersburg he was mortally wounded by a bomb thrown by a student, I. Grinevitskii, a member of the revolutionary organisation "The National Will". The Cathedral of the Resurrection on Blood was erected on the site of the murder. Alexander II was buried in the Cathedral of the St Peter and St Paul Fortress in St. Petersburg.

ALEXANDER III (ALEXANDER ALEXANDROVICH)

✤

1845-1894

EMPEROR OF ALL RUSSIA 1881-1894

The second son of Alexander II, born in St. Petersburg on February 26 1845, Alexander III became official heir to the throne after the death of his elder brother Nicholas in 1865.

He came to the throne on March 1 1881, at the age of thirty-six, after the assassination of his father, and was crowned in the Dormition Cathedral of the Moscow Kremlin on May 15 1883.

Alexander's III's reign coincided with an industrial revolution in Russia and the strengthening of capitalism. His domestic policy was particularly harsh, directed not only against revolutionaries but also other liberal movements. Fearing an attempt on his life, he refused to live in the Winter Palace; instead, he lived away from St. Petersburg in Gatchina, the palace of his great-grandfather Paul I, which was designed like a medieval fortress surrounded by ditches and watchtowers.

He married the Danish Princess Dagmar (Maria Feodorovna) and had six children.

Alexander III died on October 20 1894 in Livadia, Crimea, and was buried in the Cathedral of the St Peter and St Paul Fortress in St. Petersburg.

NICHOLAS II (NIKOLAI ALEXANDROVICH)

✤

1868-1918

EMPEROR OF ALL RUSSIA 1894-1917

Nicholas II, the last Russian Emperor, was the eldest son of Alexander III, and was born on May 6 1868 in Czarskoe Selo. He ascended the throne after the death of his father on October 20 1894, and was crowned on May 14 1896. The ceremony in Moscow was overshadowed by a catastrophe on Khodynskoe Field, where more than a thousand spectators were crushed to death.

He married the daughter of Grand Duke Ludwig of Hessen, Alice Victoria Eleanor Louisa Beatrice (Alexandra Feodorovna) and had five children. The Czarevich, Alexei, suffered from haemophilia and was a permanent invalid. There were four daughters, Olga, Tatiana, Maria, and Anastasia.

According to contemporaries, Nicholas was gentle and approachable. Those who met him easily forgot that they were face to face with the Emperor. In private life he was undemanding but had contradictions in his character, tending to weakness and inconsistency. A stubborn supporter of the right of the sovereign, despite growing pressure for revolution he did not give way on a single issue, even when common sense and circumstances demanded it. He struggled desperately to hold on to power during both the 1905 and 1917 revolutions. Freedoms accorded to people in his manifesto of October 17 1905 were soon annulled.

In foreign policy, Nicholas II took steps to stabilize the international situation, initiating two peace congresses at The Hague. During his reign Russia was involved in two wars. In 1904-5 the country suffered a heavy defeat by Japan — 400,000 men were killed, wounded or captured, and material losses were valued at 2.5 billion gold roubles. Even greater losses, however, were suffered in the First World War which Russia entered on the Allied side on August 1 1914.

Loss of territory, massive casualties, and confusion at home were the main reasons for the Second Russian Revolution in February 1917. On March 2 1917 Nicholas II abdicated.

After the abdication the royal family first remained in Czarskoe Selo then, by decision of the interim government, were transported to Tobolsk in Siberia. In April 1918 the Bolshevik government decided to move the Imperial family to Ekaterinburg in the Urals. Here they were all shot on July 17 1918. The bodies were hidden and have only recently been found and identified.

THE CONSECRATION
OF THE CZAR

✣

On July 11 1613 the solemn ceremony of the consecration of the Czar was held in the Moscow Kremlin, ancient residence of the Russian sovereigns. The new Czar was the first member of the new ruling dynasty, sixteen-year-old Mikhail Feodorovich Romanov.

The night before the ceremony long services were held in churches and monasteries. In the morning brightly dressed crowds filled the streets and squares of the Kremlin to witness the spectacle. At midday Mikhail made his way to the Gold Chamber. This was one of the ceremonial halls of the royal residence, renowned for its bright wall hangings. Here his retinue put on their golden robes. Then he summoned his closest boyars to await the moment when the young man would receive the blessing of the Church and become the ruler of the great Orthodox state.

Preparations for the ceremony were under way in the gold-domed Dormition (Uspenskii) Cathedral; this was the most important religious edifice in all Russia, the scene of ceremonies of state. The way was laid with broadcloth and red velvet. A lectern draped in rich cloth stood in the center of the cathedral for the royal regalia. Beside it on a dais was a throne, faced with gold and studded with precious stones, presented to Czar Boris Godunov by the Persian Sheikh Abbas. The Metropolitan's chair was placed nearby, and two benches for the clergy flanked the dais.

The festive decoration of the cathedral was now complete: brilliant frescoes, icons in glittering frames, cloth of gold, golden sacred vessels inlaid with enamel and jewels.

The first to enter the cathedral were senior clerics in heavy vestments. The Metropolitan, arrayed in his most sacred robes, approached the altar and began to prepare for the solemn act. A second group of holy men processed slowly to the Royal Treasury and collected the royal regalia. They, too, were attired in luxurious robes embroidered with pearls. The procession was led by the Czar's confessor, supported on either side by two deacons. The post of confessor was traditionally held by the senior priest of the Annunciation (Blagoveshchenskii) Cathedral, the private church of the royal family. On his head he bore a golden paten draped with rich cloth, and containing the Cross of Life, the crown and the *barmy* (regalia collar). Behind him, holding the jeweled sceptre, came Prince Dmitrii Mikhailovich Pozharskii, who had recently led the Russian people in their struggle against foreign oppressors. He was followed by boyars bearing the orb and other articles of the royal regalia. In the Dormition Cathedral these were placed on the lectern and covered with a rich cloth.

On the square outside, orderly columns of *strel'tsy* (royal guards) cleared a path through the crowd from the royal residence to the cathedral. The air was filled with the joyful ringing of the Kremlin bells as the Czar and his retinue emerged from the Gold Chamber and the solemn procession moved slowly towards the cathedral. As he entered, Mikhail kissed the ancient icons and the tombs of the saints. Solemn prayers were said to the Holy Trinity and the Mother of God. This was followed by a prayer to St Peter, the first Moscow Metropolitan, who in 1325 had moved to Moscow from the ancient Russian town of Vladimir. He had supported the claims of the Muscovy Princes to be rulers of the lands of Russia. From that time the saint was considered the defender of the Muscovy state: the consecration ceremony began with an appeal to

✣

Procession with regalia to the Dormition Cathedral

him for protection and patronage

After the prayers Mikhail mounted the dais. Reverently the people listened to the words of the young Czar. He spoke of the sanctity and inviolability of the Russian throne which, from the time of the legendary Riurik, had been occupied by his ancestors, the Kiev, Vladimir and Muscovy Great Princes. In accordance with the ancient custom of all ruling dynasties, Mikhail asserted the legitimacy of his sacred right to the throne. He reminded the people of his hereditary links with the family of Ivan the Terrible and that, as nephew of the childless Czar Feodor Ivanovich, he had been elected to the throne "by a nephew's rights."

The Czar's words were followed by those of the Metropolitan. He recognized the legitimacy of the election of Mikhail Feodorovich Romanov. With anguish in his voice, the Metropolitan spoke of the recent profanation of Russian soil by the enemy, and the destruction of the Royal Treasury which had contained royal articles acquired from ancient times by the sovereigns of Russia. Turning to the young Mikhail, the Metropolitan called on him to defend the Christian faith and to be "pure and steadfast" in his rule, to love and

respect his brothers, and to be "gracious, welcoming and candid towards his subjects."

The solemn ceremony of the consecration now began. It was, in the words of the young Czar, to be conducted "according to our royal rank and property" – that is, according to ancient custom.

The ritual dated to the end of the fifteenth century, the time of the Great Prince Ivan III (1462–1505), whose long reign had seen the final liberation of Rus´ from the yoke of the Mongol Tartars. The unification of the Russian lands around Moscow, which had begun at the end of the fourteenth century, was now completed with the formation of a single state. Moscow's claim of supremacy over all the lands of Russia was reflected in the title of Ivan III, who named himself "Sovereign of All Rus´." In this way he underlined that he was not only the eldest brother of the appanage princes but also their ruler.

The fifteenth century also witnessed another important historical event that influenced the young Russian state. In 1453 Byzantium fell to the Turks, and Rus´ declared itself the direct and legitimate inheritor of the Byzantine Empire. This claim was strength-

ened when, in 1472, Ivan III married Sophia Palaeologus, the niece of the last Byzantine Emperor. In 1497 the Byzantine emblem of the two-headed eagle was added to the seal of the Great Prince. This was to remain the emblem of the Russian state for more than four hundred years.

The ceremony of the consecration followed the Byzantine mode, which itself had its roots in the ceremony of the accession to the throne of the Roman Emperors. The coronation of the Byzantine Emperors had undergone a significant change in the middle of the fifth century, when the Patriarch began to participate in the ceremony; later, from the tenth century, it became a purely religious ceremony. The first celebration in Russia took place in 1498 under Ivan III when the Great Prince, who had lost his eldest son from his first marriage, declared his grandson Dmitrii as his heir. In order to secure Dmitrii's succession, Ivan deposed Prince Vasilii, son of Sophia Palaeologus. Dmitrii, however, was soon removed from real power and two years later, together with his mother, was put in prison, where he remained to his death. Despite this inauspicious end to his reign, the consecration

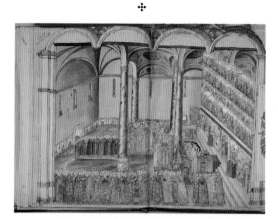

Consecration of Czar Mikhail Feodorovich in the Dormition Cathedral

of Dmitrii remained significant as the first of its kind in Russian history.

The first ceremony was conducted by the Metropolitan in the Dormition Cathedral of the Moscow Kremlin. Having made the sign of the cross over Dmitrii, he handed the crown and *barmy* to Ivan III, who placed them on his grandson Dmitrii. From then on, these precious objects came to symbolize supreme power in the Muscovy state. According to literature of the time, these were reputed to be gifts from the Byzantine Emperor Constantine Monomachus to his grandson, the Kiev Prince Vladimir Monomach, as a reward for a successful campaign in Thrace.

This legend was of particular relevance during the reign of Ivan III, as it embodied the Muscovy state's claim to be the inheritor of Byzantium, and consequently of the Roman Empire – which was expressed in the dictum "Moscow is the third Rome." The legend was also a means of connecting the Moscow dynasty of the Riuriks with its predecessors, the Kiev Princes and Vladimir Monomach. Thus it gave the Riuriks a claim to all the Old Russian lands.

From a historical point of view,

however, the legend is clearly inauthentic, since Constantine died when his grandson was two years old; he could hardly have rewarded his grandson for a military victory. The legend, however, lived on in the name of the crown of the Russian sovereigns, which became known as the "Cap of Monomach."

The source of the legend is not known. The first mention of the Cap of Monomach as a gift from the Byzantine Emperor comes in the deeds of Ivan IV. It is possible, however, that the golden cap had been the property of the Muscovy Prince Ivan Kalita from the beginning of the fourteenth century, and had been passed down through the line of the Muscovy Princes.

The ceremony of the consecration of the Czar developed over subsequent centuries without any significant changes. During the consecration of the first Russian Czar, Ivan the Terrible, in addition to the *barmy* and the Cap of Monomach, the Czar was presented with a cross, also said to be Constantine's, and a golden chain. Thereafter the sceptre became part of the royal regalia, and under Boris Godunov the regalia was also supplemented by the orb.

The consecration of Czar Mikhail

Feodorovich began when the Cross of Life was hung around his neck. During the reading of the prayers the Czar was adorned with the *barmy*, made of large badges with portraits of the saints; the Cap of Monomach was placed on his head, the sceptre in his right hand and the orb in his left. During the ceremony the Czar wore full royal costume. In accordance with Russian tradition, in which it was considered inappropriate to wear only one garment, the royal attire always consisted of several pieces of clothing worn one on top of the other. The garments were made of brocade, velvet, and satin, and were richly encrusted with pearls and other precious stones.

Documents of the time enable us to recreate the attire of the Russian Czar in the seventeenth century. We know that during his passage from the Granovitaya Palace (Palace of Facets) to the Dormition Cathedral for the consecration ceremony, Feodor Alexeevich wore a tall fur cap and a cloak with sleeves stretching to the ground over his shoulders. The cloak was made of light silver brocade with gold braid, decorated with emerald buttons, and bordered and hemmed with rows of pearls. A caftan of rich gold silk, decorated with red satin and embroidered with pearls, was visible beneath the cloak. The sleeves of the caftan were short and broad, bordered with pearls and gold badges set with diamonds, rubies, and emeralds. A coat of light snow-white taffeta was worn beneath the caftan. Diamonds in gold mounts decorated the borders of its long, narrow sleeves. The silver and gold cloth of the Czar's trousers matched the brocade of the cloak. The costume was completed by boots of bright red velvet decorated with pearls and studs containing diamonds, rubies, and emeralds. In the Dormition Cathedral, instead of his cloak, the Czar wore a *platno*, or state robe, of orange velvet with flowers in high relief; this too was decorated with pearls and precious stones. In place of the fur cap the Czar wore a golden crown set with diamonds, rubies, emeralds, and pearls.

In describing the attire of the Russian Czar during the ceremony, a foreign guest wrote, "one small part of this magnificence would have been enough to adorn ten sovereigns." The ceremonial attire of the Czar was also remarkable for its immense weight. Attendants supported the sovereign under his arms as he made his way into the cathedral.

The ceremony concluded with the anointing, which signified the holy patronage of the new Czar and the sacred nature of his power.

After the consecration, Mikhail emerged onto the square and walked towards the Archangel Cathedral, the necropolis of the Russian Great Princes and Czars. Here he kissed the graves of his ancestors, vowing to protect the ancient foundations of the Russian land. He then visited his private church, the Annunciation Cathedral, and on his way was showered with golden coins.

The young Mikhail Feodorovich was now Czar, and his descendants were destined to hold sway over this mighty country for more than three centuries.

M. V. Martynova

SAKKOS (DALMATIC) OF THE PATRIARCH FILARET
(PATRIARCH 1619-1633)

✛

LOOPED BROCADE: ITALY 17TH CENTURY

EMBROIDERY: MOSCOW, KREMLIN WORKSHOPS,

FIRST HALF OF 17TH CENTURY

BROCADE, VELVET, PEARLS, GOLD THREAD, GOLD

L. 134 CM

INV. NO TK-18

The patriarch Filaret is a figure of particular importance among the leading members of the Russian clergy, since he was not only the head of the Russian Orthodox Church under Czar Alexei Mikhailovich, but was also the Czar's natural father. After he assumed the office of Patriarch in 1619, Filaret became joint ruler with his son, the young Czar. He took an active role in decisions of both internal and foreign policy of the Russian state. Decrees and resolutions of the supreme powers at this time were issued jointly by the Czar and the Patriarch, and both had the title of "Great Sovereign". Documents concerning state affairs were also heard by both the Czar and the Patriarch, while the latter sat at the right hand of the Czar during receptions for foreign emissaries. The Patriarch Filaret had great political experience, and was also a gifted statesman. Not only did he participate directly in the affairs of state, he was also largely responsible for Czar Mikhail Feodorovich's becoming head of the Russian state. It is possible that one of the ways in which the Czar expressed his gratitude to his father was through the creation of a range of church vestments, undertaken in the Czarina's workshops especially for the Patriarch by royal decree. This *sakkos*, or dalmatic, was part of this collection from 1631, as is indicated by the inscription, woven in small pearls along the upper rim of the shoulder piece.

Later, during the renovation of the Patriarch's vestry undertaken by the Patriarch Nikon in the 1650s, the pearl embroidery which adorns the shoulders, armlets, sides and hem of the dalmatic was reapplied to new cloth. This new cloth was gilt looped brocade, with a rich design of stylized acanthus leaves and stems with flowers. It is in this renovated form that we see the dalmatic today.

PORTRAIT OF CZAR MIKHAIL FEODOROVICH

✥

RUSSIA, MID-18TH CENTURY

UNKNOWN ARTIST

OIL ON CANVAS

INV. NO. ZH-1960

This portrait of Czar Mikhail Feodorovich in a *platno* (robe) with *barmy* (regalia collar), holding an orb and sceptre, was painted in the middle of the eighteenth century. In style it might be said to be archaic for its time. Portraits of this type, which first appeared at the court of the early Romanovs, are known in the history of Russian art by the term *parsuna* (a corruption of the Latin *persona*). The style of this *parsuna* of Mikhail Feodorovich is closely linked with the techniques of icon painting. This is shown by the conventional composition of the work, the lack of movement in the pose, the general lack of perspective, and the dominance of outline over modeling. There are, however, clear differences between this portrait and an icon.

The work of the icon painter is oriented towards the spiritual world; he creates religious images of Christian saints, ignoring their actual features. This painter, on the other hand, portrays his contemporary, and tries to convey a likeness of his model. This change in approach was brought about by the many commissions for *parsuny* from members of the royal court and high-ranking boyars. As a result, the secular portrait became a very widespread and popular genre of Russian art from the end of the Middle Ages.

The grand royal portrait also glorified its subject, another reason for commissioning such a work. Portraits were painted not only of Mikhail Feodorovich and his son Alexei Mikhailovich, but also of their predecessors on the Russian throne. Many examples exist of the iconographic group to which this portrait belongs: miniatures for heraldic and genealogical books and nineteenth-century albums of lithographs; illustrations for calendars which are still printed to this day; paintings for the decoration of royal palaces, the homes of nobles, and public buildings. A nineteenth-century exhibition of royal regalia in the Armory is known to have contained, among other royal paintings, a portrait of Mikhail Feodorovich similar to this one.

The commemorative nature of such portraits upheld the idea of the supremacy of the rule of the Russian sovereigns; they also formed a political chronicle "in faces," adding a personal touch to the history of the state.

PECTORAL CROSS
✤

MOSCOW, KREMLIN WORKSHOPS, 1662
GOLD, PRECIOUS STONES, ENAMEL
H. 15.6 CM, W.10.7 CM
INV. NO. R-13/1-2

In the seventeenth century the pectoral cross was an integral part of royal dress worn at solemn state ceremonies, including the consecration of the Czar. The face of the cross is decorated with fine diamonds in beautiful mounts, and with images of Christian feast days. These are made from strikingly colored translucent enamel, so that the cross seems to sparkle like a mosaic. The cool luster of the diamonds set in the monogram of Christ and the frame of the cross are brought out by the wide range of colors in the enamel. There are also enamel compositions beneath the diamond cross. In the middle of these is the date 1662, evidently that of the manufacture of the cross. On the reverse side of the cross there is a figure of St Theodore the Recruit, the patron saint of Czar Feodor Alexeevich, set in an enamel design. This portrait was presumably added to the cross during Feodor's reign.

Of particular interest is the presence on the cross of both Russian and Greek inscriptions, which is evidence of the participation of foreign craftsmen in its manufacture. Documents show that in the 1670s Greek jewelers were invited to Moscow from Istanbul. They worked in the Kremlin workshops for several years, undertaking commissions from the royal court.

ICON AND CROSS
✤

CROSS: MOSCOW, 16TH CENTURY (?)
ICON: MOSCOW, KREMLIN WORKSHOPS,
FIRST QUARTER OF 17TH CENTURY
SILVER-GILT, PRECIOUS STONES, PEARLS, WOOD
H. 28.3 CM, W. 19.7 CM
INV. NO. MR-1059/1-3

This silver-gilt icon is, with good reason, given pride of place in the 1642 description of the "Great Treasury," where the most historic and artistically important articles for use in court ceremony were kept. It holds an Orthodox double-armed cross in a frame of gold set with precious stones and pearls. This cross was among the most highly valued artefacts in the Treasury since, according to legend, it was made of the wood of the True Cross. It was presented to Czar Mikhail Feodorovich on his accession to the throne, and it may have been used at the coronations of the Moscow Sovereigns in the sixteenth century.

At the beginning of the seventeenth century an icon was made to protect the cross. The icon contains blackened images of Christian feast days, along with carved figures of the Byzantine Emperor Constantine the Great and his mother Helena who, according to legend, discovered the True Cross. Thereafter, according to official Russian accounts, part of the sacred wood was sent to Rus´.

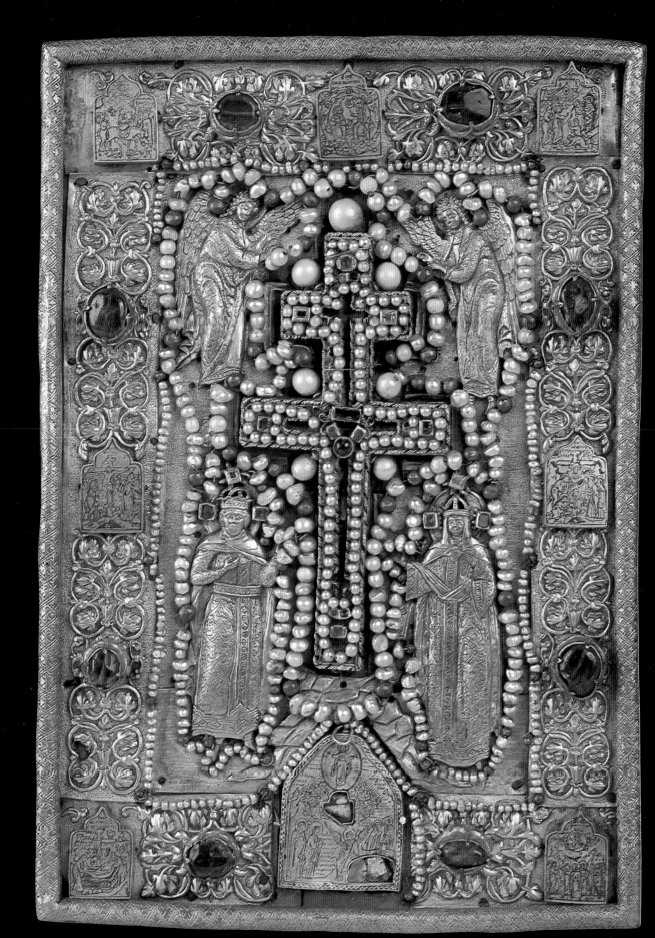

STATE ROBE OF PETER THE GREAT: PLATNO

✛

MOSCOW, KREMLIN WORKSHOPS, 17TH CENTURY

BROCADE: ITALY, 17TH CENTURY

LACE: WESTERN EUROPE, 17TH CENTURY

BROCADE, LACE, TAFFETA, BRAID

L. 158 CM

TK-2849

The *platno* or state robe – the most important article of royal ceremonial dress – is first referred to in 1628; thereafter, until the end of the seventeenth century, it was used at the most important of official ceremonies, the consecration of the Czar. The basic cut of the robe is directly comparable to that of the dalmatic, the ceremonial dress of Byzantine Emperors. After the Moscow Czars declared themselves the inheritors of the Byzantine imperial dynasty, they adopted the form of its ceremonial dress along with its rites. Royal state robes were made of brocade, predominantly gold in color as a symbol of royal power and wealth.

The state robe of Peter the Great was the last of the state robes to be made. It is reputed to have been remade from the robe of his father Czar Alexei Mikhailovich. The material is Italian brocade, which was known in Russia as *aksamit*. The gold cloth of the robe bears striking foliate ornament, containing images of crowns. This is set off by a red border. Appliqué ornaments punctuate the smooth gold surface. Originally, according to documents, the robe had golden buttons inlaid with emeralds and rubies, and a sable border. Now only the gold lace that runs along the hem and cuffs of the robe remains. Traditionally, the state robe did not reach to the floor, allowing the richly decorated ceremonial shoes of the Czar to remain visible. The robe, 158 cm in length, gives a good idea of the height of the young Peter, who was unusually tall for his time and who grew to 6ft 8in (2.04m).

Barmy (regalia collar) of
Czar Alexei Mikhailovich

Moscow, Kremlin Workshops, 17th century
Silk, gold and silk thread,
l. 171.5 cm, w. 24 cm
Inv. No. TK-2858

The *barmy*, a broad detachable collar, was worn over the ceremonial robe. It was part of the official dress of the Moscow Princes, and later of the Czars. As a mark of honor, the *barmy* was first used for the accession to the throne in 1498 of Dmitrii, the youngest grandson of the great Muscovy Prince Ivan III. There were two main types: the more traditional *barmy* consisted of separate badges, sewn together or attached to a textile backing; another type was made of a single piece of embroidered cloth.

The *barmy* of Czar Alexei Mikhailovich is made of violet-gray satin, now faded; it is in the shape of a gorget (shoulder guard), with a slit at the right shoulder, and embroidered with gold and silk thread. The badges are in the form of icon frames, and portray the Deesis – Christ flanked by the Mother of God and John the Baptist, a traditional composition in Christian iconography, symbolizing prayer and intercession. The smaller round badges have half-length portraits of the saints whose namesakes were members of the

Romanov dynasty. St Alexis, 'Man of God', for Czar Alexei, and St Michael Malein for the Czar's father, Mikhail Feodorovich. A wide ornamental band runs around the edge of the *barmy*. The faces and arms of the saints are embroidered in silk, the remainder in gold thread with brightly colored applique work. Originally the band running around the bottom edge of the *barmy* was decorated with pearls and diamond-shaped studs.

STAFF

✠

MOSCOW, KREMLIN WORKSHOPS,
FIRST QUARTER OF 17TH CENTURY
SILVER-GILT, PRECIOUS STONES, WOOD
L. 137 CM
INV. NO. MR-5789

The staff was an integral part of the regalia of the Muscovy Princes, and later of the Czars. In the sixteenth and seventeenth centuries it became an essential element in court ceremonies. In 1613 Mikhail Romanov signalled his acceptance of the Russian throne by receiving the royal staff from the hands of the Archimandrite Feodorit of Riazan in the cathedral church of the Ipatievskii Monastery.

During the ceremony of the consecration of the Czar the staff was given to the monarch on his passage from the Granovitaya Palace to the Dormition Cathedral, and when he visited the Annunciation and Archangel Cathedrals after putting on the royal regalia. A large number of different royal staffs were kept in the Kremlin Treasury, among the articles of "ancient royal rank." This staff is mentioned as among their number. It is made of silver-gilt, decorated with fine sapphires and trefoils flat-chased on a smooth ground. The first owner of the staff may have been Czar Mikhail Feodorovich Romanov. It is also possible that this is the staff which is mentioned in records for May 16 1613, where an order is given for the manufacture of several precious articles to be supplied to the Czar including "a staff to be covered with silver; the silver work should be finely gilded."

CROWN OF PETER THE GREAT:
"THE CAP OF MONOMACH
OF THE SECOND ORDER"

✠

MOSCOW, KREMLIN WORKSHOPS, 1682
GOLD, SILVER, PRECIOUS STONES, CLOTH, SABLE
H. 20.3 CM
INV. NO. R-7

The title of the crown stems from an episode at the end of the seventeenth century. After Czar Feodor Alexeevich died without issue in April 1682, the throne should have passed to his brother, the fourteen-year-old Ivan Alexeevich. The Czarevich, however, was mentally incompetent, and the Boyars' Duma therefore proclaimed Peter Alexeevich Czar at the age of ten. Peter Alexeevich was the younger brother of Feodor and Ivan. Ivan, however, had the support of the armed forces and one of the most powerful groups of nobles; they decided that both brothers should be crowned together, and forced the Boyars' Duma to declare Ivan Czar alongside Peter. At the coronation of the Czareviches the ancient Cap of Monomach was placed on the head of the elder Ivan, and a "Cap of Monomach of the Second Order" was specially made for the younger Peter.

The craftsmen who made this second crown closely recreated the original. The form of both the new and the old crowns is reminiscent of Eastern headgear. Both are made of eight gold plates, and are topped with a hemispherical knop with a cross. Like all Russian royal crowns they are trimmed with sable, a fur with an ancient ritual significance and a symbol of prosperity and wealth.

CHAIN

✛

MOSCOW, KREMLIN WORKSHOPS, 17TH CENTURY

GOLD

DIAM. OF RING 36 MM

INV. NO. R-23

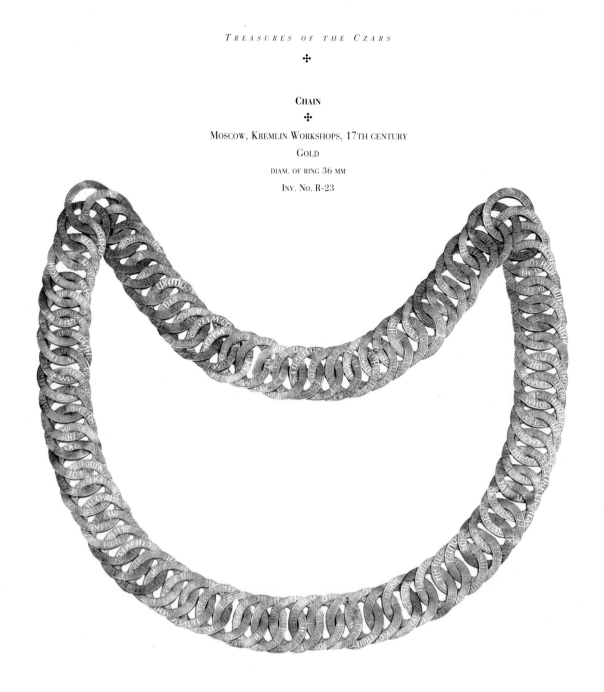

In the Middle Ages, long gold chains were an essential part of parade attire for Princes and Czars. According to Russian legends, the first royal chain was brought to Rus´ among the regalia presented to the Russian sovereign by the Byzantine Emperor Constantine Monomachus. It is clear from ancient ecclesiastical writings and from wills made by the Princes of the Riurik dynasty that by the beginning of the fourteenth century gold chains were one of the first items to be passed on to the eldest son. In the sixteenth and seventeenth centuries chains were an essential part of the 'Grand Regalia' – the ceremonial articles used at the consecration of the Czar and at other solemn state ceremonies.

Surviving seventeenth-century chains consist of great flat rings, often decorated with niello, filigree, and enamel. The gold chain of Czar Mikhail Feodorovich is perhaps the most interesting among them. The title of the first member of the Romanov dynasty, and the date of his accession to the throne, is engraved on each of its eighty-eight rings.

ORB

✛

ISTANBUL, 1662

GOLD, PRECIOUS STONES, ENAMEL

H. 29.2 CM

INV. NO. R-16

The orb was an important article in the state regalia, symbolizing earthly power. The globe is set with elegant designs of sapphires, rubies, and diamonds. This orb was made in Istanbul on the orders of Czar Alexei Mikhailovich, at the same time as the wonderful *barmy* (regalia collar) (see page 45).

The making of these articles was decreed by an act of state. By the middle of the seventeenth century Russia was becoming a mighty power. At the same time, a political theory which had originated in the fifteenth century, and which saw Muscovite Rus´ as successor to the Byzantine Empire, was gaining popularity. Czar Alexei Mikhailovich, who came to the throne in 1645, saw his mission as the unification of the Orthodox world.

Alexei considered himself the rightful successor of the Byzantine Emperors, and strove to re-enact their rituals at his court. He insisted that the sacred book used in the coronations of Byzantine Emperors be brought to Moscow. Clearly the same political motive led him to commission an orb and *barmy* from Istanbul, to be copied from the regalia of "the devout Greek King Constantine." This commission was assigned to the Greek Ivan Iur´ev, who had spent many years in the diplomatic service of the Russian court. The making of such valuable items was vastly expensive; Ivan Iur´ev informed the Czar that he would have not only to take out an enormous loan, but also to mortgage his home and all his property. The artefacts were the work of Greek craftsmen, who combined the forms and decorative motifs of Turkish design with the delicacy of Byzantine jewelry.

EAGLE PENDANT

✣

MOSCOW, KREMLIN WORKSHOPS,
SECOND HALF OF 17TH CENTURY
GOLD, PRECIOUS STONES, ENAMEL
11 x 9.5 CM
INV. NO. MR-2456

This gold pendant is in the form of a two-headed eagle, the emblem of Russia, wearing a coronation crown. The front is decorated with emeralds and rubies, and the plumage on the reverse side is made of white and black enamel. Gold rings are soldered on to the heads of the eagle, showing that it was hung on a chain over ceremonial robes.

Several features suggest that this is the work of Kremlin jewelers of the second half of the seventeenth century. These include the combination of green and red semiprecious stones, the use of painted enamel alongside translucent colored enamel, and the way the stones are mounted. There are no other surviving pendants from the seventeenth century or, indeed, from the preceding or following cen-

turies. The unique nature of the object, and the richness of its artistry and materials, suggest that it belonged to a member of the royal family.

The Byzantine two-headed eagle, first used as a Russian state emblem at the end of the fifteenth century, underwent several changes. The position of its wings altered, the number of crowns above the heads was increased from one to three, and it gained an orb and sceptre in its claws, and a shield with the figure of St George, the emblem of Moscow, on its breast. Even eagles of the same period

sometimes differed from one another. In 1856 the emblem underwent significant reworking, and from that time until 1917 the representation of the eagle was strictly regulated. It became the centerpiece of a new state emblem of extreme complexity, which included other emblems such as the griffin of the Romanov family, and symbols of newly-acquired states and lands of Russia.

The transitional government which came to power after the February revolution of 1917 and the abdication of Nicholas II continued to use the two-headed eagle as the state emblem, but the symbols of monarchy – the crowns, orb and sceptre – were removed. After the October revolution of 1917 the eagle was abolished until 1993, when once again it became the emblem of Russia.

TAPESTRY: THE ELECTION OF
MIKHAIL FEODOROVICH AS CZAR

✣

RUSSIA, ST. PETERSBURG TAPESTRY
MANUFACTORY, BEFORE 1828
MASTER S. GRIGORIEV, AFTER A PAINTING
BY G. I. UGRIUMOV
WOOL, SILK
276 X 355 CM
INV. NO. TK-2970

This magnificent work is one of the finest examples of Russian tapestry weaving.

Grigorii Ivanovich Ugriumov (1764-1823) was a leading Russian historical painter. His original painting was executed in 1799-1800 by order of Paul I for the Mikhailovskii Fortress in St. Petersburg. The artist painted the sixteen-year-old Mikhail in the center of the composition, inside a church with the iconostasis in the background. Mikhail's mother, Martha the Nun, stands beside him, and the Archbishop Feodorit of Murom-Riazan faces him, dressed in sacred robes. In the foreground are the historical figures who persuaded the unwilling Mikhail to become Czar: F. I. Sheremetev, who brings the Cap of Monomach, the sceptre, and the gold cross to the Czar; and Prince V. I. Bekhtiarov-Rostovskii, who carries the orb. The Archimandrite Avraamii of the Chudov Monastery in a mitre and chasuble, and the abbot Avraamii Palitsyn of the Troitse-Sergiev Monastery, stand on the right of the composition. On the left stands a group of people of different ranks, in clothes of classical style to which the artist has introduced elements of seventeenth-century Russian national dress.

Tapestry weaving in Russia dates from 1715-16, when master craftsmen from the Gobelins tapestry workshops in Paris came to St. Petersburg. Established in 1717 by Peter I, the St. Petersburg Tapestry Manufactory was also a school for Russian apprentices, and by 1730 all the work at the workshop – which included descriptive and ornamental tapestries, portraits, emblems, fire screens, and covers for furniture – was being done by Russian weavers.

The tapestry was made in St. Petersburg by Stepan Grigoriev during the years of patriotic fervour which followed victory over Napoleon in 1812. At this time themes from Russian history and images of the unity of the Czar and his people were particularly popular. In 1831 it was sent to Moscow as decoration for the interior of the Petrovskii fortress. There is a copy of this tapestry in the Württemberg Museum in Germany.

PRIVATE LIFE OF THE CZARS IN THE SEVENTEENTH CENTURY

✤

The private life of members of the royal household in the seventeenth century was strictly regimented. Events in the life of the royal family were considered of great significance to the state, and were accompanied by a ceremonial which had been carefully established in the preceding centuries.

The birth of royal offspring, and most of all of the Czareviches – the heirs to the throne – was a particularly solemn event. In ancient Rus´ a woman's principal role was to produce children. There was no greater misfortune for a royal wife than the lack of an heir, and particular a male heir. Inability to conceive was considered shameful and sinful, and often brought personal disaster: Czarinas who did not have children were forcibly committed to nunneries. Royal wives who were unable to have children used to wear themselves out with fasting while "with mighty weeping and wailing and frenzy" they prayed God to deliver them of a son. One can imagine, then, what rejoicing greeted the birth of a child, and particularly of a son.

According to Russian tradition, immediately after the birth of a Czarevich his measurements were taken; an icon of his patron saint was then commissioned in this exact size. This work was normally undertaken by a well known icon painter from the Kremlin workshops. A few hours after the birth of the Czarevich the whole court, in brightly colored clothes suitable for the occasion, gathered to give thanks in the Dormition Cathedral. The Czar then made a tour of the Kremlin churches and monasteries to receive congratulations. A few days later, a "Birth Feast" was held in the Granovitaya Palace. This was notable for its abundance of sweet dishes, meats and vegetables. An inordinate amount of imagination and craftsmanship went into the preparation of this feast. Thus, for example, at the birth of Peter I, the table was laid with "a large sugar honey cake in the form of the emblem of the Muscovy State, a big sugar head with colored decoration weighing 2 poods and 20 pounds, a large white molded sugar eagle, and a large red sugar eagle with orbs weighing 1.5 poods each, a molded sugar swan weighing 2 poods, a molded sugar duck weighing 20 pounds, a molded sugar tortoise weighing 10 pounds, a molded sugar dove weighing 8 pounds, a sugar model of the Kremlin with horsemen and footsoldiers, a large tower with an eagle, a smaller tower with an eagle, and a four-cornered town with cannon", and many other wonders of the culinary art. A pood was roughly 36 lb (16 kg), so the sugar head weighed 92 lb (42 kg).

The christening of the Czarevich was also attended by considerable extravagance. Historical sources give conflicting accounts as to how many days after the birth this took place. In the fourteenth and fifteenth centuries the Czarevich was normally christened when he was five to fourteen days old. In the seventeenth century it is clear that the time of the christening was not strictly defined; some writers say that it took place on the eighth day and others on the fortieth day.

The ceremony normally took place in the church of the Chudov monastery in the Kremlin. The royal children were brought here in a fine sleigh or carriage with seat and cushions bordered with gold brocade. The godparents were the child's nursemaid and his elder sister or aunt. After the christening, according to Orthodox tradition, a few locks of the baby's hair were wound up in a piece of wax and placed for safekeeping in the cathedral to preserve the newborn from grief and suffering. The christening, like the birth, was marked by

✤

Wedding procession of Mikhail Feodorovich and Evdokia Lukianovna

a ceremonial feast and the presentation of gifts.

From his first days until the age of seven, the Czarevich was surrounded by a whole retinue of female servants who followed his every step. A wetnurse was selected from women of differing ranks, "kind, clean, healthy and rich in milk." The wetnurse lived permanently at court, feeding the child up to the age of two and a half. In return for this service her husband was awarded lands and estates, and to the end of his days was accorded various privileges.

In the seventeenth century the life of the young Czarevich was one of extreme luxury. Within a month of his birth, clothes of rich fabrics were made for him. To judge by documents of the time, by his third year he owned an enormous wardrobe consisting of clothing which, in cut and materials, corresponded exactly to adult costume. As the Czarevich grew he acquired a large number of toys. Among these were toy wooden horses on wheels covered in foal skin, drums, bells, and other miniature musical instruments such as cymbals and clavichords. Miniature carriages were also built for the royal children in which they not only traveled through the streets, but

also played in their rooms. Artists from the Kremlin drew picture books. The personal taste of the child influenced his selection of toys. Peter I, for example, from an early age, owned many weapons. According to documents of the time, he had miniature axes, maces, cannon, knives, and bows and arrows. Little banners were made for him from multicolored taffeta decorated on both sides with pictures of the sun, moon, and stars. As the Czarevich grew and began to surround himself with other young boys from the court, his collection of weapons increased considerably. These playmates were to be Peter's future companions in arms and soldiers.

Most of these toys were made in the Kremlin workshops; others were bought from foreign traders. It is known, for example, that in 1679 "a little boat, studded with stones" was bought for the seven year old Peter from a foreign tradesman. Valuable toys were also used to decorate the dressers in the child's rooms. These included silver figurines of every imaginable animal, figures of acrobats and other entertainers, and little silver ships.

At the age of six or seven the Czarevich ceased to be looked after by women

and began to live under the guardianship of men. As G. Kotoshikhin wrote in his seventeenth-century work *The Russian State*, his education and wardship was undertaken by a "high-minded, gentle and intelligent" boyar; later his teachers were "talented people, not given to insobriety," and deacons from the ambassadorial office taught him to read and write.

Up to the age of fifteen the Czarevich was surrounded only by relatives, royalty, and his tutors. He never appeared before the people. Even when the Czarevich and Czarevna went to church they were hidden from view by a linen cloth. Only when the Czarevich reached the age of fifteen was he solemnly "declared", and the people made special visits to the capital in order to look upon the future sovereign.

In ancient Rus' a man did not reach adulthood by virtue of age, but was accorded those rights only on marriage. The marriage of the Czarevich was therefore all the more important. In addition, the marriage of the heir to the throne had particular political significance in ancient Rus', since in the sixteenth and seventeenth centuries the group of people close to the Czar played a large role in the governing of the state, and these people were often relatives of the Czarina.

Until the fifteenth century the Muscovy rulers had usually married the daughters of princes, sometimes of regional origin, of noble boyars, men at arms, or Novgorod vicegerents. When the Muscovy prince declared himself the sovereign of all Rus´ such marriages became impossible, since the protocol of the time did not allow marriage with a subject. Ivan III, therefore, made his second marriage to a Greek princess, married his eldest son to the daughter of a Moldavian *voevoda* (provincial governor), and gave his daughter Elena in marriage to a Lithuanian great prince. He attempted to arrange the marriages of his other children with representatives of European ruling dynasties. This, however, turned out to be far from simple. The difference in faith represented a particular obstacle and, importantly, Europe at that time was still unfamiliar with the Muscovy state. Therefore the Muscovy rulers were forced to choose brides from among their subjects.

In such circumstances it would have been natural to marry representatives of noble families. This, however, would have led to one such family being elevated above the rest and would have created a rival to the royal family. As a result, following the tradition of the Byzantine emperors, the Russian Czars began to choose their brides from among the people. They would select from the daughters of landed gentry, paying attention only to the personal qualities of the prospective bride. By entering such a union the sovereign did not diminish his royal dignity; indeed, he placed himself above his subjects since none apart from him was able to choose his bride in this way.

The selection of the bride usually took place in several stages. First, royal representatives were sent about the country to look for suitable candidates. The most worthy of these were brought to court. Here they were viewed by those close to the sovereign; only a chosen few were brought before the groom himself.

It is known that, for his second marriage, Czar Alexei Mikhailovich chose his bride from among twenty young women. The examination lasted for more than six months until the Czar conferred his choice upon Natalia Kirillovna Naryshkina, the future mother of Peter the Great. The groom presented the girl who pleased him with a golden ring and a woven cloth which represented the act of selection. Thereafter, the girl was named the Czarevna and took her place at court. From this moment she had a special status; even her father did not have the right to call her his daughter.

The choice of the bride led to the arrival at court of relatives of the Czarevna, often members of a previously obscure family. Their arrival often brought complications; there might be a storm of intrigues, plots and disputes at court. Favorites of the royal family would try to inflict violence on the royal fiancée, particularly when she arrived at court to await the marriage ceremony. They might attempt to destroy her health or make her seem sickly, turning not only to poison but to other, more ingenious, methods. For example, when Czar Alexei Mikhailovich was preparing to marry for the first time, the boyars' wives braided the hair of the preferred girl so tightly and rammed the crown on her head with such force that she fainted. Such aspersions were then cast on the health of the bride that she was exiled from court.

The young sovereigns were often genuinely attracted to their brides, and when those around them succeeded in destroying the marriage, they often suffered great distress. Mikhail Feodorovich fell in love with a young beauty, Maria Khlopova. When courtiers declared her unhealthy after attempts to poison her, he was unable to forget her, and even seven years later had not given up hope of marrying her.

Marriage ceremonies at the Russian court were remarkable for their extreme opulence; in form they followed national traditions established over many centuries. The role of courtiers in all stages of the ceremony was carefully set out in marriage records of the seventeenth century. Particular significance was attached to the servants of honor at the marriage ceremony, since this position testified to the closeness of the courtier's relationship to the head of state.

Before the ceremony the young couple were solemnly blessed by their parents with icons of the Mother of God and the Saviour. Attendants and noblewomen dressed the bride for the ceremony and placed on her head a golden crown inlaid with precious stones and

pearls – a symbol of virginity. The regalia of the bridegroom for the ceremony was no less fine than for a coronation. Czar Mikhail Feodorovich, for example, wore a half-length sable caftan with gold brocade and a velvet coat lined with sable, with flaps thrown back over the shoulders; his belt was of solid gold. The boyars who accompanied the Czar wore silver fox fur hats and gold robes with standing or folded collars studded with pearls.

The wedding day did not simply represent a means of continuing the royal line; it was also a time of hope for a life of love and concord, particularly since the Czar had chosen his bride according to his own inclination. The state rooms were decorated for the occasion: every wall was hung with icons draped with pearl veils. These icons contained images of the saints, and the bride and groom prayed to them for a happy marriage.

Before the wedding ceremony, the Czar and Czarevna went to the Granovitaya Palace where, according to Russian tradition, their hair was combed and dipped in liquid honey. A wedding headdress was placed on the Czarevna's head and her face was covered with a veil woven with pearls and precious stones.

The young couple were then showered with golden coins, and grain and hops symbolizing fertility.

A special seat covered in sable and with a velvet canopy was set up in the Granovitaya Palace for the bride and groom. According to folk custom, sitting on fur promised wealth and plenty to the young couple. Nearby stood a table covered with three tablecloths; at given moments during the ceremony, the cloths were removed one by one. On the table stood a special loaf which was offered to the bridegroom and boyars before the marriage, and a saltcellar.

A large number of courtiers took part in the marriage ceremony, each with his or her own particular role. These included the matchmakers, the confidants of the bride and groom, the wedding sponsors, the so-called "sitting" boyars and boyarinas who formed a special honorary council in the state rooms. Another group of boyars made up the wedding train and accompanied the bride and groom on their procession. The entourage also included the loaf carriers, who bore special round loaves wrapped in precious cloth on velvet-covered trays; the candle bearers with delicate wedding

Bedchamber of the newly-wed Mikhail Feodorovich and Evdokia Lukianovna

candles and the heavy candles of the sovereign and his bride, decorated with gilded rings; lamplighters; and others.

Particular significance was attached to the role of those who guarded the route of the bride and groom, ensuring that no one could cross it. Superstition was widespread in Rus´. For this reason, as one foreign visitor wrote at the beginning of the seventeenth century, "no wedding may be conducted without the help of the most skilled sorcerers who abound in this country, where anyone wishing to harm another always turns to wizardry. The wedding is seen as a particular opportunity for causing harm to the newlyweds and their friends. This is why the newlyweds always have a sorceress at their side who never leaves them and tries to undo the evil spells of their enemies."

The bride was carried to the Dormition Cathedral in a sleigh, while the Czar rode on a horse of the Argamak breed. The place of each participant in the ceremony was strictly defined.

After the wedding the young couple and their guests were entertained in the Granovitaya Palace. The bride and groom sat at a table without eating anything, although, at the beginning of the third course, a chicken was placed in front of them. For Russians, as for other nations, a swan or chicken was a symbol of wedded love. The Czar's witness then wrapped up the chicken in a cloth, together with some salt and bread, and carried it into the bedroom.

The bridal bed, in simple folk tradition, was made of sheaves of rye, wheat, and barley. In the royal palace, however, these were covered with a carpet and a down quilt. The sheaves augured wealth and plenty in the home. Two thick candles were placed on the bedhead, one for the sovereign and one for his bride. A tub filled with wheat was placed by the bed, along with a large cross and icons of the birth of Christ and the birth of the Virgin. A horseguard rode all night outside the bedchamber with drawn sword to protect the young people from harm and evil spells.

In the days following the wedding, tables were set up in the chambers of the Czar and Czarina. Here were displayed the many gifts presented to the couple by their subjects.

Sad events in the life of the ruling dynasty were also marked with a carefully defined ritual. When a member of the royal family "left this earthly kingdom for the eternal happiness of the kingdom of heaven," the event was signalled by a slow ringing of the church bells. This tolling had particular significance for the Russian people and was regarded with extreme reverence. Joyful ceremonies were accompanied by ceaseless peals which so filled the air that, according to visitors, it was impossible to hear one's own voice.

When a Czar died, his courtiers kissed his hand and bade him farewell. His body was then wrapped in costly cloth and placed in a coffin lined with cloth of gold. Those closest to the Czar, the "Chamber Boyars," then bore the coffin away and placed it on a specially prepared sleigh which was covered with a rich pall and strewn with branches. It was carried to the necropolis of the Moscow sovereigns at the Archangel Cathedral. Several hundred monks and priests holding candles lined the funeral route. Clergy walked in front of the coffin carrying crosses and icons. A precious icon was carried on top of the coffin and was then placed beside the tomb. The icon painted at the time of the Czar's birth (the so-called "measured icon") was brought to

✜

the tomb, along with an icon of the Czar's patron saint. The latter icon was normally painted after the consecration of the Czar and until his death was held in the Annunciation Cathedral, the royal family's private church.

The Czar's widow took part in the funeral procession. She was carried on a special litter and was followed by relatives and other courtiers dressed in mourning. Until the end of the seventeenth century, mourning weeds in Rus´ were of dark cerise, deep violet and dark green. By the end of the century black robes were increasingly common at funeral ceremonies.

Large crowds of ordinary people, "with great sobbing and wailing," accompanied the Czar on his final journey. Violent expressions of grief not only reflected the emotional character of the Russian people but were also dictated by custom. Women and girls wept; some beat their breasts, others clutched their foreheads as they fell on the tomb chanting ancient folk lamentations. In 1715, however, on the death of his sister-in-law Martha Matveevna, Peter the Great forbade chanting, howling, and wailing on the tomb of the deceased.

A large number of singers took part in the funeral procession. Their mournful, protracted melodies accompanied the Czar on his final journey and resounded about the Cathedral during the requiem. On the third day after the funeral, memorial feasts were held in all the monasteries and churches of Russia. For forty days after the funeral courtiers stood guard over the Czar's tomb day and night, and memorial services were held.

The wake for the dead was a custom strictly observed by the Romanovs. Homage was paid to the memory not only of members of the family but also of all past Muscovy rulers. Particular reverence was accorded to the murdered son of Ivan the Terrible, Czarevich Dmitrii, who had been canonized by the Russian Orthodox church.

As dictated by Orthodox tradition, a special dish was prepared for the burial and the wake: a porridge known as *kut´ia*. In ancient Rus´ this dish was made by boiling millet and wheat in sweetened water; later it was made from rice. It was served in a special vessel known as a *bratina*, several of which, made in the Kremlin workshops, were placed on the tomb. The practice of honoring the memory of

the dead, ordained by Christian law, was strictly observed in ancient Rus´. Donations were made in churches which were then used to construct memorials.

M. V. Martynova

✜

EARRINGS

✜

RUSSIA, 17TH CENTURY

GOLD, PRECIOUS STONES, PEARLS,

ENAMEL, GLASS

6.8 X 2 CM; 7.6 X 2.5 CM

INV. NOS MR-2647/1-2, MR-2649/1-2

COMB AND CASE

✜

TURKEY, 17TH CENTURY

CRYSTAL, BONE, GOLD, PRECIOUS STONES,

VELVET, GOLD THREAD

COMB: 8.6 X 11.3 CM

CASE: 11.2 X 13.4 CM

INV. NO. DK-171/1-2

Combs in use in Rus´ were made of various local materials such as wood and the bone of domestic animals; there were wonderful examples made from walrus tusks, which were sent to the Moscow court from the northern Russian lands. Combs of cypress wood or ivory were also bought for royal use. The ambassadorial gifts presented to the Russian state often included combs: in 1630, for example, the Turkish ambassador Foma Cantacuzin presented Czar Mikhail Feodorovich with "a comb of horn, covered in jasper, with gold carved into the jasper and reeds carved into the gold." This Turkish comb is similar, but with a crystal surface. The comb is in a green velvet case with a foliate design embroidered in gold thread. In Turkey itself, richly decorated combs of this type were intended for use in the highly formal bathing ceremony. In Russia, combs became part of the wedding rites. The European traveller Adam Olearius observed in his notes on Russia that on the eve of the wedding the groom would give his bride a small casket with a mirror and comb.

From the beginning of the fourteenth century earrings were a widely used female adornment in Rus´. At that time they were normally in the form of a delicate metal pendant, curved in the shape of a question mark, with a bronze, glass, or stone bead at the end. In the sixteenth and seventeenth centuries earrings were notable for the wide variety of their forms. In addition to ornamental motifs, they often included figurative elements, most frequently birds.

These earrings are notable for their use of precious metal and polychrome enamel and the detail of the jewelry work, which is typical of the Kremlin craftsmen.

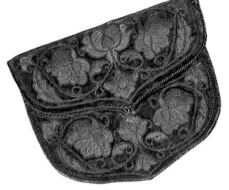

PECTORAL CROSS

✤

MOSCOW, KREMLIN WORKSHOPS,
SECOND HALF OF 16TH CENTURY
GOLD, PEARLS, PRECIOUS STONES, SILVER.
FILIGREE, ENAMEL
H. 8.3 CM, W. 5.5 CM
INV. NO. MR-129

According to royal annals, this cross was given by Czarina Evdokia Lukianovna to her elder daughter Irina during her christening ceremony in 1627.

The form of the cross and its decoration are exceptional for their extreme delicacy. A light blue sapphire is set in the centre of the cross, with an image of the Crucifixion in relief and a Greek inscription. The back of the sapphire has no mount and the stone transmits the light in a remarkable way. The circular, slightly broadened ends of the cross are decorated with delicate filigree ornament, with enamel and tiny drops of blackened gold. The stylized foliate motifs, the strong color of the enamel, the blue sapphire and the use of black gold in an enamel setting all indicate that the cross is the work of Kremlin craftsmen of the second half of the sixteenth century, evidently in the service of Ivan the Terrible. This cross, which belonged to one of the last members of the Riurik dynasty, became an inherited relic of the family of the first Romanov, Mikhail Feodorovich, who consistently stressed his links with the former Czars of Russia.

PORTRAIT OF THE CZAREVICH
PETER ALEXEEVICH

✤

RUSSIA, END OF 17TH CENTURY

UNKNOWN ARTIST

OIL ON CANVAS

INV. NO. ZH-1966

This portrait, in the traditional style of seventeenth century Muscovy Rus´, is one of the few oil paintings of the young Peter the Great.

At the end of the seventeenth century several portraits of Peter were commissioned by his family and painted on icons. These pictures, following the traditions of ancient Russian religious portraiture, show Peter in the form of Christ-Emmanuel or the Archdeacon Stephen. Portraits of Peter also began to be included in secular compositions; in these the figure of the man is free from all the disciplines of religious iconography.

This portrait nevertheless has ideological significance, underlining the prestige of the Muscovy domain. The same aim is served by the contemporary book *The Roots of the Great Sovereigns* (1672): here the young Peter is portrayed alongside state emblems and portraits of members of the Riurik and Romanov dynasties. In *The Ceremony of the Coronation of the Czars Ivan and Peter Alexeevich* (1682) the ten-year-old Peter is portrayed in a royal crown, holding an orb and sceptre in his hands. This was the model for the present portrait. Certainly this painting has none of the intimacy and privacy which the present-day observer automatically looks for in portraits. It is, nevertheless, a fine formal portrayal, in which the individual features of the young boy are just discernible through the official image of the heir to the Russian throne.

✥

PORTRAIT OF THE CZAREVNA
ELIZAVETA PETROVNA

✥

RUSSIA, 1722

A. P. ANTROPOV

OIL ON CANVAS

INV. NO. ZH-1968

This portrait of the younger daughter of Peter the Great, the future Empress Elizaveta Petrovna, was one result of a commission received by Antropov in the 1720s to make copies of royal portraits. In the absence of direct contact with the model, the artist has created an image showing a fusion of features common to the family.

The portrait has an intimate quality, a sense of psychological, poetic insight, although these qualities do not detract from the formality of the portrait of a person of high rank. The artist has paid attention to the rendering of the child's form; despite the conventionality of the almost frontal pose, and the trappings of a grown woman, the Czarevna captivates with her childlike charm. The expression of worldly reserve and seriousness dictated by court etiquette is at odds with the natural timidity and emotion which suffuse her face.

Such things were not among the qualities demanded of formal portraits. Their presence in the picture of the young Elizaveta are examples of the more intimate portraiture at which the artist excelled.

COFFIN CLOTH OF THE CZAREVICH
DMITRII ALEXEEVICH

✛

MOSCOW, KREMLIN WORKSHOPS, 1649-50
KARP TIMOFEEV
CLOTH: ITALY, FIRST HALF OF 17TH CENTURY;
EMBROIDERY: RUSSIA, 1649
VELVET, DAMASK, SILVER,
PRECIOUS STONES, PEARLS
140 X 70 CM
INV. NO. TK-2158

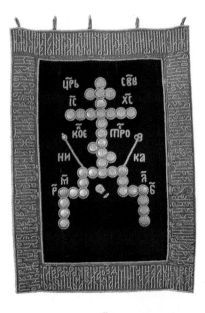

In Orthodox funeral rites, coffin cloths were laid on the coffins of the dead. Each church would make its own coffin cloth, always with a portrayal of the cross of Golgotha, a symbol of suffering, death, and the afterlife. For the burial of members of the royal household, other coffin cloths were used, often of a more personal character recalling the memory of the deceased. These were laid on the tombs of members of the royal family on the days set aside in the Orthodox calendar for mourning the dead: forty days, a year, and three years after the death.

The cloth was for the coffin of Dmitrii Alexeevich, the first son of Alexei Mikhailovich, who was born on October 22 1648 and died on October 6 the following year.

An inscription of pearls woven into the green velvet border of the cloth states that it was placed on the coffin of the Czarevich Dmitrii Alexeevich "by order of Czar Alexei Mikhailovich, on the sixth day of October 7158 [1649]." Thirty-eight silver-gilt badges are applied to the central crimson section of the cloth, forming the eight-pointed Cross of Golgotha. The badges contain carved images of Orthodox feast days and saints. They were made by smiths of the Silver and Gold Chambers of the Kremlin workshops. Mitres, scapulars from church robes, and coffin cloths were kept in the Kremlin workshops until they were used. During the days of mourning for Russian Czars and their elder sons, their coffin cloths were carried to the family tomb in the Archangel Cathedral.

The images on the badges of the coffin cloth represented the patron saints of the deceased, of his parents, of living members of the royal family, and of the dynasty in general. These cloths usually took at least a month to make: the inscription, woven with pearls, would take fifteen to twenty days, and the rest of the cloth also required a considerable time for preparation. It is known that sketches for coffin cloths were made by artists from the Kremlin workshops; often these would be well known icon painters and calligraphers, in this case the artist Karp Timofeev.

MEMORIAL SHROUD

✛

MOSCOW, KREMLIN WORKSHOPS
CLOTH: ITALY, 17TH CENTURY
EMBROIDERY: RUSSIA, 1667
BROCADE, VELVET, DAMASK, SATIN, CORD, GOLD,
SILVER, PRECIOUS STONES, PEARLS
1,05 X 77 CM
INV. NO. TK-3128

Memorial shrouds were an important part of Russian Orthodox funeral rites. They were a substantial memory of the deceased, a constant prayer for the peace of his soul. In churches shrouds were suspended from icons, and accorded particular respect. They were presented to cathedrals and churches and were used during the requiem mass for the dead; after a certain time they became the property of the church. This shroud was presented to the Dormition Cathedral of the Moscow Kremlin, in memory of the boyar Boris Ivanovich Morozov. The inscription on the shroud shows that it was made on July 20 1667, on the wishes of his wife Anna Il'inichna Morozova, the sister of the Czarina Maria Il'inichna. Morozov was brought up with Czar Mikhail Feodorovich and was "uncle", or tutor, to the Czarevich Alexei, later Czar Alexei Mikhailovich. He was undoubtedly one of the most influential figures of the first half of the seventeenth century. When he died in 1661 he was buried in the Chudov Monastery of the Moscow Kremlin, and it is known that his requiem mass was led by the Patriarch Nikon. The shroud is made of Italian cloth of gold and green velvet, decorated with threaded pearls and gold studs with precious stones. Its price, as is shown by the inscription in tiny pearl thread around the edge of the middle section of the shroud, was 7,800 roubles – a colossal sum. In comparison, the gold orb brought to Czar Alexei Mikhailovich from Constantinople in 1662 cost 7,917 roubles.

TOWEL	CANDLESTICK	PILLOW AND CASE

TOWEL

✣

MOSCOW, 17TH CENTURY

LINEN, GOLD AND SILVER THREAD

320 X 60 CM

INV. NO. TK-722

Ornamental towels made entirely by ladies' hands served as a kind of visiting card for their makers, an example of their artistic taste and craftsmanship. Female handicrafts had long been highly valued in Rus´, and the ability to embroider, thread pearls, knit, and make lace were considered feminine virtues. Embroidered towels were an important part of the marriage ceremony, since they showed the bride's ability to make and decorate essential articles of daily life. This towel is remarkable for its delicacy and grace of form. Its creator has used only gold and silver thread and the purest white linen. Fantastical flowers and branches are spread thickly across the surface and united by a background of golden sweet peas. The towel is embroidered in a special two-sided technique, so that the decoration is the same seen from either side.

CANDLESTICK

✣

MOSCOW, KREMLIN WORKSHOPS, 1699

SILVER, EMERALD, GLASS, ENAMEL

H. 26.4 CM, DIAM.19 CM

INV. NO. MR-3388/1-2

When royal personages died, members of their family would often make rich donations to cathedrals and monasteries. This silver candlestick decorated with 142 emeralds was one such donation. The inscription on the interior of the candlestick's base tells how the Czarina Martha Matveevna Apraxina placed it in the Archangel Cathedral of the Moscow Kremlin. The Archangel Cathedral was the resting place of the Great Princes and Czars of Russia until the end of the eighteenth century, when the state capital was moved from Moscow to St. Petersburg. In 1682 Czar Feodor Alexeevich, the elder brother of Peter the Great, was buried there. In his memory, his widow presented this candlestick to the cathedral.

PILLOW AND CASE

SWADDLING BAND: SVIVAL´NIK

✣

PILLOW AND CASE: SATIN, FRANCE (?),

END OF 17TH CENTURY

EMBROIDERY: RUSSIA, END OF 17TH CENTURY

DAMASK: RUSSIA, 19TH CENTURY

SVIVAL´NIK: RUSSIA, END OF 17TH CENTURY

SATIN, REP, DAMASK, PRECIOUS STONES, PEARLS,

GOLD THREAD, WIRE-RIBBON, LACE,

SILVER LACE, GLASS

PILLOW: 42 X 43 CM;

SVIVAL´NIK: 260.7 X 2.8 CM

INV. NOS TK-1135/1-2, TK-1794

This small child's pillow and case are made of deep gold satin, trimmed with a band of pink-gold rep with a foliate design made of gold thread, pearls and emeralds. It was probably intended as part of the "ornamental bedclothes" of a young Czarevich. Such bedclothes were particularly richly decorated, and were exhibited at family occasions such as weddings, births, and christenings. Pillows were made from expensive imported cloth; they were decorated with embroidery and often with precious stones.

Royal bedclothes were extremely carefully looked after, owing to the ancient and still widely held belief in Rus´ that the royal family needed protection from witchcraft. In view of their high value, "ornamental bedclothes" were usually kept in the Sovereign's Treasury or the Chamber of the Czarina's workshops, where most of them were made. In the nineteenth century this pillow decorated the display bedstead in the children's room of the Moscow museum known as the House of the Romanov Boyars, which had been opened on the initiative of Emperor Alexander II. The *svival´nik*, or swaddling band, was probably, together with the pillow, part of the parade bedclothes of a newborn Czarevich; it was placed over the swathing cloths of the newborn baby.

✢

JEWEL BOX, LARETS

✤

SOL´VYCHEGODSK, END OF 17TH CENTURY

SILVER, ENAMEL, FILIGREE

11 x 11 x 19.5 CM

INV. No. MR-1082

The term *larets* referred to boxes of differing size, used for storing jewelry or perfume. They were in the form of a rectangular box on small globular legs, with a tall hinged lid. Decoration varied. This silver casket is from Sol´vychegodsk, and, in the traditional style of that town, is decorated with painted enamel.

Sol´vychegodsk jewelers were experts in painting enamel, and used the technique in various ways. One method was to cover the surface of the article with white enamel; the white background would then be decorated with enamel paints of different colors. This casket is decorated differently: cartouches, flowers, and leaves are stamped into the surface and filled with colored enamel. Each stamped design is surrounded by silver wire, not purely for decorative purposes: the silver fastens the enamel to the flat surface of the casket. The enamel and the slightly raised silver edges stand out in relief on the surface, giving the whole article an unusual plasticity.

✤

✛

PATEN

✛

MOSCOW, KREMLIN WORKSHOPS, 1664

GOLD, PRECIOUS STONES,

ENAMEL

DIAM. 21 CM

INV. NO. MR-3438

This gold paten, with an
enamel image of the Virgin and Child, was
used to hold bread for the communion service.
It was part of the set of liturgical plate presented to the Chudov Monastery in the Moscow
Kremlin by the boyarina Anna Il'inichna
Morozova, in memory of her husband the
boyar Boris Ivanovich Morozov. Since Anna
Il'inichna was a sister of the Czarina, her order
was undertaken by the best Kremlin craftsmen.
All the articles in this set are decorated with a
multicolored combination of dark and
sparkling, translucent enamel. The effect is
heightened by the play of bright precious
stones, giving the whole a highly decorative
character typical of the jeweler's art in the
seventeenth century.

✛

ALTAR CROSS

❖

MOSCOW, KREMLIN WORKSHOPS, 1677

GOLD, PEARLS, PRECIOUS STONES,

ENAMEL, NIELLO

H. 37.5 CM

INV. NO. MR-4228

his gold cross is typical of Russian religious altar crosses. It has eight points and a traditional image of the Crucifixion in the center. Its decoration is an effective fusion of gold, velvety niello work, bright precious stones, and a large pearl.

According to the inscription on the cross, it was produced by order of Czar Feodor Alexeevich, the elder brother of Peter the Great, in memory of his father, Czar Alexei Mikhailovich. Feodor Alexeevich came to the throne as a fourteen-year-old boy, and ruled for six years. By contemporary accounts he was an intelligent and well-educated man, but from childhood suffered from an incurable disease. It is likely that this illness was the cause of his rich offerings to the Kremlin churches and monasteries. The many pieces of plate and the gospels ordered by Feodor Alexeevich, which have survived to this day, are remarkable for their magnificence and the beauty of their finish.

PROCESSIONAL CROSS

MOSCOW, END OF 17TH CENTURY
SILVER, GOLD, ENAMEL, FILIGREE
77.5 x 36.7 CM
INV. NO. MR-4962

Processional crosses were used in Orthodox cathedrals on one of the most important of Christian feast days – the feast of the Exaltation of the Cross of Our Lord *(Vozdvizhenie)*. The festival stems from the legend that in Jerusalem in the fourth century the Empress Helena, mother of the Emperor Constantine the Great, found the True Cross on which Jesus Christ was crucified.

According to the traditions of the feast, a service was held during which the cross was solemnly carried from the altar and raised *(vozdvigat')* above the head of the priest, so that it was visible to all the congregation.

Processional crosses were notable for their large size. In addition, their form was traditional for all Russian divine crosses, and included scenes of the Crucifixion, with the Virgin and St John the Divine standing in front, and the heavenly host and the Mount of Golgotha with Adam's skull behind. On this cross these canonical images are augmented by delicate and detailed representations of instruments of the Passion – articles connected with the events of the week preceding Christ's death. These symbolic images first appeared in the works of Russian craftsmen – and particularly of jewelers – in the last decades of the seventeenth century. Their presence points to the introduction of features from Western iconography into Russian art.

Russian written sources from the seventeenth century also refer to the use of these crosses in the marriage ceremony. Thus, in the description of the marriage of Czar Mikhail Feodorovich and Evdokia Lukianovna, we read that along with icons "a Holy Cross was placed at the head" of the matrimonial bed.

TANKARD

✤

Augsburg, 1565-70

Master Abraham I Lotter

Silver, filigree, niello

h. 25.5 cm

Inv. No. DK-254

This magnificent vessel became royal property at the beginning of the seventeenth century when it was presented to Czarevich Alexei Mikhailovich on his christening by Feodor Ivanovich Sheremetev, a member of an ancient, rich, and powerful family of boyars. The christening took place in the Chudov Monastery of the Moscow Kremlin on March 22 1629.

The tankard was made in Augsburg, one of the most important centers of gold and silver work in Germany. It is tall and cylindrical in form, with a delicate silver filigree design of late Renaissance character. Of the few surviving examples of Southern German work from the second half of the sixteenth century, this is the earliest. It is undeniably the work of a master craftsman. The combination of punched work, etching and cast details make it a particularly fine example of German applied art.

LOVING CUP: BRATINA

✤

Moscow, Kremlin Workshops,

first half of 17th century

Silver

h. 10 cm, diam. 11 cm

Inv. No. MR-4185

This *bratina* is part of a set of memorial vessels. It was filled with water sweetened with honey and placed on the tomb of the deceased. The austere decoration, consisting of chased triangles, indicates its intended use. The inscription around the rim describes how it was made after the death of the Czarevna Irina, daughter of Mikhail Feodorovich, who died soon after birth.

✛

GOBLET IN THE FORM OF A SHIP

✛

NUREMBERG, 1609-32

MASTER ESAIA ZUR LINDEN

SILVER

H. 31.3 CM

INV. NO. MZ-290

Ship goblets became fashionable in the seventeenth century, a time of geographical discoveries and nautical developments. The goldsmiths of the ancient German city of Nuremberg were considered the finest creators of these objects, whose production demanded the greatest expertise. It is believed that ship goblets were used to drink the health of sailors setting off on long voyages.

The elegant appearance of the ship, its elaborate shape and the virtuosity of its design reveal the predominantly decorative nature of the object. The model has a single mast, sails, rigging, a pennant, many armed soldiers on the deck and a beautiful stamped design of cupids and sea monsters on the hull.

A significant number of silver ships were kept in the Kremlin treasure houses. They were used as toys by children of the royal family, and as table decorations.

✛

CHILD'S GLOVES

❖

RUSSIA, END OF 17TH CENTURY

TOOLED LEATHER

9 X 7.5 CM

INV. NO. TK-642/1-2

When they left Moscow on pilgrimages with their children, Russian Czarinas would often visit local bazaars on their way where they would buy simple folk toys. It is possible that this is how these tiny leather gloves, with their stamped border, became royal property.

An essential addition to winter clothing in Rus' were mittens, *rukavki*; or gloves, *rukavki pershchatye*. They were made of leather, sometimes morocco; or wool, often broadcloth; or sometimes from silk and gold thread. Elegant mittens were decorated with rich embroidery and formed an ornamental accessory to traditional Russian clothing. "Warm" (winter) mittens were lined with fur, while "cold" mittens had a simple lining. These gloves are an exact small-scale copy of adult ones. They may have been specially made as playthings, or as an example of the work of a master currier.

RATTLE

❖

NUREMBERG, END OF 17TH CENTURY

MASTER WITH INITIALS SK

SILVER

L. 19 CM

INV. NO. MZ-1092

Toys for the royal children were made in the Kremlin Workshops or purchased abroad. They not only entertained the young Czareviches and Czarevnas, but guided their spiritual and aesthetic development, since they were often the creations of first-class jewelers and artists. This silver rattle, the work of a German master, is exceptionally refined in shape and harmonious in proportions. Its beautifully embossed decoration includes characteristically baroque motifs.

DOLLS

❖

RUSSIA, LATE 17TH-EARLY 18TH CENTURY

COTTON, LINEN, SILK, TULLE, GALLOON,

GOLD THREAD, GLASS, BRAID

H. 29 CM, 26 CM

INV. NOS TK-2466, TK-2467

The art of making cloth dolls was known in Russia from earliest times, and was widely practised in all walks of life. In the seventeenth century such dolls were designed for royal children in the Czarina's Chamber; this was a female workshop, where one of the craftswomen was the Czarina herself. In 1629 when Irina, the elder daughter of Mikhail Feodorovich, went to live with her grandmother Martha the Nun in the cells of the Voznesenskii Monastery, "twenty scraps of satin, golden and silver cloth, thick cotton, and taffeta for dolls" were sent from the Czarina's workshops.

These dolls are made of white linen, and wear Russian national costume of the seventeenth century. Their skirts are of Russian printed cloth with delicate floral ornament, and trimmed with galloon and silk thread. The *dushegrei* – short loose-fitting sleeveless jackets – are made of gold galloon; they are gathered in at the back and fastened at the waist with a magnificent ring. The dress of the dolls is completed by a *kika* and a *kokoshnik* – traditional headgear for married Russian women. The *kika* is a tall, conical headpiece, made of paper and covered with blue satin, gold braid and thread. A *kika* was presented to a bride on her wedding as a symbol of the beginning of married life. The head of the other doll is adorned with a *kokoshnik*. It is made of paper, covered with silk cloth, and finished with braid and colored glass. Two rows of small glass beads hang around the necks of the dolls.

TWO TOY CANNON

⊹

RUSSIA, 18TH CENTURY

TURNED BRASS

L. 14 CM, 11 CM

INV. NOS OR-3619, OR-3624

Working model cannon were extremely popular in Western Europe, and were also well known in Russia. Russian museum collections contain dozens of such models from the eighteenth and nineteenth centuries. Some of these could be called toys, and others teaching aids, although it is often difficult to distinguish the two.

These two cannon came to the Rust Camera (the Arsenal in St. Petersburg) from the St. Petersburg diamond workshop in 1797, along with eight others. It is most likely that they were used as playthings by the younger members of the royal family and later as educational toys.

CHILD'S RAPIER

⊹

WESTERN EUROPE, 18TH CENTURY

STEEL, GOLD, DIAMONDS

L. 49 CM; L. OF BLADE 42 CM

INV. NO. OR-3997

This rapier may have been made or bought for the Czarevich Peter Petrovich, son of Peter the Great, or for the Emperor Peter II, Peter the Great's grandson. The rapier came to the Armory in 1810 from the collection of the Rust Camera. This collection included the weapons of Peter the Great and other articles of armaments belonging on the whole to Russian Emperors and Empresses of the first half of the eighteenth century.

The blade of the rapier is of forged steel; it is engraved with gilt ornament and an inscription in German. The shape resembles that of the work of German smiths at the beginning of the eighteenth century. The hilt and guard are of gold, decorated with six silver mounts set with diamonds.

CHILD'S ARMOR

✛

MOSCOW, KREMLIN ARMORY, 1634 (?)

MASTER PETR SHASAT (?)

IRON, BRASS, LEATHER

INV. NO. OR-304

This child's armor was probably made for the Czarevich Alexei (later Czar Alexei Mikhailovich), son of Mikhail Feodorovich. Like adult armor, it consists of a helmet, cuirass, and a pair each of vambraces, cuisses with poleyns, sabatons, and gauntlets (one of which is damaged). Its decoration is characteristic of the time, with cast laps of brass, with a figured ornament in relief. This expensive toy was kept in the Armory for a long time. It may also have been used by the children of Czar Alexei Mikhailovich, including the future Emperor Peter the Great.

ICON: ALEXIS, MAN OF GOD, IN OKLAD

MOSCOW, KREMLIN WORKSHOPS
PAINTING: MID-17TH CENTURY
OKLAD: MOSCOW, 1654
GOLD, SILVER-GILT, PRECIOUS STONES, PEARLS,
WOOD, SILK, EGG TEMPERA, LEVKAS (GESSO)
48.3 X 14.5 CM
INV. NO. ZH-549/1-2

This icon was painted
on the birth of the Czarevich Alexei Alexeevich,
son of Alexei Mikhailovich. This is shown by
the portrayal of St Alexis, the Czarevich's
patron saint. He was an ascetic and hermit
who lived at the turn of the fifth century.
According to legend he was born into a Roman
patrician family, but, forgoing a life of wealth,
left his family and died in poverty.

The Czarevich Alexei Alexeevich did
not live long, dying in January 1670 at the age
of sixteen. His christening (measured) icon was
transferred to the Archangel Cathedral of the
Kremlin.

The silver-gilt *oklad* (frame) of the
icon is decorated with a wonderful foliate
design in the tradition of Russian jewelry of the
turn of the seventeenth century.

ICON: THE KAZAN MOTHER OF GOD

PAINTING AND OKLAD: MOSCOW,
BEGINNING OF 17TH CENTURY
WOOD, EGG TEMPERA, SILVER, PEARLS,
PRECIOUS STONES
32 X 28 CM
INV. NO. ZH-537/1-2

In the marriage
ceremony great significance was attached to
the icon of the Virgin, which was used to bless
the bride and groom. The icon was believed to
have miraculous and intercessionary powers:
among other things, it protected against evil
and wrongdoing, and healed illnesses.

The Kazan Mother of God was the
subject of some of the most revered Russian
benedictory icons. The first of this iconograph-
ical type is believed to have been painted in
1579 in Kazan; hence its name. Soon after, the
icon was acclaimed as miraculous, and already
in the sixteenth century manuscript copies of
the icon began to appear.

This icon was painted by Moscow
artists at the beginning of the seventeenth century; it was decorated with a jeweled *oklad*,
the work of Kremlin masters. It was placed in the
Archangel Cathedral, the resting place of the
Great Muscovy Princes and the Czars, and was
evidently a personal icon of the royal family.

The *oklad* is made of silver-gilt. It is
richly decorated with fine sapphires, emeralds,
rubies, and tourmalines, with a thread of
pearls applied along the edges of the *oklad*, the
headdress, and crown above the head of the
Virgin. The opulent decoration lends it an
extraordinary decorative quality: it is at once
festive and solemn.

✥

WEDDING CROWNS (MAN'S AND WOMAN'S)

✥

RUSSIA, 17TH CENTURY

SILVER-GILT

DIAM. 18.5 CM, H. 8.5 CM

INV. NOS MR-5070, MR-5071

Wedding crowns were an important part of the church ritual of marriage. They were made of silver-gilt, in the shape of a smooth hoop, and were decorated fairly modestly. A figured finial rises above the front part of the crown. Along the upper edge runs an undulating band of chased ornament with carved points (much damaged in these examples). The center bears carved compositions: on one crown is a half-length portrait of the Deesis – the Saviour, the Virgin and John the Baptist – on the other, Our Lady of the Sign with St Joachim and St Anne. Joachim and Anne were the parents of the Virgin, and were therefore a symbol of marital fidelity. The soft and gentle carving is particularly attractive; the assured mastery of Russian engraving of the seventeenth century is inimitable.

Wedding crowns were placed on the heads of the bride and groom on their betrothal in the church. In form they reflect ancient models made of silver, bronze, iron, and wood. The crown was a sign of secret union and the blessing of the heavenly powers, and was also part of Jewish marriage rites. In Moscow the splendid wedding ceremony of members of the royal family took place in the main cathedral of the Kremlin, the Dormition Cathedral, from which these two silver crowns have come.

✥

✛

CAP OF CZARINA MARIA DOLGORUKAYA: VOLOSNIK

✛

MOSCOW, 1624

TAFFETA, GOLD AND SILK THREAD

H. 16 CM, CIRCUM. 59 CM

INV. NO. TK-3289

From ancient times married women in Rus´ were obliged to hide their hair, and even at home did not appear bareheaded. This rule applied to all women, including Czarinas. Of all the types of female headgear which existed in the seventeenth century, the most essential and the most frequently worn was the *volosnik*, a small cap which covered the back of the head and the upper part of the forehead. As a rule, *volosniki* were either woven on bobbins or knitted from silk and gold thread with a special needle. The forehead part of the cap – the *ochel'e* – was made of colored cloth decorated with embroidery. The *volosnik* was also part of the funeral ceremony. This may be connected with the pre-Christian tradition of burying people in their wedding clothes

This *volosnik* belonged to the Czarina Maria Dolgorukaya, and comes from her tomb in the Voznesenskii Monastery which, until the end of the seventeenth century, was the resting place of the Great Muscovy Princesses and the Czarinas. Maria Dolgorukaya, the first wife of Czar Mikhail Feodorovich, was the daughter of the noble boyar Vladimir Timofeevich Dolgorukii. The marriage was not a happy one. Chronicles record that the sovereign did not want to marry her, and agreed to it only out of filial duty to his mother, Martha the Nun, who had considerable influence over him. On the second day after the wedding, which took place on September 19 1624, the young Czarina was taken ill, and less than four months later, on January 6 1625, she died.

The crown of this *volosnik* is woven from gold thread on bobbins, and gathered in at the back of the head with a silk ribbon. The *ochel'e* is of taffeta, originally scarlet in color but now very faded. Embroidered on it are images of the tree of life and a unicorn, symbols of marriage and virginity.

✛

KERCHIEF: SHIRINKA

✛

MOSCOW, KREMLIN WORKSHOPS, 17TH CENTURY
TAFFETA: ITALY, 17TH CENTURY;
LACE: RUSSIA, FIRST HALF OF 17TH CENTURY
TAFFETA, LACE, GOLD THREAD, PEARLS
45 X 46 CM
INV. NO. TK-547

The *shirinka* – a small formal kerchief – was in wide use in seventeenth-century Russia. It was both an article of daily use and an element of parade costume in which, depending on the ceremony, it had various symbolic meanings. *Shirinki* were an essential part of the marriage ceremony: the groom gave his bride one rather than a ring. *Shirinki* for royal weddings were made in the Kremlin workshops. Their design was often undertaken by professional court artists. In 1653, for example, the royal icon painter Ivan Matveev spent "a week and six days" preparing the designs for royal hats and *shirinki*. Those examples of such work that have survived are remarkable for their artistic delicacy, and for the use of both traditional embroidery and gold pillow lace. It is worth noting that for Russian seamstresses gold lacemaking was less usual than artistic embroidery. The art of bobbin lacemaking came to Rus´ from the West. It was a technique mainly used in Moscow, and for some time was practised only at court; in 1625 ten lacemakers were employed in the Kremlin workshops. Moscow lace soon took original

forms. A favorite practice of the Kremlin seamstresses was the use of river pearls in gold and silver lace. In this technique, either separate pearls were worked into the lace, or small parts of the design were filled in with pearls. The sparkle of the white pearls set off the metallic surface of the lace, and fused with the white taffeta of the central section of the *shirinka*. The overall effect was one of great elegance.

RING: PERSTEN´

✛

MOSCOW, KREMLIN WORKSHOPS,
LATE 17TH CENTURY
GOLD, PRECIOUS STONES, ENAMEL
DIAM.1.9 CM
INV. NO. MR-2672

Archaeological excavations show that early rings in Rus´ were made by twisting together thick metal wire. By the eighth or ninth centuries Slav craftsmen had already begun to make rings of solid gold and silver.

In the sixteenth and seventeenth centuries rings were cast and richly decorated with large semiprecious stones, enamel, and niello. Such rings were known in ancient documents as *perstni*. Archives also reveal that rings were worn by both women and men. Royal personages and people at court wore several rings on their hands, often one on each finger.

At court jeweled *perstni* often served as presents for christenings, name days and weddings. It is possible that the heart-shaped gold rings in the Kremlin collection were wedding gifts which the groom presented to his bride together with the traditional *shirinka*, or kerchief (left).

CHILD'S BAG

✛

RUSSIA, 17TH CENTURY
VELVET: TURKEY, 17TH CENTURY
VELVET, TAFFETA, SILK AND GOLD THREAD
8.5 X 6 CM
INV. NO. TK-645

The small bag or purse was an essential component of ancient Russian dress. It was attached to the belt or worn over the shoulder, and used to carry small articles or money, instead of a pocket. This child's bag is rectangular; it is made of Turkish velvet with a foliate ornament. It hangs from two cords woven from silk and gold thread, with a blue silk tassel at the end of each.

Bags made of cloth or leather were known as *moshchnaia* or *kalita*. The nickname Kalita ("moneybags") was given in the fourteenth century to the Muscovy Prince Ivan Danilovich. who was famed for his parsimony.

✛

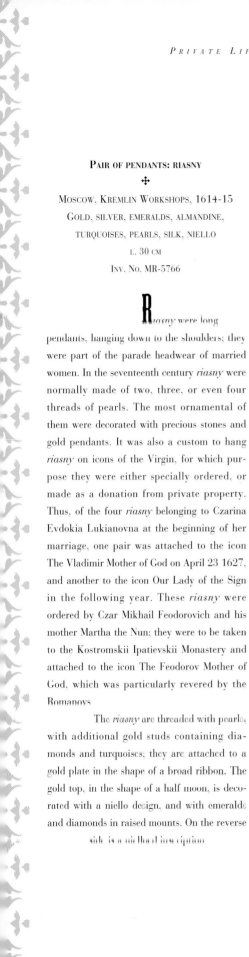

PAIR OF PENDANTS: RIASNY

❖

MOSCOW, KREMLIN WORKSHOPS, 1614-15

GOLD, SILVER, EMERALDS, ALMANDINE,

TURQUOISES, PEARLS, SILK, NIELLO

L. 30 CM

INV. NO. MR-5766

Riasny were long pendants, hanging down to the shoulders; they were part of the parade headwear of married women. In the seventeenth century *riasny* were normally made of two, three, or even four threads of pearls. The most ornamental of them were decorated with precious stones and gold pendants. It was also a custom to hang *riasny* on icons of the Virgin, for which purpose they were either specially ordered, or made as a donation from private property. Thus, of the four *riasny* belonging to Czarina Evdokia Lukianovna at the beginning of her marriage, one pair was attached to the icon The Vladimir Mother of God on April 23 1627, and another to the icon Our Lady of the Sign in the following year. These *riasny* were ordered by Czar Mikhail Feodorovich and his mother Martha the Nun; they were to be taken to the Kostromskii Ipatievskii Monastery and attached to the icon The Feodorov Mother of God, which was particularly revered by the Romanovs

The *riasny* are threaded with pearls, with additional gold studs containing diamonds and turquoises; they are attached to a gold plate in the shape of a broad ribbon. The gold top, in the shape of a half moon, is decorated with a niello design, and with emeralds and diamonds in raised mounts. On the reverse side is a niello inscription

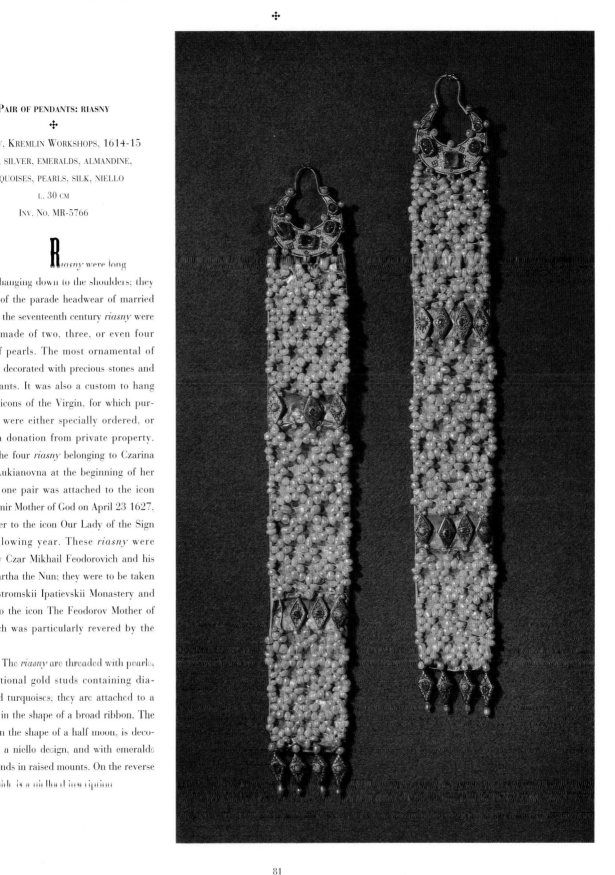

BUTTONS

✠

MOSCOW, KREMLIN WORKSHOPS, 17TH CENTURY

GOLD, PRECIOUS STONES, ENAMEL

5.5 x 3 CM

INV. NOS MR-2318. MR-2319

Buttons had a significant role in the design of old Russian clothing, both male and female. For the costumes of rich peasants and landowners, buttons were made of tin, bronze or, more rarely, of silver. The formal clothes of the Czar and his courtiers were decorated with buttons of precious metals and stones made by the craftsmen of the Gold and Silver Chambers in the Kremlin. Such buttons are remarkable not only for their beauty, but also for their great material value: quite often the buttons would cost more than the garment itself.

The form of the buttons, techniques for making them, and their decoration were extremely varied. Depending on the clothing for which they were intended, they could vary from the size of a pea to that of a hen's egg. The number of buttons also depended on the type of clothing, and would often be quite large. One of the records of the Royal Treasury describes a garment having 68 gold buttons with niello ornament. In the sixteenth and seventeenth centuries jeweled buttons were sewn onto hats as well as other clothing. The demand for buttons in court life was too great for the royal jewelers to meet; buttons were also bought at the Moscow silver market from *pugovishniki*, button makers, who sold their work by weight.

These two gold openwork buttons decorated with transparent enamel and precious stones were probably made in the Kremlin workshops, judging by the opulence of their design. In design they show the influence of Western European jewelry, which was due to Western goldsmiths who worked at the royal court in the seventeenth century.

CHILD'S WINTER SLEIGH

✠

PROPERTY OF THE CZAREVNA

EKATERINA IVANOVNA

MOSCOW, KREMLIN WORKSHOPS, 1689-92

WOOD, LEATHER, TAFFETA, COPPER

L. 200 CM, H. 100 CM, W. 100 CM

INV. NO. K-2

This closed sleigh was used for the games and entertainment of the young Czarevna Ekaterina, niece of Peter the Great. According to literary sources of the eighteenth century, Peter himself had an identical carriage in childhood.

The sleigh has two seats, and is set on runners. Five little windows are set in the front and sides. The rectangular body of the sleigh, distinguished by its elegant outline, is covered with red leather, stamped with a gold ornament showing leaves, flowers and berries. The ornamental composition also contains images of fantastic birds, beasts and *putti*. The decoration is achieved through the use of brass nails with round heads. Mica is embedded in the windows; it is attached to narrow strips of tin, decorated with nails with corrugated heads and open-worked studs in the form of stars and two-headed eagles. The whole creates the impression of lace. The upholstery inside is of scarlet Eastern taffeta of the seventeenth century.

Until recently, it was thought that the leather used in the finish of the carriage was imported from Spain. Spain was famed for the production of stamped leather, which was especially popular with craftsmen of the Baroque period. According to eighteenth century archives, however, the leather upholstery of the carriage was made by craftsmen of the Moscow Kremlin. This upholstery has not survived in full to this day. In 1959 it was supplemented by new leather with a stamped ornament, which in form and the treatment of the details was very close to the design of the original.

ICON: THE HARROWING OF HELL

✣

PAINTING AND OKLAD: MOSCOW, FIRST HALF
OF 17TH CENTURY

29.4 x 25 CM

INV. NO. ZH-540/1-2

This small icon was part of the iconostasis of the Archangel Cathedral in the Moscow Kremlin. This was the cathedral where members of the Romanov dynasty were buried. The presence of the icon in the cathedral is connected with Russian funeral rites, according to which icons were brought to the tombs of the deceased in the church, and left there. These would be family relics, a symbol of the blessing of a mother, father or grandfather, sometimes passed on from generation to generation.

The subject of the icon is Christ's defeat of the powers of darkness during the three days between the Crucifixion and the Resurrection, a symbol of the victory of life over death. Beneath his feet lie the broken gates of Hell, with its shattered locks, keys, and chains. Below, shrouded figures rise from their tombs. To either side of Christ stand Adam and Eve, whom he holds by the hand, the biblical kings Solomon and David, and Old Testament prophets, whose original sin Christ redeemed by his death.

Catholic artists often portrayed a different variation of the Resurrection, in which Christ is portrayed rising above his tomb, surrounded by astonished soldiers. Russian icon painting of the seventeenth century reveals for the first time elements of Western iconography; this work shows two iconographic variants united in one composition.

Icon: The Nativity

✢

Russia, end of 19th century (?)
Wood, egg tempera, levkas (gesso)
31 x 26.2 cm
Inv. No. KP-51690

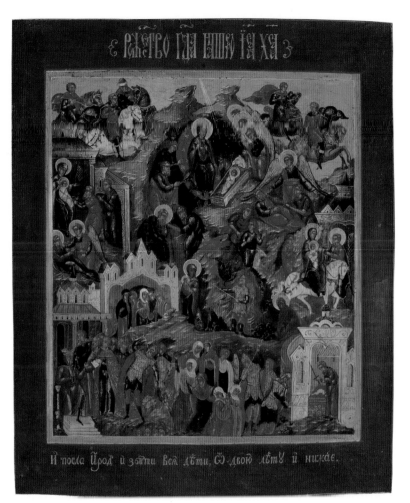

The icon painter has faithfully represented the Gospel account of the birth of Christ. In the center of the composition at the top are the confinement of the Virgin, the manger with the baby Jesus, the kneeling shepherds, and the praising angels. In the top corners are the Magi following the star. In the central section of the icon are the Magi bringing gifts to Christ, the angel warning Joseph to flee to Egypt, the doubts of Joseph and the old pastor, the appearance of the angel to the sleeping Magi, and the flight to Egypt. In the lower part of the icon are the Magi before King Herod, the massacre of the innocents, the weeping of the women of Bethlehem, St Elizabeth hiding in a cave with John the Baptist, Rachel weeping over her children, and Zacharias before the throne.

The artistic methods displayed in the icon suggest that it is the work of an icon painter at the turn of the twentieth century: the use of handwritten script, the lines of the blackened drawings, the way in which the hills are portrayed. However, the miniature details of the whole composition, the sonority of its color combinations, and the introduction and execution of architectural forms follow icon-painting traditions already perfected at the end of the seventeenth century.

ROYAL PARADES AND CEREMONIAL ARMS OF THE SEVENTEENTH CENTURY

❖

One of the most important elements of court ceremonial in Russia was the royal parade. This was the name given to ceremonial processions undertaken by the Russian Czars when they left their residence in the Kremlin and set off on military campaigns, pilgrimages, or hunting expeditions.

Court records of this era describe the preparations undertaken for each royal parade. The order of procession was carefully worked out and lists were drawn up of the participants in the ceremony, and the royal equipment and attire. Horse trappings from the office of the stables, and weapons from the Armory, were distributed for use in the parade. The type of each item was dictated by the purpose and significance of the excursion. The number of horses, carriages and other vehicles was carefully calculated. Only the most high-ranking boyars, *stol'niki (courtiers)* and noblemen from the Duma were allowed to accompany the Czar, while the Czarina was escorted by wives and widows of boyars. Boyars and noblemen were obliged to present themselves at the Kremlin in their finest robes, armed, and mounted on richly caparisoned horses.

There were three principal types of royal parade in seventeenth-century Russia: military reviews, royal campaigns and expeditions (normally of a religious nature) and hunting trips (often undertaken at the same time as royal campaigns).

Military reviews were significant events, generally preceding a declaration of war or a campaign by the Czar's forces. The sovereign's regiment (Bolshoi Gosudarev) played the most important role; it was made up of the finest representatives of the Russian gentry and was directly under the sovereign's orders. Military reviews lasted for several days and were held on the Devich'ii Field near the Novodevich'ii Monastery just outside Moscow. Banners, armor and weaponry were distributed to the regiments from the Armory for use in the review. A "campaign" armory of the Czar was set up, which contained the finest examples of sidearms, firearms, and other weapons: sabers, broadswords, and *konchary* (cavalry swords) with jeweled hilts and silver-gilt scabbards; valuable pistols in embroidered holsters; arquebuses with barrels and stocks inlaid with gold and encrusted with ivory and mother-of-pearl; fine armor with chased gold ornament. Most important were the Czar's ceremonial weapons, which consisted of three *saadaki* (bow sets), lances, spears, pikes, and arquebuses. These were carried in front of the sovereign by the royal weapon bearers, or *ryndy*, dressed in white or scarlet caftans. The armor bearer rode behind the sovereign with the royal helmet in his hands.

When a military review signalled the beginning of a campaign, the army paraded from the Devich'ii Field right through the city of Moscow, and processed through the Kremlin. One witness wrote of the review of Alexei Mikhailovich, before the Riga campaign: "What a day of spectacle, the like of which I shall not see again!"

A ceremony was also arranged for the return of forces from a military campaign, which was particularly splendid after a victory. Accounts of Alexei Mikhailovich's entry to Moscow after the successful Polish campaign describe the royal procession glittering with gold and precious stones: the richly attired army bearing banners as they formed two columns to line the route to the Kremlin. All the bells of Moscow's many churches rang out. The boyars headed the procession, followed by 24 royal parade horses with jeweled harnesses

❖

Royal Parade of Ivan the Terrible

and horsecloths, and saddles embroidered with gold and pearls. Next came the royal chariots and carriages. The Czar himself entered the Kremlin on foot preceded by the *strel'tsy* (guards).

The second type of ceremonial procession was the royal pilgrimage to monasteries. These processions were timed to coincide with religious holidays, and were named after the monastery or town to which the pilgrimage was directed. Some of the best known were the Trinity, Mozhaisk, Nicholas, Rubtsovskoe and Pokrovskoe pilgrimages. Particular events in the life of the state and of the royal family were always marked by pilgrimages: these included the consecration of the Czar, a royal marriage, and the birth of an heir.

Every year on September 25, the feast day of St Sergius of Radonezh, and sometimes at other times as well, a pilgrimage was made to the Troitse-Sergiev (St Sergius) monastery, a political as well as a religious center, 43 miles from Moscow. In 1675 Adolf Lizek, secretary at the Embassy of the Holy Roman Empire, wrote a detailed description of the pilgrimage. The procession was led by the infantry: first came a cannon with two gunners

at either side, followed by two grooms leading the magnificent skewbald horse of the commander. The commander sat astride his horse flanked by bodyguards in red uniform. He was followed by the standard bearer and a band of trumpets and drums. Twenty companies of *strel'tsy*, with arquebuses in their hands and ceremonial axes on their shoulders, brought up the rear. The procession moved slowly into the field where an army, 14,000 strong, stood awaiting the arrival of the Czar. This was the advance guard which prepared the sovereign's route and pitched camps along the way. The cavalry arrived at midday, armed with arquebuses; 432 of these weapons, with gilt locks and ebony stocks and butts, had been distributed from the royal treasury. The Czar's two favorite mounts were led in the middle of the cavalry. Behind the cavalry came a long row of carriages containing the royal bedclothes, dresses, linen, articles from the Czar's bathroom, furniture, domestic tableware, icons, weapons, and other items. A special carriage was put aside for gifts presented to the Czar during the journey. The Czar's retinue was made up of many different servants, from sentries and stokers to a doctor and a watchmak-

er. The long line of carriages was drawn by 62 horses, each wearing a cloth embroidered with gold and silver. On either side of the route, 200 *strel'tsy* cleared the way. Finally, a row of carriages appeared bearing the Czar, the boyars, and all those who had been ordered to take part in the expedition. An equally opulent procession of the Czarina and her daughters then emerged from a different gate of the Kremlin. The procession moved slowly, making its first stop only just beyond the boundaries of the city, where a whole fortress had been erected with ditches, ramparts and towers. Grand marquees and tents had been set up within, where participants could rest and change their clothing. The whole journey to the Troitse-Sergiev monastery took five days or more. After prayers, the distribution of alms, and solemn feasts in the monastery, the procession returned to Moscow to an equally magnificent greeting.

When the Czar set off on a pilgrimage with his family, the Czarina and Czarevnas were escorted by their own no less magnificent procession, with all the necessary ceremonial elements. The procession included troops of cavalry at the head and the rear, horses led on foot, the carriages of the Czarina and the Czarevna, carriages for the wives and widows of the boyars, the boyars themselves, and crowds of ordinary people who had rushed to see the dazzling spectacle. The windows of all the carriages were heavily curtained, so that no one could see the Czarina, the Czarevna, or the boyars' ladies. But there was a magnificent spectacle of rouged ladies in red dresses, white ribboned hats and yellow boots sitting astride white chargers. These were the chambermaids and seamstresses who lived with the Czarina in the Terem Palace. From 25 to 35 horses were sent from the office of the stables for each such procession.

The Russian Czarinas made their own pilgrimages to monasteries and churches. Many documents have been preserved describing the pilgrimages of Czarina Evdokia Lukianovna, wife of Czar Mikhail Feodorovich Romanov. As many as 40 carriages and over 1,000 horses were used in her processions. The carriage drivers wore caftans of cerise velvet with pearls, and green velvet caps trimmed with sable.

Life at the Russian court also involved some smaller expeditions. A detailed description has survived of one of these expeditions, when Czar Alexei Mikhailovich went to the village of Pokrovskoe-Streshnevo, in the northern part of present-day Moscow. This was the site of a country estate and church belonging to his mother, the Czarina Evdokia Lukianovna, who came from the Streshnev family. Small expeditions of this kind did not differ greatly from expeditions to the Troitse-Sergiev monastery, but they were less solemn. Fewer soldiers took part in ceremonies of this kind; there were no banners or cannon, and no icons were carried.

Processions which accompanied royal hunting trips were formed quite differently. Members of the royal hunt – huntsmen on horseback and on foot, falconers, and so on – always accompanied the Czar on his pilgrimages and even on his military reviews, so that he could hunt during halts. But royal excursions were also undertaken with the specific aim of hunting. When the Czars went out to hunt "unofficially" their retinue was very small. Only those servants directly involved with the royal hunt, and a few invited guests, accompanied the Czar.

When a hunting trip was undertaken for the amusement of the whole royal family, or when foreign emissaries had been invited to take part, the excursion was particularly ceremonious. The procession consisted of ranks of soldiers, horses sparkling with jewels, huntsmen with hounds and hawks, grooms, hundreds of servants, and finally an enormous convoy of carts containing everything needed for the hunt and for the ceremonial feast. The whole procession moved slowly to the scene of the hunt, where everything had been prepared. Game birds were enclosed in pens, and tents were erected. Samuel Collins, an English doctor in the service of Czar Alexei Mikhailovich, described the scene as the most magnificent he had ever seen. The tents of the Czar, the Czarina, and their children stood in a circle, in the center of which a temporary church had been erected. Barriers and guards stood a rifle shot away from the tents, preventing onlookers from entering the scene of the hunt.

One unifying element was traditionally present in all Russian ceremonial processions. Both the parades of the Czar and Czarina themselves and the processions in which the Czar did not take part (such as ambassadorial meetings), always featured the "horses of the royal saddle," led by members of the office of the stables. They were of an Eastern breed and were the principal decorative element of the procession. The "Grand Horse Attire" – the valuable trappings of the horses, distributed from the office of the stables for ceremonial processions – delighted and amazed onlookers. Saddles, stirrups, and harnesses were faced with gold and silver and covered in precious stones, and the horsecloths were studded with pearls. The horses also bore forehead pendants (*reshmy*), tassels hanging from the neck (*nauzy*), silver hoops, or knee cops on the legs (*nakolenniki*), and clanking chains stretching from bridle to saddle which jangled as the horses moved.

The ceremonial royal parade continued to be a feature of Russian life until the end of the seventeenth century, when Peter the Great replaced it with a different type of procession based on a Western European model.

O. B. Melnikova

MAIL SHIRT

⁜

MOSCOW, KREMLIN ARMORY, 17TH CENTURY
IRON
L. 91 CM
INV. NO. OR-4714

The mail shirt is formed of interlocking wire rings which allow the wearer easy movement. Shirts of this type appeared in Russia in the thirteenth century and gradually replaced the heavier chainmail, so that by the sixteenth or seventeenth centuries they had become the most widely used armor in the Russian noble cavalry. The flexibility of the shirt meant that it could be used with other protective covering. A thick quilted garment was normally worn beneath it. The breast and back were protected by additional lames (plates); the upper arm was protected by a short rerebrace, and the lower arm by a vambrace.

This mail shirt is a fine example of traditional metal-weaving techniques of the Moscow masters. Its cut shows that it was designed for a horseman – the hem was shortened at the back so as not to hinder sitting in the saddle, and the lengthened front section protected the upper part of the cavalryman's legs. Mail shirts made in Moscow were the heaviest of all the mail shirts of seventeenth-century Russia. This example weighs about 20 lb (over 9 kg).

✣

SUPPLEMENTARY ARMOR: ZERTSALA

✣

MOSCOW, KREMLIN ARMORY, 17TH CENTURY

IRON, BRAID

28.5 x 25 CM

INV. NO. OR-4183/1-4

In sixteenth- and seventeenth-century Russia, supplementary armor was used to strengthen chainmail and mail shirts. Known as *zertsala*, this usually consisted of four plates: a breastplate, back-plate and two sideplates. These were joined by straps, laces, or chains of metal rings.

The plates were made of highly polished steel, often gilded or silvered, and sometimes decorated with precious stones. The mirror-like shine of the armor explains its name, which comes from the same root as the Russian word for mirror, *zerkalo*.

The lames of the *zertsala* are particularly interesting for their decoration. Small heart-shaped badges of a two-headed eagle, the emblem of Russia, are in relief in the center of the breast and back plates. It is clear, however, that the decorative qualities of the emblems are more significant than their symbolic meaning. The body of the eagle follows the contour of the badge, while the feathers are almost deliberately unrealistic, pointing upwards, and not downwards. The tongue which should protrude threateningly from the beak has been transformed into a plant tendril. Particularly remarkable is the way the armorer has portrayed the emblem's Christian symbols: the crosses on the crowns – including even the cross of Golgotha between the heads of the eagles – have been replaced with flowers.

According to descriptions in the Inventory of 1606–07, this *zertsala* was originally even more brightly decorated: the white silver and silver-gilt of the images and of the ornamental bands shone out from the rich blue background of the plates, which were lined with red and green cloth and joined by green silk braid.

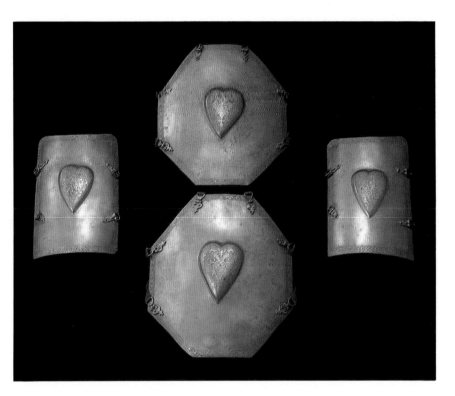

✣

BROADSWORD AND SCABBARD

✛

RUSSIA, FIRST HALF OF 17TH CENTURY

STEEL, WOOD, SILVER, TURQUOISES, CLOTH,

PRECIOUS STONES

L. OVERALL 101 CM, L. OF BLADE 88 CM

INV. NO. OR-4445/1-2

This broadsword is typical of the bladed sidearms in wide use in Eastern Europe and Russia during the sixteenth and seventeenth centuries, which originated in the Near and Middle East. This example differs from Western European broadswords in the wider double-edged blade and the saber-like shape of the hilt. The decoration of the scabbard is also different, with its silver-gilt chased and flat-chased ornamentation, turquoises and precious stones. In Russia broadswords of this type were especially popular among the richest and most noble of the military class, and were used as parade weapons. In battle they were used mostly as a supplementary, in which case they were carried not on the sword belt, but attached to the left side of the saddle. For this reason broadswords were considered as part of horse armor in the seventeenth century.

Broadswords occupied an important place in the Royal Treasury, with their skillfully ornamented blades of fine Damascus steel, and their rich decoration of precious stones and metals. Such swords first came to the country as military trophies, as gifts from ambassadors, or as trade imports; they often became models for Russian armorers.

This sword is first recorded in the inventory of the Armory of 1686–87 among royal broadswords under the number 1, which indicates the high value accorded it by the compilers.

The blade is straight and double-edged. In the upper part, near the hilt, is a hallmark of two sickle-like semicircles. In the sixteenth century these sickle hallmarks were used by Italian armorers from Genoa. Their weapons were as widely known in the East as in Europe. This popularity led to the hall-

mark's being used by armorers from other countries.

The hilt is silver. The quillons and the pommel are in the shape of dragons' heads. Similar decorations had already appeared in eastern countries (Central Asia, Turkey, and Persia) in the fourteenth and fifteenth centuries. In these countries the dragon was considered as a symbol of war.

The scabbard is covered in silver-gilt with chased floral ornament; it is decorated with turquoises and rubies, set in high mounts.

It is quite possible that this broadsword was produced in the workshops of the Armory of the Moscow Kremlin in the middle of the seventeenth century. Judging by the wording of the inventory of 1686–87 – "as for previous inventories" – it was already part of the main Armory in 1664.

KONCHAR AND SCABBARD

✠

RUSSIA, SECOND HALF OF 17TH CENTURY

STEEL, WOOD, SILVER, BONE

L. 118 CM

INV. NO. OR-4545/1-2

According to academics, the name *konchar* comes from the Turkish word *kandzar*, meaning sword or dagger. The word, however, is also consonant with the Slavic word *konets* or *konez*, in its meaning of sharp. Thus, for example, in Russian, *konchatyi* is the adjective for a sharp knife, and in Czech a *koneiz* is a foil (a sidearm with a long narrow blade). The Hungarian word for this weapon – *hegyestorok*, "cutting edge" – is also extremely close in meaning.

There are two types of *konchar*: the fighting *konchar*, with a long blade and, as a rule, a saber hilt; and the parade *konchar*, decorated with precious metals and stones, and with a smaller blade. The distinctive feature of the weapon is that it was not carried on the swordbelt, but was attached to the saddle. Therefore the decorative character of the ceremonial *konchar* had to correspond to the richness of the horse trappings.

This *konchar* is smaller than other known examples. It may have been made for one of the Czareviches. The form of the hilt is also different. Its grip is extended, ending in a pommel in the form of a dragon's head. The cross-guard with its dragon-head quillons is reminiscent of a saber hilt.

The scabbard is wooden, covered in cerise velvet. The chape, mouth-locket, and suspension rings are of silver, decorated with delicate stylized niello and turquoises.

The decoration resembles the work of armorers of the Moscow Kremlin in the second half of the seventeenth century. However, this sword came to the Armory collection from the Rust Camera in St. Petersburg in 1810.

PAIR OF SADDLE PISTOLS

✣

MOSCOW, KREMLIN ARMORY, 17TH CENTURY

IRON, WOOD, SILVER, COPPER

L. 58.8 CM, 59 CM; BORE OF EACH 15 MM

INV. NOS OR-2843, OR-2844

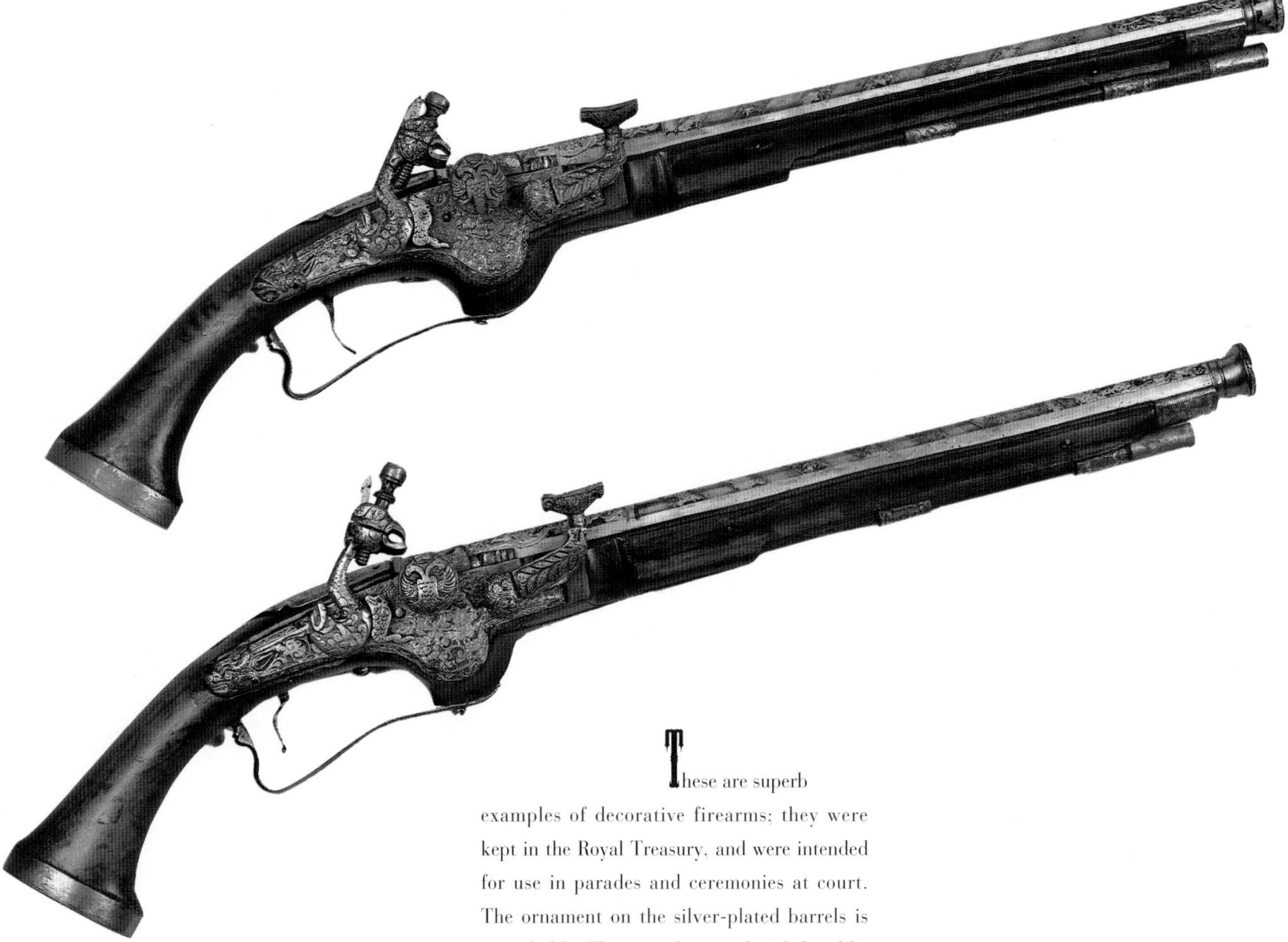

These are superb examples of decorative firearms; they were kept in the Royal Treasury, and were intended for use in parades and ceremonies at court. The ornament on the silver-plated barrels is remarkable. They are decorated with heraldic griffins and two-headed eagles, and the flint-locks have a flat-chased foliate design with fantastic dragons. The priming pan fences have sliding disc covers decorated with two-headed eagles. Parade pistols and other firearms usually had silver fittings decorated with filigree, gilt, niello, and enamel. The ramrod recess, the forepart of the stock and the muzzle plates of these pistols are brightly gilded and covered with a delicate flat-chased foliate design.

✢

HOLSTER

✢

MOSCOW, WORKSHOPS OF THE KREMLIN
STABLES OFFICE , 17TH CENTURY
LEATHER, VELVET, GOLD AND SILVER THREAD,
PEARLS, BRAID, GOLD, PRECIOUS STONES
33 x 19 CM
INV. NO. OR-4902

Such holsters were designed for a pair of saddle pistols (see left): they were attached to the pommel. Russian holsters were used in court ceremonies in the seventeenth century. The holsters in the Kremlin Armory collection were made in various workshops of the Moscow Kremlin: those of the Armory and the Stables Office, as well as the workshops of the Czarina's Chamber. This holster is clearly the work of the Czar's harness makers. Much of its decoration is similar to that of the saddles and caparisons from the Treasury of the Royal Stables.

The leather holster is covered with smooth green velvet. The velvet lapels and the flaps covering the cartridges are embroidered with gold and silver thread and studded with pearls. Rubies and emeralds are set in raised mounts. In the middle of the flap is a two-headed eagle under a crown, embroidered in pearls; this shows that the holster was the property of the Moscow sovereigns.

DOUBLE-BARRELED ARQUEBUS

✛

MOSCOW, KREMLIN ARMORY,

SECOND HALF OF 17TH CENTURY

IRON, WOOD, BONE,

MOTHER-OF-PEARL

L. 152 CM, BORE 10 MM

INV. NO. OR-4995

This double-barreled arquebus is an interesting example of a seventeenth-century hunting firearm. The barrels are positioned one above the other; on pressure being applied to a staple, they would change position by rotating on a pivot in the butt. One barrel is rifled with eight lands; the other is smooth. They have cut decoration on the breech and muzzle. A heraldic two-headed eagle is portrayed on a flat-chased foliate ground.

The flintlock, characteristic of the second half of the seventeenth century, is also of interest. Only part of the lock – the cock and the mainspring – is attached to the neck of the butt, while each barrel has a separate frizzle (steel), powder pan and steel spring.

QUIVER AND BOW CASE: SAADAK

❖

MOSCOW, KREMLIN ARMORY, 1666

MASTER DMITRII ASTAF′EV

LEATHER, CLOTH, SILVER, PRECIOUS STONES,

ENAMEL, FILIGREE

L. OF BOW CASE 68 CM

L. OF QUIVER 38 CM

INV. NO. OR-4471/1-2

In the sixteenth and seventeenth centuries the term *saadak* referred to the complete set of armaments for a horseman. This included the bow, its case or *naluch*, and the quiver and arrows. Until the sixteenth century this was the principal weapon of the feudal forces. In the seventeenth century it was replaced by firearms: saddle pistols and carbines. Thereafter bows were used as offensive weapons only by the national militia. They continued in use for hunting. But from the middle of the sixteenth century and throughout the seventeenth century a set of three *saadaki* was the most important item of royal Russian ceremonial armaments. These form the basis of the small and unique collection kept in the Kremlin Armory. The most important features of Russian royal *saadaki* of the seventeenth century were the richness of their ornamentation, the precision of their finish, and the portrayal of state emblems. Each ceremonial assemblage consisted of the bow and arrows themselves, a quiver, bow case, and *takhtui* (cover for the bow case), and a cover for the complete *saadak*.

The three *saadaki* were graded in importance; this is an example of a "tertiary" *saadak*. It was made by Master Dmitrii Astaf′ev as an Easter gift for Czar Alexei Mikhailovich. In documents from the seventeenth century it is referred to as "*saadak* quiver and *lub′e* [quiver and bow case]"; that is, it did not include other elements – the cover, bow and arrows. The *saadak* originally included a *takhtui* made of yellow silk from Shemakha, a region of the Caucasus and part of the state of Persia. The *takhtui* was the work of Pronka Andreev, a student of Astaf′ev. This, however, has not survived. In the 1686–87 inventory, this *saadak* is entered under the number 8.

The *lub′e* is made from red Persian leather. Both the quiver and the bow case are embroidered with stylized foliate ornament in silver thread. The Russian emblem of a two-headed eagle under three crowns is portrayed in the center. In the upper corner of the bow case is a silver plate decorated with precious stones and enamel. A similar plate in the upper corner of the quiver bears a heraldic lion rampant.

The belt of the *saadak* is of silk, with silver and enamel fittings. Seventeenth-century documents indicate that the silver decoration of the *saadak* was prepared in the Silver Chamber of the Moscow Kremlin.

MACE

✠

EASTERN EUROPE, BEGINNING OF 17TH CENTURY

SILVER-GILT, WOOD, BRONZE

L. 77 CM

INV. NO. OR-3790

The mace is one of the oldest types of weapon, and was widely used both in Europe and the East. From the sixteenth century military use of the mace began to decrease, and the weapon became a symbol of military power. In the seventeenth century maces of this type from the Armory were often presented to military leaders on their promotion to a post of command in the Russian army.

This weapon belonged to the boyar Boris Mikhailovich Lykov, a well known political figure of the early seventeenth century. He was a distant relative of the Romanovs on his mother's side, and a personal friend of Feodor Nikitich Romanov (the Patriarch Filaret). It is known that he played a significant role in the election of the young Mikhail Feodorovich Romanov as Czar in 1613. The ownership of the mace was established by the monogram on the smooth plate at the end of the shaft: *BKBML*, standing for "Boyar Prince *(Kniaz)* Boris Mikhailovich Lykov." However, in the inventory of the weapons collection at the Rust Camera, from where it came to the Armory in 1810, it is described as "belonging to a *hetman*" (a Cossack military commander).

The body and shaft of the mace are entirely covered with turquoises and silver-gilt, the latter decorated with flat-chased stylized ornament. This decoration is similar to the work of Eastern European armorers, who in the sixteenth and seventeenth centuries were strongly influenced by the Turkish school.

✠

FOREHEAD ORNAMENT FOR A HORSE: RESHMA

✣

TURKEY, FIRST HALF OF 17TH CENTURY

GOLD, SILVER, RUBIES, EMERALDS,

NEPHRITE

H. 11.5 CM, DIAM. 22.5 CM

INV. NO. K-1087

DECORATIVE BRIDLE: OGOLOV´

✣

TURKEY, 17TH CENTURY

GOLD, SILVER, RUBIES, TURQUOISES, NEPHRITE,

LEATHER, COPPER

L. OF STRAPS 101 CM, 51 CM

INV. NO. K-235

The decorative bridle was an essential part of royal horse trappings for ceremonial processions. The leather straps of the *ogolov´* were attached to the horse's head and further strengthened by an iron bit and reins made of silk (not shown). Sometimes a plume of feathers or strung pearls would be added, or a forehead decoration – the *reshma*. For parades of horses from the royal stables, two types of bridle were used: those decorated in the workshops of the Kremlin stables, and imported ones, usually from Turkey. Turkish horse trappings were highly valued in Russia before the time of Peter the Great, and were widely used by the Czars and the nobility. Turkish bridles are recognizable by the extreme richness of the trimmings, and the abundance of precious stones.

The straps for this bridle are made of soft red morocco leather entirely hidden beneath silver-gilt plates studded with rubies and turquoises. Flowers and trefoils are chased on the plates, many of which contain roundels of nephrite, also inlaid with rubies and turquoises.

Several different types of bridle were used, and in descriptions of the royal stables from the seventeenth to the nineteenth century they were given distinct names. This is an *ogolov´* with an *osheik* – an additional strap which tied around the horse's neck. Its use was purely decorative, and it was entirely covered in silver.

The fine central pendant, which was attached to the forehead of the horse, is also unusual. A nephrite mount holds a six-pointed star encrusted with gold and precious stones.

The *reshma* is a jeweled silver or gold plate which was placed on the Czar's horse (on the bridge of the nose) for ceremonial processions. It was attached to the bridle by silver chains.

The surface of this silver *reshma* is entirely covered in a delicate ornament on a blackened ground. This was a favorite device in Turkish precious metalwork of the sixteenth and seventeenth centuries. The gifts of ambassadors, tradesmen and representatives of the Orthodox Church would often include elements of a horse's harness – *reshmy*, breast ornaments, bridles and saddles – and might also include weapons in silver cases with carved decoration on a blackened ground. These articles became part of the Royal Treasury, and many have come down to us in the collection of the Kremlin Armory.

The mountings of bright nephrite, encrusted with rubies and emeralds framed by gold petals, lend particular brilliance to the *reshma*. They are continued along its silver-gilt chains.

✛

BREAST ORNAMENT FOR A HORSE: PAPERST′

✛

TURKEY, 17TH CENTURY

GOLD, SILVER, RUBIES, TURQUOISES, NEPHRITE,

LEATHER, BRAID

L. OF STRAPS 74 CM, 64 CM, 54 CM

INV. NO. K-414

The *ogolov′*
(see previous page) and the *paperst′* – the head
and breast trappings of the horse – were
always made in matching style. The silver-gilt
plates which cover the straps of the *paperst′*
are similar to those on the *ogolov′*. The
paperst′ consists of three straps which were
attached to the saddle by hooks.

The smiths who produced the
ogolov′ and *paperst′* set would pay particular
attention to the decoration of the forehead pendant of the former and the central plate of the
latter. This example has rubies and turquoises
set in nephrite mounts covering most of the
surface of the figured silver plate.

HELMET: ERIKHONSKAYA SHAPKA

TURKEY, 16TH CENTURY
STEEL, WHITE METAL, PRECIOUS STONES,
TURQUOISES, SILK CLOTH
DIAM. 21.3 CM
INV. No. OR-118

Royal military headgear occupies a special place in the Armory collection of Russian ceremonial armaments. During processions (particularly royal military reviews) the orushnichii, or head of the Kremlin Armory, would carry the helmet immediately behind the Czar. In seventeenth-century Russia a particular type of ceremonial helmet, which had first appeared in Turkey at the end of the sixteenth century, was often used. This had a sliding nasal bar to protect the face, ear guards, and a neck guard. It was known as an *erikhonskaya shapka*, from the Russian word *erikhonit´sia*, meaning "to stand out, impress by one's beauty".

This beautiful helmet apparently of sixteenth-century Turkish origin, came to the Royal Armory in 1622. After Prince Feodor Ivanovich Mstislavskii died without heir, valuable articles – including weapons – which had belonged to the ancient and powerful line of the Mstislavskiis became the property of the Sovereign.

This helmet has always been highly valued and carefully guarded by the Armory. In the inventory of 1654–56 it was named as the second most important of three helmets belonging to the royal ceremonial collection.

It is made from Damascus steel. Vertical flutes are carved in the crown, which accentuate the beauty of its shape. The terminal is attached to a flat-chased patterned plate studded with red rubies and blue turquoises. The surface is richly damascened in gold. A sapphire in a high mount lies in the center of the flat, chased nasal bar. The interior is lined with soft red silk cloth.

CAPARISON

✣

TURKEY, 17TH CENTURY

VELVET, SILVER-GILT, RUBIES, PEARLS

174 X 155 CM

INV. NO. TK-2620

Caparisons, or horse cloths, were an important part of ceremonial horse trappings. Their purpose and form varied: some covered the breast and crupper of the horse, some were placed beneath the saddle, and others covered the saddle. Parade caparisons were generally made in the Stables workshops from imported cloth, embroidered with pearls and decorated with precious stones.

This caparison, according to documents of the time, came to the Stables Treasury in the middle of the seventeenth century from Turkey as a gift to Czar Alexei Mikhailovich. Similar articles are mentioned in a description of the gifts made by the Greek Dmitrii Astaf'ev, who was a member of the Turkish Embassy in 1654.

This caparison is made of dark red velvet, and decorated with silver-gilt studs set with rubies on a ground of stylized pomegranates and toothed leaves, embroidered with pearls.

SADDLE

TURKEY, ISTANBUL, MID-17TH CENTURY

SILVER, EMERALDS, PEARLS, VELVET,

WOOD, GOLD THREAD, LEATHER, ALTABAS

H. TO POMMEL 31 CM,

H. TO CANTLE 16 CM, L. 41 CM

INV. NO. K-230

This saddle, from the Treasury of Czar Alexei Mikhailovich, is remarkable for its beautiful shape and delicate decoration. It has a low, round cantle rising to a narrow pommel at the front, flanked by oval wings. This shape is seen in the work of the finest saddlers of Istanbul in the middle of the seventeenth century. Documents from the old palace archives show that such saddles were brought to the Russian Czar from Istanbul by ambassadors of the Turkish Sultan, and by Greek traders. Royal saddles had mounts of gold or silver, and were richly decorated with precious stones.

The saddle is covered with velvet in the Czar's color, red. Leaves, tulips and carnations are embroidered on the seat in fine silver thread. Intertwined leaves and pomegranate flowers are embroidered on the side flaps in gold thread. The border of the saddle seems from a distance to be of gold, but is in fact covered with Turkish *altabas* – silk cloth interwoven with silver. The carnations and tulips on the border are of pearl, and the calyces of the flowers are made of fine pierced emeralds sewn onto the cloth.

TASSEL FOR A HORSE: NAUZ

✥

MOSCOW, KREMLIN WORKSHOPS, 17TH CENTURY
SILVER, GOLD, SILVER-GILT
AND SILK THREAD
L. 78 CM
INV. NO. K-103

Those who attended the Moscow Czars during ceremonial processions were obliged to present themselves at the Kremlin in bright ceremonial clothing and on horseback; their horses had to be attired in the most luxurious finery. One of the essential elements of parade horse trappings in the sixteenth and seventeenth centuries was the long tassel hanging beneath the horse's neck – the *nauz*.

This *nauz*, which belonged to Nikita Ivanovich Chulkov-Bol'shii, is particularly fine. The tassel is made from two types of thread: red silk, and gold intertwined with fine silver. The top of the tassel is covered in open-worked gauze, woven from silver-gilt thread.

The upper part of the tassel has a silver plate with a flat-chased ornament. The strips which border the plate are decorated with a foliate design, and the owner's name is engraved on a circular panel. It was common for Russian silversmiths to engrave inscriptions on valuable utensils such as *kovshi* (drinking ladles), *bratiny* (loving cups), or dishes. It is, however, extremely rare to find horse trappings with the name of the owner. In the old inventories of the Stables Treasury there is only one mention, in 1589, of a saddle inscribed with the owner's name – that of a powerful cavalry boyar, followed by the name of the Czar, Boris Feodorovich Godunov.

This tassel is one of the many exhibits at the Armory about which much still remains unknown. Clearly it came to the Royal Treasury from the chattels of a boyar; this was common when a boyar was disgraced or died without leaving an heir. Nothing is known of the owner of the tassel. Members of the ancient line of Chulkov are often mentioned in historical documents of the sixteenth and seventeenth centuries, and the family emblem of two six-pointed stars and two arrows is well known.

BRIDLE CHAIN

✥

MOSCOW, KREMLIN STABLES WORKSHOPS,
17TH CENTURY
SILVER
L. 286 CM
INV. NO. K-107/15

This massive silver chain is almost 10ft (3m) in length. The fifteen broad, curved links are decorated with magnificent flat-chased ornament of undulating stems, flowers and leaves.

In the sixteenth and seventeenth centuries chains of this type were a special feature of royal parade horse trappings. They were attached to the horse's neck to act as a leading rein, and were held by an attendant who either walked beside the parade horse or rode on another horse. Bridle chains were part of the "Grand Attire"; that is, they were used on the most solemn occasions. In the "Court Rankings" (*Razriad*) – daily records which were kept at the royal court – special reference is made to the use of bridle chains at court ceremonies. For example, when on April 16 1651 Czar Alexei Mikhailovich began the royal procession to the village of Pokrovskoe, with forty parade horses, "the attire was of the grandest, with clanking chains, reins and *nauzy* (tassels)."

Silver bridle chains were much admired by onlookers at ceremonial processions, particularly by foreign observers, many of whom referred to them in their accounts of Russia. Adam Olearius, a member of the Holstein Embassy to Moscow in 1634, wrote: "Instead of reins, the horses wore enormous silver chains. The links of the chain were more than two inches in width, but the silver was no thicker than the blunt edge of a knife, so that it was almost possible to pass your hand through the great rings; these chains made a mighty noise when the horses moved."

✛

STIRRUPS

✛

TURKEY, BEFORE 1636
IRON, SILVER-GILT, RUBIES,
TURQUOISES, LEATHER, CORD
H. 14 CM, W. 12.5 CM
INV. NO. K-541/1-2

Stirrups from Turkey were large and particularly fine, and were highly valued in Russia in the seventeenth century. They were used with both Turkish and Russian saddles. The shape of these stirrups is typical of Turkish design: with their broad rectangular bases and figured bell-shaped arcs they were very comfortable for the horseman. They are made of iron; small stars are flat-chased on the base, beneath the horseman's foot. The outer edges are trimmed with silver-gilt. The stirrups are decorated with an ornament of gilded flowers and trefoils chased on silver, set with brightly sparkling rubies and turquoises. The stirrup straps are of blue cord, matching the color of the turquoises.

These stirrups are an interesting example of the way in which Turkish horse trappings came to the Royal Treasury not always from Turkey itself. According to seventeenth-century documents they were among gifts from the ambassador of the Moldavian *voevoda* (governor) Vasilii, who visited Czar Mikhail Feodorovich in 1636.

✛

✛

KNEE-COPS FOR A HORSE

✛

MOSCOW, KREMLIN STABLES WORKSHOPS,
SECOND HALF OF 17TH CENTURY
SILVER
H. 10.5 CM
INV. NOS K-129, 130, 131, 132

In sixteenth- and seventeenth-century Russian ceremonial processions, royal horses wore silver "knee-cops" on their legs. These were like wide hoops made in halves attached by hinges and pins. In order not to harm the horses' legs, the interior of the knee-cops was cushioned with red silk or velvet. Documents of the time show that many knee-cops were produced in the Stables workshops, and in the Silver and Gold Chambers of the Kremlin. For example, "silver-gilt hoops for 100 horses" were commissioned from the Silver Chamber in preparation for the procession of Czar Feodor Alexeevich. The Soviet researcher M. M. Denisova considered that the knee-cops in the Armory collection might have been part of this commission.

They are made of pure silver, with a flat-chased undulating foliate ornament. The holes along the edges were for the attachment of the cloth lining.

AMBASSADORIAL CEREMONY IN THE SEVENTEENTH CENTURY

✣

Court ceremonies for ambassadors developed from the end of the fifteenth century, reaching their final form in the seventeenth. The ritual of meetings, receptions and negotiations for foreign emissaries, the sending abroad of Russian emissaries, and so on, played a particularly important role in the young Russian state at the turn of the sixteenth century. There were good reasons for this. Links with European and eastern countries had been largely destroyed in the years under the Mongol yoke. Now, therefore, Russia had to rebuild these links completely. At the same time foreign states were making overtures towards the Russian state, hoping to find in Muscovy a friend and ally.

The resident emissary, permanently living at his post, became part of diplomatic practice in the second half of the sixteenth century. Nevertheless, throughout the seventeenth century, alongside this new type of diplomatic representative, the "occasional diplomacy" usual in former times continued. This was the establishment of *ad hoc* embassies in response to important events. Ambassadors, emissaries and heralds were assigned to conduct peacetime negotiations and settle questions of trade

privileges, to conclude union agreements and to establish borders, often at the accession of a new monarch or the birth of a royal heir, or after military victories over neighboring states.

Hundreds of ambassadors from the four corners of the world could be found in the streets of Moscow in the Middle Ages: they made a rich and solemn spectacle, a wonderful parade of national dress and customs.

Many foreign visitors wrote about diplomatic etiquette at the Moscow court. In addition, Russian records exist – the "Ambassadorial Books" – in which the arrival of a foreign mission in Russia was carefully recorded. These ancient documents survive to this day and allow us to recreate Russian ambassadorial custom in minute detail.

Foreign ambassadors were obliged to inform the *voevoda* (provincial governor) of the relevant Russian border town in advance of their imminent arrival in Russia. The *voevoda* would then send his representative to meet the foreigners at the border. At this stage the foreigners had to declare where the embassy came from, the rank of the emissary, and the size of his retinue. The information was immediately relayed to the capital by heralds. The *voevoda*

would keep the emissaries with him until further orders were received. Finally, permission for entry would arrive from Moscow and the emissaries' lengthy journey began. Their itinerary from the border to the capital was carefully worked out. Special policemen were assigned for the "protection" of the ambassadors and were also charged with the sustenance of the embassy throughout the journey. This might be far from an easy task: some embassies numbered up to 1,000 people.

The procession made its final stop outside Moscow. Here the emissaries were met by two or three courtiers on behalf of the Czar. Each of these made ceremonial greetings, asking formal questions about the envoys' health, the health of their sovereign, their journey, and so on. The embassy was also informed of the day of its entry into the capital. The time of entry depended on the weather and time of year, but as a rule it was fixed for the morning.

Special representatives – usually up to 200 men – were selected to meet the emissaries in Moscow. The ambassadorial train, headed by the "chief ambassador," and the "welcoming party" moved slowly towards each other, meeting at an agreed place. The retinue

✣

Banquet in the Granovitaya Palace

lined up beside the ambassadors and the principal Russian participants, and everyone was required to dismount.

The ambassadors had then to remove their hats and listen to a ceremonial royal greeting conveyed by the senior member of the welcoming party. After an exchange of greetings and speeches, everyone remounted their horses and the procession moved sedately to the residence allotted to the ambassadors and their retinue, where everything had been made ready for them.

In Moscow, as during the journey, the foreign guests were provided for out of funds from the treasury, and each day abundant provisions were delivered to the ambassadorial residence from the royal kitchens. Notes from the ambassadors give a wonderful account of these provisions. One ambassador wrote that "the food provided for the embassy would have been enough for 300 men, let alone 30." Another's account shows that, during a stay of 16 weeks in the capital, his embassy of 33 men consumed "48 bulls, 336 rams, 1,680 chickens, 112 geese, 224 ducks, 11,200 eggs, 10 deer and 336 lb of butter."

The audience with the Czar was the culmination of the ceremonial. The pomp and wealth which accompanied it (and which was remarked upon by all foreigners) took on a deep symbolic meaning, since it represented the well-being and prosperity of the state itself. Ambassadors were informed in advance of the date of the audience and the rules of court etiquette, and how they should conduct themselves on the road to the Kremlin. The royal audience was both an honor for the ambassador and a sign of respect for his monarch; it was, therefore, a public event which took place in front of a large crowd of people. On entering the Kremlin, and before they reached the steps of the royal palace, the ambassadors were required to dismount. This was a strict rule of the audience. It was also a custom in private Russian life of the sixteenth and seventeenth century: to come right up to a house on horseback was to show disrespect to the host.

Ambassadorial gifts played a large role in the ritual of the ceremonial procession. They were open to public view, since their richness reflected the honor of the Czar. One remarkable account has been preserved, describing how one Western ambassador, who had suffered many mishaps and been robbed on his journey, had nothing to present to the Czar apart from a chiming clock which had miraculously been preserved. For the public procession, however, the clock alone was clearly insufficient. A number of valuable articles were therefore lent from the Royal Treasury, which the ambassador presented to the Czar in his own name.

The foreign diplomats were led into the Granovitaya Palace, part of the royal residence, where the "royal place" stood, a dais with a throne.

"The Czar sits in his royal place in all his royal finery. At his right hand, by the window, is a stand on a base. Below the Czar on either side stand the *ryndy* – four bodyguards, members of noble families, dressed in ermine robes, tall hats and boots, each holding a decorative axe."

Royal dress described in seventeenth century accounts was remarkable for its opulence. The Czar wore a precious crown and held a sceptre and orb. The sceptre remained in the Czar's hands throughout the ceremony, but it was extremely difficult to hold the massive jewelled golden orb for a long time. There was a stand next to the throne on which the

Czar would place the orb from time to time. On a bench beside the throne stood a hand-basin on a silver-gilt dish covered with a towel. The Czar rinsed his hands after he had offered them to be kissed by the ambassadors and members of the ambassadors' retinue because, in the words of one foreign writer, "the Russian sovereign, when offering his hand to an ambassador of the Roman faith, considered that he had been touched by a profane and unclean man." In the seventeenth century this custom, which aroused great interest in foreign diplomats and was always commented on, gradually became little more than a curiosity.

The boyars were essential participants in the ambassadorial audience. These were representatives of the highest aristocracy of Russia in the Middle Ages. In long robes of notable opulence, they sat on benches along the walls of the chamber, in silence and almost motionless, only occasionally standing up and taking off their tall fur hats at the mention of the Czar's name. These figures, reminiscent of stage extras, underlined the theatricality of the whole spectacle, making it seem carefully choreographed. The words and gestures of the participants had but one aim: to underline the

prestige of the sovereign and his domain. The exchange of gifts was an essential element of the ceremonial. Eastern emissaries brought rich garments, carpets and other textiles, and precious stones. Most significant of the gifts sent by Western monarchs were gold and silver utensils. Western European diplomats often presented the Russian sovereign with goblets. These might be extremely unusual: sometimes in the shape of exotic fruits, of real or fantastical beasts and birds; sometimes they were made in the form of ships with tiny figures of sailors, or allegorical figures or quaint fairytale characters. There were amusing goblets, double and triple goblets, goblets with moving parts driven by a concealed mechanism. Silver and gold, rock crystal, mother-of-pearl and coconut shells, elephant tusks and even ostrich eggs were used in these works. Gifts presented to the Czar were carefully recorded and put into the Treasury for safekeeping.

Foreign diplomats also received gifts of corresponding value in return; these usually consisted of furs, most often sable. When he had received his gifts, the Czar would order the ambassadors to approach the royal hand. The kissing of the royal hand was the

next stage in the ceremonial of the royal audience, although Muslim ambassadors were not allowed to kiss the hand and instead the Czar placed his palm on their head.

The ceremonial feast, which the sovereign hosted for foreign diplomats, was as essential an element of the ceremony as the feast given in honor of guests in private life. At the same time, the ambassador considered an invitation to the royal table as "an honor."

In comparison with other aspects of the ceremonial at the Moscow court, foreign tradition had less influence on the ceremonial feast. On the whole it showed the influence of national folk customs. The idea of "ambassadorial honor" at court was undoubtedly closely connected to that of the "honor of the guest" in ordinary life. The feast generally took place in the Granovitaya Palace. For this reason the palace, which in any event was one of the most striking of the royal buildings, was particularly finely decorated. Several foreign guests commented on this:

"The Granovitaya Palace is an enormous hall, splendidly decorated, with beautifully painted arches. In the middle of the hall is an enormous column, surrounded from

Reception of foreign ambassadors in the Royal Palace

top to bottom by shelves. These contain such a multitude of gold and silver goblets and utensils that it is impossible not to be awestruck at the sight. On the lower shelves stand a vast number of enormous dishes and cups of pure gold, and also a life-size silver lion. There are also many silver cups and vessels, each one of such a size that one man alone could not carry them and too large to think of drinking from."

The ambassadors were led into the palace, where the Czar and his courtiers were already sitting at their places. The sovereign sat at a separate table raised above the rest. No one, apart from the Czar's son, was allowed to sit at this table, a fact which underlined the position of the Czar and his heirs. The closer the placement to the Czar the more honorable; in addition, it was more auspicious to sit beside the royal table than opposite it, and more honored to sit on the Czar's right than on his left. The ambassadors did not all sit down at the same time, but separately, in the company of those whose official status was equal to their own. In accordance with their positions at the tables, the guests received from the sovereign "presentations of wine and food." To receive dishes from the hands of the Czar was considered the highest favor and represented a solemn act; the name of the dish was announced and all those who were to partake of it had to stand. Most honorable of all were the "remains", goblets from which the Czar had taken a sip and dishes which he had tasted, since these were considered to provide a direct link with the sovereign.

Before the feast the Czar distributed bread to all those present to symbolize hospitality. This custom had its parallel, and possibly its origin, in national life, as the host of a private Moscow feast would do the same. In contrast to the giving of bread, salt was not distributed to everyone: as one ambassador wrote, "to receive a saltcellar from the sovereign is a high honor indeed, since salt expresses not only favor but love." The large number of royal "presentations" meant that the ambassadorial feast continued for five or six hours; throughout this time nobody was allowed to leave the table. The unusual length of the dinner was also a result of the many toasts in honor of the sovereign, members of his family, and guests. Each guest on whom the Czar conferred attention had to stand as a mark of gratitude and everyone else then stood after him.

All bowed and then sat down again. In the course of a feast, guests stood over and over again: one ambassador went through this process sixty-five times. "We stood so often," wrote another ambassador, "that from hour to hour the movement increased my appetite."

After the first royal audience and the feast, negotiations were held which might last for more than a week, ending with a formal leave-taking. This ceremony was also conducted by the Czar himself, who conveyed his compliments or a petition to each diplomat's monarch, and offered the ambassadors a cup of mead or wine. The drinking of the beverage signalled the end of the ambassadors' stay at the court of the sovereign. This custom also originated in everyday life. Such ceremonies, rooted in national tradition, were gradually formalized; they lost their ritual significance and became part of court protocol. They remained in force until the end of the eighteenth century, when they were partly abolished and partly renewed by the reforms of Peter the Great.

I. A. Bobrovnitskaya

CAFTAN

MOSCOW, KREMLIN WORKSHOPS,
SECOND HALF OF 17TH CENTURY
VELVET: ITALY, SEVENTEENTH CENTURY
VELVET, TAFFETA, SILK THREAD
L. 153 CM
INV. NO. TK-2242

Caftans are first mentioned in Russian documents of the fifteenth century. Thereafter, and particularly in the seventeenth century, the name caftan referred to any loose-fitting, ankle-length, secular garment, with many buttons, long sleeves, and a lining. It could be worn as either an undergarment or an outer garment, in summer or winter. Caftans varied in the cloth from which they were made, and in minor details of cut. This garment was for indoor use, of a type worn by members of the aristocracy on official occasions. It is made from smooth cerise velvet, with a braid edging and long tapered sleeves. It is fastened from top to bottom by 47 pear-shaped buttons covered with cerise silk and attached by dark purple thread. The caftan was a particularly elegant and sedate garment, with its flowing, loose form and its length, stretching almost to the floor. It encouraged a smooth and dignified gait, as was considered fitting in the Middle Ages. The full costume included a high fur hat and a staff in the right hand.

FORMAL CAFTAN: TERLIK

MOSCOW, KREMLIN WORKSHOPS,
SECOND HALF OF 17TH CENTURY
SMOOTH VELVET AND DAMASK:
ITALY, 17TH CENTURY
UNCUT VELVET: GDANSK, 17TH CENTURY
VELVET, DAMASK, SILK AND GOLD THREAD,
GALLOON
L. 123 CM
INV. NO. TK-2616

The *terlik* was the rarest kind of Old Russian court uniform; it was kept in the State Treasury, and given out only for official ceremonies. In the seventeenth century it was worn by many of those in service at court: the *ryndy*, who stood by the throne and accompanied the Czar on ceremonial processions, the noble *zhil'tsy*, who met foreign emissaries and stood at official receptions bearing halberds and partizans (ceremonial staff-weapons), the *voznichie*, who were part of the royal entourage, and others. Seventeenth-century documents refer to garments made from velvet and various figured cloths of different colors. Normally, the purpose of the dress would dictate the manner in which the *terlik* was decorated. Only four examples of the *terlik*, including this one, have survived to this day. They are all made of smooth crimson velvet with two-headed eagles embroidered on the front and back. The cut of the *terlik* was very varied, and was not typical of Old Russian dress in general. It is a knee-length caftan consisting of two main sections: a detachable, tight-fitting bodice and a lower part in the form of a wide skirt, gathered in at the waist, with a central overlap. The collar is small and round. The sleeves are in two parts; the upper arm is wide and gathered in at the elbow; from the elbow to the hand the sleeve is narrow, with a small reversed cuff at the wrist. The fastening on the front of the bodice is concealed behind a broad figured flap, fastened with hooks on the left side and on the shoulder.

A wide strip of uncut long-napped velvet, golden in color, runs around the hem of the skirt, imitating fur. The external lining of the lapels, the cuffs, and the collar is finely decorated with interwoven thread in two colors. On the bodice of the *terlik* two-headed eagles with three crowns are embroidered in shallow relief with gold and silk thread. On the breast of each eagle is a shield with St. George, the emblem of Moscow. The garment has a certain theatricality. On more than one occasion Nicholas II, the last Russian Czar, chose a *terlik* as his costume when attending masked balls at court.

TOWEL

MOSCOW, KREMLIN WORKSHOPS,
SECOND HALF OF 17TH CENTURY
CALICO, SILK AND GOLD THREAD
210 X 60 CM
INV. NO. TK-544

The towel is typical of decorative articles where practical purpose was less relevant than richness of design. Made of linen, it is ornamented with embroidery in different colored silk and gold thread. The bright colors of the fantastic foliate designs and the richness of the trimming make this example particularly decorative. Such towels were used during the ceremony of the presentation of gifts, and at banquets and other formal receptions. It is known that towels of this kind were brought to the royal court from Turkey and the Crimea; Russian versions were also made in the workshops of the Kremlin. There was a special workshop known as the Czarina's Chamber, where the Czarina herself took an active part in the production of items of royal dress and other small pieces, including parade towels.

BOOT: SAPOZHOK

❖

MOSCOW, KREMLIN WORKSHOPS,
17TH CENTURY
VELVET, LEATHER, PEARLS
L. 20.7 CM
INV. NO. TK-2878

Made of dark red velvet and decorated with pearls, this boot is an extremely rare example of Old Russian parade footwear. In seventeenth-century Russia, as in all European countries, there was none of the wide variety of footwear so characteristic of the modern day. The basic type of ancient Russian footwear was the *sapog*. There were two types: the short *sapog* to the ankle, and the long *sapog* which sometimes reached to the knee. Boots were made of leather for outdoor wear, or of various smooth or decorated textiles for wear in the home. Parade footwear, and particularly royal footwear, was decorated with gold or pearl embroidery, and precious stones, and trimmed with gold braid. Right and left boots were identical. The sole was wide, and the heel raised but quite solid. There was no fastening. Footwear for men and women was essentially the same. It is known, for example, that the Czarina Evdokia Lukianovna had a pair of short boots of red velvet, decorated with pearls and colored stones; when the pearls were removed to decorate a new pair of boots for the Czarina, the original boots were given to her father Lukian Stepanovich Streshnev.

AMBASSADORIAL AXE

✛

TURKEY (?), BEGINNING OF 17TH CENTURY

STEEL, SILVER, WOOD

L. 126 CM

INV. NO. OR-2235

The *ryndy* (weapon bearers and bodyguards of the Czar) are first described as being armed with axes in documents dating from the middle of the sixteenth century. From the end of the sixteenth and throughout the seventeenth century, the guard of honour of *ryndy* armed with axes was an essential element of all ambassadorial ceremonies. Axes of both Turkish and Russian manufacture are mentioned in Armory documents. Their purpose and basic construction were identical, but the form and character of

their heraldic decoration varied. This axe is probably the work of Turkish craftsmen. It is made of Damascus steel in the shape of a half moon, as was traditional for such axes. It differs from examples of Russian work in the slightly smaller size and greater curvature of the blade. A damascened foliate design decorates the edge of the blade. The status of this weapon is underlined by the damascened representation of the Russian two-headed eagle with three crowns.

The handle of the axe is wooden

and covered in silver, ending in a spherical pommel. The silver is engraved in the manner of leather used in the manufacture of hilts and scabbards for side weapons. In Russian documents of the seventeenth century such engraved silver is referred to as *khoz serebro*. Further decoration consists of two silver rings, each with flat-chased, stylized foliate ornament.

EWER OF CZAREVICH IVAN ALEXEEVICH
✦

MOSCOW, KREMLIN WORKSHOPS, 1676
SILVER, ENAMEL, FILIGREE
H. 32.1 CM
INV. NO. MR-3420

TABLECLOTH
✦

DENMARK, MANUFACTORY OF KARL TISSEN,
1621
SILK, CANVAS
408 X 218 CM
INV. NO. TK-2184

Washbasin sets, consisting of an ewer and bowl, were used to rinse the hands at table. They were already known at court in Moscow in the sixteenth century. The sets which are kept in the museums of the Kremlin are mostly of foreign origin: often they were presented to the state as ambassadorial gifts. Among the work of Moscow silversmiths are two ewers which were commissioned for the young Czareviches Ivan and Peter by their older brother Feodor Alexeevich soon after his accession to the throne. The two bowls which were part of the sets have not survived. Documents from the time show that the Czar Feodor even dictated their decorative character, stipulating that "the sides of the bowls should be decorated with silver badges with enamel designs, and the basins should be engraved with grasses." The shape of the ewer is traditional and, as was usual at that time, the handle is reminiscent of handles on German vessels of this type. It is quite likely that in creating the set the craftsmen used imported, readymade components. At this time the work of German jewelers was widely exported to Russia.

In seventeenth-century Russia decorative tablecloths were an important adornment to the Royal Chambers. This wonderful blue and white silk tablecloth with woven thematic illustrations, a gift from King Christian IV of Denmark to Czar Mikhail Feodorovich, was brought to Moscow by the Russian ambassador Prince Alexei Mikhailovich L´vov and his scribe, Zhdan Shipov. The delicate design on the central panel of the tablecloth represents a laid table: the design consists of large dishes with wildfowl, sturgeon, and turtles; smaller dishes with lobsters, herrings, various fruits, berries, and vegetables; and twelve empty plates set between knives and two-tined forks. This central panel is bordered by two narrow bands: the first is decorated with a garland of small flowers, leaves, and fruits; the second shows *putti* flying in pairs, supporting shields with the inscription "Gloria." Various scenes are woven into the border: a royal hunt with hounds and gamebirds; a sea battle between sailing ships under various European flags; views of a medieval town, with the cathedral, town hall, and tall houses. The border at the ends of the tablecloth includes heraldic badges with the coat of arms of Christian IV, and the emblems of Denmark and its constituent lands and regions. The inscription "Anno 1621" and the initials "KT" are woven beneath the emblem of Denmark. Figures representing the seasons occupy the four corners.

The tablecloth is executed in double-sided embroidery, where the design on the face of the cloth is visible in negative on the reverse side. It is a unique example of European weaving, highly valued at the time of its manufacture, and carefully preserved.

WINE VESSEL IN THE FORM OF A LEOPARD

✣

LONDON, 1600-01

SILVER

H. 98 CM, WT. 29.32 KG

INV. NO. MZ-693

This leopard, with a heraldic shield in its paws, sits on a massive square base. The detachable head of the figure is attached by a heavy chain to rings in the mouths of two lion *mascaron* applied to its shoulders. The heraldic shield bears a *mascaron* in the form of a female face, and is flat-chased in the Renaissance style. The base is decorated with chased grasses and engraved pendants of fruit. The surface of the vessel is covered in hatching, to represent the beast's coat. The image of the leopard was widespread in English decorative art, but this example and

its pair also in the Armory collection, are unique in English silverwork of the turn of the seventeenth century. These vessels, originally from the English royal treasury, are among the most valuable acquisitions made for the Royal Treasury; they were bought by state officials in Archangel in 1629.

DISH: LOKHAN´

✣

AMSTERDAM, 1664

MASTER KONRAD BERGVELDT

SILVER

DIAM. 50 CM

INV. NO. MZ-114

Such was the size and wealth of decoration of dishes like this *lokhan´* that in Rus´ they were often treated as decorative panels and hung on walls; they were also placed on dressers in the royal apartments.

This deep round dish was presented to Czar Alexei Mikhailovich in 1665 by the Dutch States. It has a low base, a smooth, gently convex interior, decorated with crests, and a wide border with eight palmettes. Each of these is decorated with engravings of tulips and daffodils on short undulating stems, a popular decorative motif in Dutch silverwork of the 1650s and 1660s. The palmettes and crests are further decorated with *knorpelwerk* (auricular) ornament, widely used in Dutch decoration up to the end of the seventeenth century.

INCENSE BURNER IN THE FORM
OF A MOUNTAIN: GORA-KURILNITSA

✚

HAMBURG (?), BEFORE 1629
SILVER-GILT
H. 53 CM, L. OF BASE 40 CM
INV. NO. MZ-246/1-4

This remarkable
silver-gilt object was both a practical vessel for
burning incense and a superbly lavish table
decoration. It was a gift from the Danish King
Christian IV to Czar Mikhail Feodorovich.
It is in the form of a steep mountain crowned
by a castle with watchtowers; paths and
stairways run down the mountain's sides. The
castle is a model of the famous fortress of
Kronborg at Helsingör, the seat of the Danish
kings (and also the scene of the action in
Shakespeare's *Hamlet*).

Incense burners were already being
produced in Italy in the fifteenth century. The
Victoria and Albert Museum in London contains two bronze examples, the work of the
Italian Bartolomeo Bellano, and in a private
collection in Baden-Baden there is another
made by the celebrated Nuremberg master
Albrecht Janitzer in 1590. The Armory contains two other similar vessels in the form of
mountains by Dierik Utermark from Hamburg,
which also came from the treasury of King
Christian IV of Denmark.

TANKARD: STOPA

✚

LONDON, 1617-18
SILVER
H. 41.5 CM
INV. NO. MZ-666

This *stopa* was
presented to Czar Mikhail Feodorovich by
Charles I of England in 1636. It is one of nine
English tankards dating from 1585 to 1663
in the Kremlin Armory collection. With one
exception they are of the "Hanseatic" type: tall
cylindrical vessels of this type were widely produced in the towns of the Hanseatic League up
to the end of the eighteenth century, and also
in other regions around the Baltic and North
Sea. The lid, body and base of the *stopa* are

engraved with fantastic sea creatures in oval,
rhomboid, and circular cartouches, showing
the influence of Dutch ornamentation.
Elsewhere, the pomegranate seeds and roses
and sweetbriar flowers on thick stems are
characteristic of English decorative
art. The body is also engraved with
the emblem of James I of England.
The different types of scrolling
which decorate the cartouches, and
the combination of a flat-chased
gloss subject on a matt ground, are
characteristic of late Renaissance English
silver.

DISH

✚

AUGSBURG, 1645-50
JAKOB II PLANCK
SILVER
75 X 88 CM
INV. NO. MZ-1222

Augsburg was one
of the principal sources of fine metalwork in
seventeenth-century Europe. The center of this
dish (of the *lokhan'* type) contains an ornately
chased allegorical composition depicting the
Triumph of Peace and set in a wide scrollwork
border. The female figures on the bottom of
the bowl represent Peace, Glory, Plenty, and
History. The *putti* astride the eagle, the dragon,
lion, and sea creature in cartouches on the side
of the dish symbolize the four elements.

✚

COVERED GOBLET

✤

NUREMBERG, 1637

MASTER WITH MAKER'S MARK OF A KNIFE

SILVER-GILT

H. 85 CM

INV. NO. MZ-1081/1-2

West European goblets of varying shape and decoration were used in Russian life as dresser ornaments. They were also awarded to *voevody* (provincial governors) and merchants for faithful service or successful campaigns, and were popular as gifts, often presented on solemn occasions and ceremonies, such as the consecration of the Czar, weddings, namedays and christenings. Czar Alexei Mikhailovich, on his accession to the throne in 1646, received nearly 200 standing cups, the majority of which were of German origin.

This tall, elegant, bell-shaped cup was made in Nuremberg, the most important center of gold- and silversmithing in Germany in the sixteenth and seventeenth centuries, and is typical of the type of wine goblet in use at that time. Its most striking features are the large convex bosses which both give it a massive appearance and show off the reflective qualities of the surface. This style of molding reminded Russians of apples; such standing cups are referred to in Old Russian documents as *yablochnyi* or "apple-like."

PITCHER

✤

AUGSBURG, C. 1690

MASTER LORENZ II BILLER

SILVER, FILIGREE

H. 51.5 CM

INV. NO. MZ-1621

Vessels of this type were traditionally used to decorate the dressers in the Granovitaya Palace up to the end of the nineteenth century. In form the pitcher is reminiscent of classical vessels, with its long neck, arched handle, and circular base. The body and lid of the vessel show a gilded ornament of densely interwoven acanthus leaves and pendants of fruit; such ornamentation was characteristic of European art of the turn of the eighteenth century, as was this vessel's filigree technique. The stamped roundels on the long neck and the delicately pearled beading on the lid contribute greatly to the decorative effect. This pitcher is a typical example of the mature Augsburg baroque style.

DRINKING VESSELS: CHARKI

✥

MOSCOW, KREMLIN WORKSHOPS, 17TH CENTURY

GOLD, ROCK CRYSTAL, PRECIOUS STONES

H. 4.8 CM, DIAM. 9.1 CM (BELOW LEFT)

SILVER, GOLD, PRECIOUS STONES

H. 2.2.CM, DIAM. 6.4 CM (BELOW RIGHT)

INV. NOS DK-19, MR-5157

In descriptions of the Royal Treasury in the seventeenth century, a large number of different vessels made up the garnish which adorned tables and dressers during official banquets. These vessels included standing cups *(kubki)*, loving cups *(bratiny)*, goblets *(kovshi)*, drinking vessels *(charki)* and saltcellars; they might be made of gold and silver or other valuable materials. Reference is often made to vessels made from semiprecious stones: crystal, agate, cornelian, or jasper. Also mentioned are utensils of such exotic materials as coral, mother-of-pearl, coconut shells, and ostrich eggs. Many of these articles were of foreign manufacture, and were brought to the sovereign by foreign traders or purchased abroad for the Russian court.

The Armory collection also contains several examples of Russian national vessels made from stone, ivory, and rare woods. The *charka* on the left, made from rock crystal, is such a vessel. The delicacy of the translucent stone and its striking beauty are brought out by the lavish gold surround. Its handle is particularly fine, enriched with brilliant green and white enamel and decorated with sparkling precious stones – emeralds and tourmalines. An inscription showing that the *charka* was the property of Czar Mikhail Feodorovich is set on a dark blue enamel ground on the crown of the *charka*.

The decoration on the second *charka* is no less interesting. The luster of the gilt and precious stones, the velvety smoothness of the niello work, and the ebullient intricacy of the ornament all combine to turn a utilitarian vessel into a work of art.

**TABLE CENTERPIECE OF
A WARRIOR ON HORSEBACK**

❖

AUGSBURG,
SECOND HALF OF 17TH CENTURY

SILVER

H. 47 CM

INV. NO. MZ-2020

In the seventeenth century striking and theatrical ornamental silverwork was used to decorate dressers. The metalworkers of Augsburg were particularly renowned in this field. They produced figures of European monarchs on horseback, including Gustavus Adolphus of Sweden, Charles I of England, and Christian V of Denmark, as well as various German dukes. The craftsmen also created other figures of warriors on horseback which were not portraits, as with this centerpiece, which was presented to Peter I in 1684 by the Swedish King Charles XII.

In this work the horseman wears classical dress and a helmet; he has a sword at his side. He sits on a rearing horse, set on a tall base. This baroque composition is extraordinarily dynamic: the horse and rider seem to be in motion, an impression reinforced by many details of the design. The quality of this table sculpture lies in the fusion of composition and expressive power, while it is also highly representative of the style of its age.

DRINKING LADLE: KOVSH

✛

MOSCOW, KREMLIN WORKSHOPS,
FIRST HALF OF 17TH CENTURY

SILVER

L. WITH HANDLE 29 CM,

W. 21.5 CM

INV. NO. MR-4156

The *kovsh*, or drinking ladle, is one of the most distinctive articles of Old Russian tableware. Archaeological excavations have revealed that wooden vessels of this type were in use in Rus´ by the eleventh century. Later, in the fourteenth century, the first metal *kovshi* were produced. Both gold and silver were used. This example belonged to Czar Mikhail Feodorovich.

The wonderfully graceful outline recalls that of a boat or a water bird. Mead, a popular beverage in Old Russian times, was drunk from a *kovsh*. There were many different recipes for mead, which was flavored with various fruits and berries. White mead was drunk from a silver *kovsh*, and red mead from a golden one.

✢

DRINKING LADLE: KOVSH

✢

MOSCOW, KREMLIN WORKSHOPS,
FIRST HALF OF 17TH CENTURY
GOLD, PRECIOUS STONES, PEARLS, NIELLO
H. WITH HANDLE 14.5 CM, L. WITH HANDLE 29.5 CM
INV. NO. MR-4126

This gold *kovsh*, also the property of Czar Mikhail Feodorovich, is notable for the beauty of its shape and the exceptional lavishness of its finish. Plates set with pearls and bearing delicate niello ornament decorate the spout and the handle. Precious stones in high-relief mounts sparkle brightly on the smooth and gleaming surface. These vessels, along with the regalia and other articles of the court ceremonial, were kept in the Great Treasury, and were used on ceremonial occasions. Displayed on dressers, they demonstrated to foreign visitors the wealth of the Moscow sovereign and the artistry and skill of Russian goldsmiths. Only the most honored guests were served from such *kovshi*. Documents recount how in 1621 during dinner at the Patriarch's palace, the Patriarch was brought mead in three *"kovshi* decorated with pearls and jewels" from the sovereign's dresser.

✢

POURING VESSEL: ENDOVA

✛

MOSCOW, KREMLIN WORKSHOPS, 1644
SILVER
H. 17 CM
INV. NO. MR-4189

Vessels similar in form to a large *bratina* with a spout were used in Rus′ over many centuries. The collection of Old Russian tableware in the Armory is unique both in size and in the value of its components; this, however, is the only *endova* in the collection. It would be filled with mead, beer, or wine and used to replenish smaller vessels. The decoration of the *endova* is based on the alternation of smooth, polished ovoli and ovoli with a flat-chased foliate ornament. Around the top of the spherical, bulbous vessel runs a smooth band with an inscription which describes how the *endova* was made for the boyar Vasilii Ivanovich Streshnev, who was one of the relatives of the Czarina Evdokia Lukianovna, the second wife of Mikhail Feodorovich. Streshnev was the head of the Silver and Gold Chambers of the Moscow Kremlin in the middle of the seventeenth century, where court jewelers used precious metals to create wonderful objects for the royal court.

LOVING CUP: BRATINA

✛

MOSCOW, KREMLIN WORKSHOPS, 1642
MASTER FEODOR EVSTIGNEEV
GOLD
H. 17.7 CM
INV. NO. MR-4133/1-2

This *bratina* has a pointed lid; the smooth join to the body of the vessel makes the whole reminiscent of the cupola of a Russian church. These loving cups usually bore inscriptions with the name of the owner or with some Russian proverb or motto. The inscription on this vessel reads: "True love is like a vessel of gold: it can never be broken. and if it should ever bend, then reason will mend it." In the work of the Russian masters. the inscription always had a decorative as well as a moral purpose, forming the basis of a distinctive ornament for the object.

LOVING CUP: BRATINA

✛

MOSCOW, KREMLIN WORKSHOPS, 17TH CENTURY
SILVER-GILT
H. 11 CM, DIAM. 12 CM
INV. NO. MR-5079

The *bratina* is a ceremonial cup whose form, as with the *kovsh,* is based on that of an Old Russian utensil. These vessels were widely used in royal and noble circles, and were an essential part of the feast-day tableware. The *bratina* was filled with *kvass* (rye beer), wine, or beer, and was passed from one guest to the next. The comparative simplicity in form is combined with unusually intricate ornament. Often the surface would be covered with chased or flat-chased foliate design.

BOWL: CHASHA

✢

SOL´VYCHEGODSK, END OF 17TH CENTURY

SILVER, ENAMEL, FILIGREE

H. 15.7 CM

INV. NO. MR-1206

In the seventeenth century silverware with painted enamel – the work of craftsmen from Sol´vychegodsk – was extremely popular in both the royal and Patriarch's households.

The particular feature of enamel work from Sol´vychegodsk is the combination of multicolored painted designs on a smooth white background. Foliate ornament predominates in the decoration. This type of decoration was an important part of the jeweler's art from early times. Until the seventeenth century foliate ornaments on enamel were treated conventionally and symmetrically; at the end of the century, however, new features began to appear. Many of the enamel flowers are easily recognizable – tulips, poppies, irises, and cornflowers. It is not only the form, but also the scale of the flowers that makes them so lifelike.

The ornamentation is full of vitality: the flowers, with their long, smoothly curved details, seem almost to braid the surface of the vessel.

Changes in the character of foliate designs did not come about by chance. To some extent their appearance is explained by the influence of floral designs in Western European baroque style. More, however, they are the result of a process of secularization evident in Russian art of the seventeenth century, and a consequent interest in the real world and a striving for verisimilitude of form and design. Particular emphasis was laid on the charm and beauty of the natural world; where enamel ornamentation had previously been somewhat harsh, it now became exuberant and joyful.

PLATE

✢

MOSCOW, KREMLIN WORKSHOPS,

1670-80

SILVER, NIELLO

DIAM. 30.2 CM

INV. NO. MR-4205

Vessels of this type in Rus´ were more decorative than practical. The beauty of the finish of this plate lies in the contrast of the sparkling silver-gilt surface with the velvety smoothness of the niello work and in the juxtaposition of light background with dark ornament and vice versa. Floral motifs including stylized pomegranate seeds adorn the plate; this type of decoration appeared in Russian work in the second half of the seventeenth century, influenced by Eastern decoration. A thin gilt inlay is applied to the bottom of the plate, bearing a laurel wreath roundel with a coat of arms consisting of a pair of arms holding a sword crossed with two sabers.

In comparison with Western Europe, coats of arms appeared in Russia relatively late, in the last quarter of the seventeenth century. At the beginning of the 1670s, at the behest of Czar Alexei Mikhailovich, the master of heraldry of the Austrian Emperor Leopold I came to Moscow. In 1673 he designed a special form of heraldry to be used in the creation of coats of arms for Russian families. The device on this plate belonged to Bogdan Matveevich Khitrovo, a Russian aristocrat who for a quarter of a century was in charge of the artistic workshops of the Moscow Kremlin.

BEAKER: STAKAN

✣

MOSCOW, END OF 17TH CENTURY

SILVER, NIELLO

H. 20.1 CM

INV. NO. MR-1773

From the beginning of the sixteenth century tall, bell-mouthed beakers were depicted in Russian miniatures as part of the official feast garnish. In the second half of the seventeenth century vessels of this type were decorated with a combination of niello work and engraving. The surface of the silver *stakan* is covered with delicate nielloed grasses on a lustrous damascened ground of long undulating stems with magnificent leaves and flowers. In contrast with the work of previous centuries, in the second half of the seventeenth century Russian foliate designs began to lose their stylized character, and became more natural and lifelike. The ornament on the sides of the *stakan* portrays birds sitting on branches; also shown are dynamic figures of running beasts – a unicorn, a deer, and a ram.

GOBLET

✣

MOSCOW, KREMLIN WORKSHOPS, 1628

MASTER JAKOB FRICK

GOLD, PRECIOUS STONES, ENAMEL

H. 17 CM, DIAM. OF CUP 11.5 CM

INV. NO. MR-1046

This harmonious, elegant gold vessel, decorated in multicolored enamel and precious stones, is a rare example of Old Russian secular tableware of the seventeenth century. Although goblets existed in Russian life from early times, they were usually of Western European origin. In form, this goblet, which belonged to Czar Mikhail Feodorovich, is reminiscent of a church chalice or *potir*; the traditional liturgical inscription, however, has been replaced by the name of the Czar. Seventeenth-century documents attest that the vessel was the work of Master Jakob Frick. This craftsman was involved in the creation of a number of masterpieces, including the lavishly bejeweled crown of Mikhail Feodorovich, which occupies a central place in the Armory collection of state regalia.

THE ROYAL COURT AND THE ORTHODOX CHURCH IN THE SEVENTEENTH CENTURY

✥

At the turn of the seventeenth century and shortly before the accession to the throne of the first Czar of the Romanov dynasty, a significant event took place in the history of the Russian Orthodox Church: the establishment of the Patriarchate. The Russian Orthodox Church had been effectively independent since the middle of the fifteenth century (after the fall of Constantinople to the Turks in 1453 and the Florentine Union); now, however, the Church became fully separated from the Constantinople Patriarchate.

The proposal to establish a Patriarchate was first put forward by Czar Feodor Ivanovich, the last of Ivan Kalita's descendents to rule in Moscow. After permission had been granted by all the hierarchies of the Eastern Church, Feodor Ivanovich ratified the election of a new head of the Russian Church. Alongside the Czar, the leader of secular life, the Patriarch now became the leader of ecclesiastical life. Thus was demonstrated the inextricable link between the two supreme political powers in Russia, the monarchy and the Church.

The principle of the "Two chosen by God" – that is, the indissoluble union of Church and state – was adopted by Russia from Byzantium along with Christianity in the tenth century. Over several centuries relations between Church and state were sometimes complicated and conflicting; at all times, however, they were governed by this principle.

The Russian Orthodox Church played a leading role in the unification of the disparate lands under the power of Moscow, and in the gaining of political independence from the yoke of the Golden Horde. In particular, the transfer of the center of power from Vladimir to Moscow at the beginning of the fourteenth century was politically beneficial to the Muscovy Princes. By so doing, the Church effectively gave its blessing to their internal and foreign policy measures. Consequently, any obstinate princes from other lands who indulged in excessive behaviour could expect not only military reprisals; they might also be expelled from the Church, a punishment no less feared. As Moscow became a political power, and one of Eastern Europe's most potent centralized states, the significance of the Russian Orthodox Church also increased. The voice of the Metropolitan of Rus´ began to be

heard more and more loudly. So it was that when, after the bloodless struggle with the Turks, Byzantium and the Constantinople Patriarch were forced to enter a Union with Catholic Rome, Moscow declared itself the true defender of the Orthodox faith. Around the turn of the sixteenth century, a new political idea arose in the monasteries of Russia: "Moscow, the third Rome." For several centuries it endured as the ideological core of the internal and foreign policy of the Russian autocracy.

The essence of autocracy, however, is sole power, and the Sovereign of All Russia was not willing to share it with anyone – not even with the Church. For this reason, during the political terror under Ivan the Terrible, not only innumerable secular victims, but also many ecclesiastical ones were put to the sword. Only the defeat of the interventionists and the restoration of nationhood after the Time of Troubles resurrected the authority of the Russian Orthodox Church. "The Sovereigns of All Russia" – the Patriarchs Filaret and Nikon – not only gave their blessing to state policy, but were also active in conducting it. It was the Patriarch Filaret – the father of the first Czar

✥

of the Romanov dynasty – who in the view of many researchers was the real head of state at the time. In the middle of the seventeenth century the Patriarch Nikon did not simply conduct ecclesiastical affairs, and undertake the significant reforms that led to the schism in the Church; he also ruled the state while Czar Alexei Mikhailovich was away on military campaigns. The secular powers, however, watched the erosion of their rights with dismay, until eventually the ecclesiastical council gave way to pressure from Alexei Mikhailovich. The once all-powerful patriarch was deposed, and sent to one of the northern monasteries as a simple monk. Several more decades were to pass before Peter the Great issued a decree dissolving the Patriarchate, 150 years after its establishment. Russia was now under the power of a sole ruler.

The ancient Byzantine tenet of the "Two chosen by God" found symbolic expression in the two residences in the Moscow Kremlin – the Czar's and the Patriarch's. As early as the beginning of the fourteenth century Ivan Danilovich Kalita, the founder of the first Moscow royal dynasty, had set aside some land within the Kremlin for the Metropolitan's

court, where wooden, and later stone buildings were constructed. In the middle of the seventeenth century, by order of the Patriarch Nikon, a new stone Patriarch's Palace was founded, with a private church that has survived to this day. The vast riches of the Church and the personal wealth of the Patriarch allowed that the finest stonemasons of the time were employed in the building's construction. The finished ensemble was magnificent, and greatly influenced Russian architecture of the time; in the words of contemporaries, the Patriarch's Palace "filled them with wonder." The principal room of the palace was particularly striking. Called the Cross Chamber (Krestovaya Palata), it was a rectangular hall of 280 sq m, with a roof in the form of a groined vault with no central support. The Cross Chamber served much the same purpose for the Patriarch as did the Granovitaya Palace for the Czar. Here the Patriarch received the Czar, foreign emissaries and visiting priests; it was also the scene of meetings of the Church Council.

In most respects the customs surrounding the life of the Patriarch were similar to those of the Czar; often, indeed, the Patriarch's court matched the royal court in

opulence and luxury. One foreigner visiting Russia in the middle of the seventeenth century observed accurately that "after the Great Prince, the greatest power in the land belongs to the Patriarch." The ceremonial processions of the Patriarch on foot and by carriage were reminiscent of the processions of the Czar.

The Patriarch had his own staff of attendants, of the same rank as those at the royal court, as well as boyars, *okol'nichie* (of status below a boyar), *stol'niki* (lesser nobles) and *deti boiarskie* ("boyars' sons" – of inferior rank still). Like the Czar, the Patriarch had his own artistic workshops, where precious utensils and clothes were made. Along with foreign treasures, these were kept in the Patriarch's Treasury, no less luxurious and opulent than the Royal Treasury.

The Patriarch's Treasury consisted of the Secret Treasury, which contained his personal belongings, and the Patriarch's Sacristy, the treasure house of the Russian Orthodox Church. The Sacristy, housed in the Dormition Cathedral, was particularly magnificent. This was where the splendid ceremonial vestments of the Patriarch were kept, made from expensive imported cloth and embroi-

Dormition Cathedral of the Moscow Kremlin

dered with pearls and precious stones. Here, too, was kept church plate for various purposes, made of gold and silver and decorated with bright enamel and semiprecious stones, and intricate nielloed and stamped designs. In addition to church plate and ecclesiastical robes, many secular articles were also stored here. When banquets were hosted by the Patriarch in the Cross Chamber, the ceremonial table service contained an enormous quantity of gold and silver vessels: goblets, *chashi* (bowls), *kovshi* (drinking ladles), *charki* (drinking vessels), and *bratiny* (loving cups).

In addition to the chambers of the Patriarch, the Moscow Kremlin also contained the most important place of worship in Russia – the Dormition Cathedral. Founded in 1479 by the Great Prince Ivan III, it was altered and enriched by practically all the Romanov Czars, who took great care in its construction and decoration. It is the supreme, but still typical, example of an Orthodox place of worship, containing a complex synthesis of the various fields of artistic creativity – architecture, icon and fresco painting, and decorative and applied art of all kinds. Everything in the cathedral has symbolic significance, and is

subject to strict rules and canons. A religious building is a house of God, a symbol of heaven on earth. Every fresco has a theological basis, and each has a strictly defined position in the cathedral. The most significant of the Orthodox images are portrayed in the most important parts of the church: on the ceilings of the cupolas or under the vaults. These include Christ the Almighty, the Lord of Hosts, The Saviour Not Made with Hands, the Saviour Emmanuel, and Our Lady of the Sign. Prophets and evangelists are portrayed in the drums and squinches of the domes, while the vaults and lower parts of the walls show scenes from the Gospels relating to the life of Christ. On the west wall, as dictated by tradition, is a portrayal of the Day of Judgment. The columns are covered with portraits of saints and martyrs, who were considered the building's "pillars." The role and significance of the frescoes in the cathedral were not purely didactic, setting out the dogma of the faith. The artistic quality of medieval frescoes, with their delicate coloring set off by a gold ground, played a significant role in inspiring the devotion of worshippers at the cathedral.

Icons were even more important.

These were the most essential elements of a church, since Orthodox theology considered sculptures of the saints as heathen idols: consequently, sculptures were rare in religious buildings. An icon was "a book for the illiterate," assisting the "spiritual ascent" of believers. This distinct and symbolic purpose of the icon was achieved by artistic techniques which were characteristic of ancient Russian art and endured to the end of the seventeenth century. At first glance these techniques may not appear complex; they are, however, extraordinarily expressive. The symbolic center of the icon was the countenance of the saint, portrayed in various spiritual states. The eyes and mouth of the saint were the focus of the spiritual state, along with the gestures of the arms and, in particular, the position of the hands. In order that these elements should be as visible as possible, figures on icons were usually portrayed full face or three-quarter face. The spirituality of the figures is underlined by the absence of material attributes, and by the way in which they are portrayed on a flat plane without perspective, so that graphic quality predominates over the pictorial.

Russian icons are unique not only

✣

Interior of the Dormition Cathedral

for their distinct artistic language, but also because of the way in which they are positioned in the church. Apart from some individual icons, most were set in the iconostasis, a unique feature of Russian churches. This was a wall of icons which separated the altar from the rest of the cathedral. The iconostasis, which became an essential part of ecclesiastical architecture at the beginning of the fifteenth century, consisted of several rows. The first row, on the level of the "royal door" in the middle of the iconostasis, contained the "local icon," set amid other icons. The local icon was connected with the particular subject or saint to whom the cathedral was dedicated. Above the royal door were the icons portraying the Deesis: in the center the icon of Christ and on either side, turned towards him in devotional poses, the Mother of God, John the Baptist, and the Archangels Michael and Gabriel. The row above the Deesis was the "festal row," containing icons illustrating the main Christian feast days. Higher still, in the two upper rows, were portraits of the prophets, while the highest row held pictures of the Christian patriarchs.

The elements of the Orthodox service combined to rich effect: the chanting of prayers and congregational singing, the measured rhythm of the priests' movements, the sparkle of the icon lamps, the flames of the candles and the delicate wisps of fragrant smoke from the censers. The senses of the faithful were overwhelmed with sights, sounds, and odors. The purpose was to lead the congregation into a religious state of grace; to bring them from worldly cares to divine rebirth.

The Moscow Czars made pilgrimages on every church holiday, and took part in all the rituals and ceremonies that marked the church year. These royal processions were considered among the most important of court ceremonies; the Czar, therefore, would appear in parade dress, with a pectoral cross, a baldric chain on his chest, and a silver staff in his hand. He would be supported under the arms by "the chosen ones" – boyars and *stol'niki*. In the eyes of his subjects, the pilgrimages of the Czar were of national significance, for the prayers of the Czar would save the state and its people. The Czar's piety was an expression of the piety of his people. For this reason, the Czars were rigorous in their observance of the full cycle of church services and prayers. They would attend in ceremonial dress, as befitted the head of the Orthodox state. During Lent, for example, Czar Alexei Mikhailovich, known for his extreme piety, would stand in church for five or six hours, making as many as a thousand prostrations to the ground.

The ceremonies which marked the principal feast days of the church calendar, and in which the Czar participated, were modelled on the solemn religious rites of the Byzantine Church. Each feast day had its own particular significance, and all took place in the Kremlin with great display and solemnity. On Christmas Eve, for example, the Czar would traditionally make a secret journey, accompanied only by his *strel'tsy* and officials of the Privy Council, to prisons and almshouses, where he would distribute alms with his own hands. Later that day, choristers would come to the palace to sing praises to Christ. At the end of the ceremony the Czar would offer them red and white mead, brought in by one of the courtiers in gold and silver *kovshii*. On Christmas Day itself, after the early service of prime, when the bells summoned the congregation to the liturgy, the Czar would go to the Dining Chamber of the palace, where awaited the Patriarch and the clergy. For this occa-

✣

sion the hall was decorated with carpets and broadcloth. In the near corner was the seat for the Czar, and alongside it the chair of the Patriarch. The Czar took his seat in the Dining Chamber and commanded his boyars and other nobles to be seated on the benches, while junior courtiers normally remained standing. In the vestibule he then greeted his guests: the Patriarch, accompanied by metropolitans, archbishops, bishops, archimandrites, and abbots, who carried a cross and holy water. After the prayers the choristers wished the Czar long life, and the Patriarch gave an official greeting and blessed the Czar. Then the Patriarch went to greet the Czaritsa and other members of the royal family. From there he made his way to the service in the Dormition Cathedral where, by now, the Czar was already in his place, dressed in all his parade finery. At the end of the service the Czar returned to his palace, where he prepared for the feast day banquet.

No less solemn was the feast of the Epiphany, which was marked by the Procession of the Cross from the palace to the Moscow River. Here a hole was cut in the ice, through which the Patriarch blessed the water. The procession from the palace to the river often stretched for several miles. It began from the portals of the Dormition Cathedral, from where the procession moved through the Secret (Tainitskie) Gates of the Kremlin to the river. A description of this procession written in 1680 has survived. Courtiers in golden costumes preceded the Czar in his parade finery, three abreast, with the lower ranks at the front. Behind the Czar came the senior courtiers, also in gold caftans, and behind them more junior ranks "not in gold." A guard processed on either side of the Czar, made up of Moscow *strel'tsy* dressed in colored parade caftans, and armed with gilt arquebuses and halberds, which had been specially distributed from the Armory for the occasion. The leaders of the regiments of *strel'tsy* were dressed in an outer vestment of velvet, with colored caftans beneath. In addition, *strel'tsy* with banners and drums in "full military order" lined the royal route through the Kremlin. "Large regimental arquebuses" – heavy cannon – were placed along the route, surrounded by carved spiked railings painted in different colors. Alongside these stood gunners dressed in colored robes and holding banners.

During the ceremony of the blessing of the water, the Patriarch read a prayer, threw salt into the water, and swung an incense burner over it. After the ceremony Muscovites would distribute the water around the town in buckets, and later would bring their horses to the ice hole to drink the holy water.

On the Sunday before the beginning of Lent, a ceremony was held in which the Czar and Patriarch both took part: the feast of the Day of Judgment. The ceremony was held in the Dormition Cathedral, in the middle of which was hung the icon of the Day of Judgment. After reading from the four Gospels the Patriarch blessed water and used it to wipe the icon with a sponge. At the end of the service he made a sign of the cross and sprinkled water over the Czar and the other members of the congregation.

One particular church festival, which embodied the power of the Patriarch, was Palm Sunday. This was both a ceremony and a performance, recounting the entry of Christ into Jerusalem. The ceremony began with two processions from the Dormition and Annunciation Cathedrals, which joined up and moved together to the Cathedral of the Veil on Red Square. The procession was headed by a

✣

low wagon, drawn by six horses, on which stood an artificial tree richly decorated with flowers and berries. Boys clothed in white stood beneath the tree, singing "Hosanna" and "God save us." Behind the wagon came clergy in rich vestments, carrying banners, crosses, icons, and censers; they were followed by the boyars and others close to the Czar, who walked three abreast and carried real or artificial palm leaves. As the bells of the town rang out, the Czar came next in all his parade finery. In one hand he held a palm branch; in the other he held the reins of an "ass," in fact a white horse draped with broadcloth and with special extensions to its ears. The Patriarch sat sidesaddle on this animal, dressed in his sacred robes. In his right hand he held the Gospels, while in his left he held a cross with which he blessed the crowds lining the way. Dozens of children in clothes of broadcloth ran in front of him. Some of them removed these garments and spread them out on the road, while others scattered pieces of red broadcloth beneath the feet of the horse. The Patriarch was escorted on either side by metropolitans, archbishops, bishops, archimandrites, and abbots, who carried large candles. Behind the clergy came representa-

tatives of the merchants and traders of the city. A prayer was said at the Place of Execution on Red Square, after which the Patriarch again blessed the people; the whole procession then returned once more to the Kremlin.

Another special ceremony in which the Patriarch participated was the New Year festival, celebrated in seventeenth-century Russia on September 1, calculated from the supposed date of the Creation. A special dais covered with red broadcloth was erected in Cathedral Square between the Archangel Cathedral and the royal palace. On this three richly decorated lecterns were placed. The first of these was for the icon of St Simon Stylites, whose feast day was celebrated on September 1; the second was for the Patriarch to read from the Gospels; the third was for the archdeacon. A large goblet of holy water stood on a table behind the lecterns, covered with a parade cloth. Two special places were set opposite the icon: the seat of the Czar, on three raised steps, and covered with a canopy of gold cloth; and the seat of the Patriarch, on two raised steps, covered with a colored carpet. As the bells rang out, the Czar, escorted by courtiers, and a procession of the clergy carrying religious images

would make their way from the Dormition Cathedral. After blessing the water, the Patriarch would make the sign of the cross and sprinkle water over the Czar and the people, and would then make a speech of greeting. For this occasion more than 20,000 people would gather in Cathedral Square.

This ceremony was abolished by Peter the Great, who moved the New Year festival to January 1, and decreed that years should be dated from the time of the birth of Christ. Ten days after his decree, on January 1 1700, a celebratory service was held in the Dormition Cathedral "for a prosperous start to the year", with the traditional wishing of long life to the Czar. As before, the Kremlin was filled with people. Regiments of soldiers were positioned around the square and, as the church bells began to peal, an artillery salute rang out. That evening Moscow witnessed an unprecented spectacle – fireworks. A new year and a new century had begun, and with it a new epoch in the history of the Russian state and the Church.

I. I. Vishnevskaya

✣

✣

OKLAD (FRAME) FOR THE ICON
THE TIKHVIN MOTHER OF GOD

✣

MOSCOW, BEGINNING OF 17TH CENTURY
ROBES OF THE VIRGIN AND CHRIST:
RUSSIA, 19TH CENTURY
SILVER, GOLD, PRECIOUS STONES, PEARLS
91 X 71 CM
INV. NO. MR-9016/1-6

The silver-gilt *oklad* for the Tikhvin Mother of God icon came to the Armory from the Kirillo-Beloozero Monastery. The richness of the decoration and the variety of techniques used in the precious metalwork are typical of the seventeenth century. It is a marvelously lavish and ceremonial piece of work: the crown of the Virgin contains large sapphires and rubies weighing 90 and 30 carats; two 40 carat sapphires and an enormous gilded topaz of 700 carats are set in the *tsata* (pendant); the *ubrus* (head-dress) is woven with *kafimskii* (river) pearls, and the stamped foliate design is especially delicate.

This exquisite *oklad* once decorated an example of one of the most revered icons of the Church. The chief characteristic of the Tikhvin Mother of God was that the Child was held in Mary's left arm. The original icon was reputed to have been painted by the apostle Luke, and up to the end of the fourteenth century was kept in the Church of the Blachernae in Constantinople. In 1383 this holy relic disappeared from the city and, according to Russian annals, surfaced near Novgorod in the town of Tikhvin, from where it got its name. A church was built here dedicated to the Virgin and later, in the middle of the sixteenth century, the Tikhvin Monastery was founded on the initiative of Ivan the Terrible. Legend has it that the icon worked many miracles. In 1613 the Swedes had seized much of the land around Novgorod; the Tikhvin Monastery, and the local inhabitants who had gathered within its walls, were saved from the Swedes by the protection of the icon. Soon after this event a holiday was instituted in honor of the Tikhvin Mother of God. Copies were made of the miraculous icon. It was in the presence of one of them that Russia concluded the significant Stolbov Peace with Sweden.

Icons of the Tikhvin Mother of God were very popular in Rus´, and few churches did not have one among their collection. It would be a particular honor to commission an *oklad* for such a revered icon. In the case of this icon, judging by the valuable work on the *oklad* which is clearly the work of a Moscow master, the commission may have come from a member of the royal family.

✣

ROYAL DOOR

MOSCOW, FIRST HALF OF 17TH CENTURY
FRAME: RUSSIA, 19TH CENTURY
SILVER, WOOD, TEMPERA
157 X 40 CM
Inv. No. ZH 151/1-2

The royal door was set in the middle of the iconostasis, and led to the central part of the altar, where the altar table was situated. During the liturgy the Gospels and the holy articles symbolizing Jesus Christ, the King of Glory, were brought out through the royal door. Compositions of the Annunciation and the four Evangelists were usually depicted on the door.

The form of this royal door, with its characteristic figured outline, was widespread in Rus´ in the sixteenth and seventeenth centuries. The artist's signature is hidden beneath the inscription and a dried coating of holy oil. Several elements of the composition, however, suggest that it is the work of a Moscow icon painter of the first half of the seventeenth century. These include the lack of perspective in the treatment of the architectural forms, and the brown hills with characteristic bleached edges, as well as the heavy build and large heads of the figures. This view is confirmed by the work's provenance from the Nikola Gostunskii Church in the Moscow Kremlin.

The stamped metal frame, dating from the nineteenth century, is decorated with a foliate ornament in the tradition of seventeenth-century work.

ALTAR CROSS

✢

MOSCOW, 1659

SILVER, PEARLS, PRECIOUS STONES

H. 36 CM

INV. NO. MR-4977

The altar cross was one of the most important of all religious articles. As its name suggests, it was kept on the church altar. During services it was raised to bless the congregation, and the faithful kissed it. At the feast of the Epiphany it was used to sanctify the holy water.

Altar crosses had different forms. In the Orthodox church the most popular form was that of the eight-pointed cross. The particular feature of such crosses was the additional lower bar set at an angle. In theological literature, the following symbolic explanation is given for this feature of Russian crosses: when Christ came down to earth, man began a process of spiritual regeneration, a passage from darkness to the light of heaven. The salvation of man, his ascent to heaven from earth, is symbolized by the slanting bar.

This cross was commissioned by the Czarevna Irina Mikhailovna, the eldest daughter of Czar Mikhail Feodorovich. Irina Mikhailovna was the godmother of Peter the Great, and on July 29 1672 she carried the newborn Peter from the font.

CENSER: KADILO

✢

MOSCOW, 1620

SILVER

H. WITH CROSS 34 CM, DIAM. 14 CM

INV. NO. MR-9959

The *kadilo* was a religious vessel for the burning of incense, used in Christian church services for the censing ritual. This ritual, which symbolized the prayers of the faithful ascending towards God, had its roots in Biblical times. The temples of the ancient Israelites had special censing altars with incense burners.

In Orthodox churches the censing ritual was carried out in front of icons as a mark of particular reverence, and in front of the congregation to symbolize the grace of the Holy Spirit descending upon them.

Old Russian censers were designed to reflect church architectural styles, and varied greatly in shape and size. Sometimes they were made in the shape of a square temple topped by a cylindrical drum with an onion dome, crowned by a cross. In addition to censers with direct associations with religious buildings, there were also spherical censers made of two joined cups, the upper of which was shaped like the roof of an old Russian church. This censer is an excellent example of the latter type, which was especially popular in Russia in the seventeenth century.

ALTAR GOSPELS

✛

TEXT: MOSCOW, 1648

COVER: MOSCOW, 17TH CENTURY

COVER FRAME: MOSCOW, 1814

GOLD, SILVER, PRECIOUS STONES,

PEARLS, GLASS, WOOD, BROCADE, PAPER,

CLOTH, NIELLO

37 X 53 X 10 CM

INV. NO. KN-195

This set of gospels comes from the Convent of the Ascension in the Moscow Kremlin, from the vestry of the Church of the Ascension of Our Lord. The convent, founded by the wife of Dmitrii Donskoi at the end of the fourteenth century, was the burial place for Great Princesses, Czaritsas and Czarevnas.

Printed in the time of Peter the Great and the last Patriarch Adrian, the book is remarkable for its highly decorative nature: the silver-gilt cover, the brocade binding, the plethora of precious stones, and the pearl lining.

A niello portrayal of the three-figured Deesis occupies the center of the cover. This and the symbols on the corner brackets show many of the characteristic features of late seventeenth-century art: the detailed working of architectural backgrounds, and the free treatment of the clothes of the Evangelists. The portraits of the Evangelists include the symbols of each: the Angel for Matthew, the Lion for Mark, the Calf for Luke, and the Eagle for John; all these symbols personify the essence of Christ. The hasp of the cover bears full-length portraits of Christ's favorites, the Apostles Peter and Paul.

The artistic mastery of this article suggests that it is the work of Kremlin silversmiths. The abundance of precious metals – more than 2 lb (1 kg) of gold and 4 lb (nearly 2 kg) of silver – indicates that it was commissioned by a very rich person. Despite the absence of a dedication, which may have been destroyed during restoration at the beginning of the nineteenth century, there is no doubt that the commission was undertaken on behalf of a member of the royal family.

CHALICE

✣

MOSCOW, 1681

SILVER, NIELLO

H. 30 CM, DIAM. 17.5 CM

INV. NO. MR-4428

This chalice was placed in the Nila Stolbenskii Monastery near Tver´ by Czar Feodor Alexeevich. It was part of the set of church plate that included the paten with *zvezditsa* (star-shaped cover), plates, and utensils for cutting the Communion bread. It is a splendid example of the work of jewelers in the capital in the second half of the seventeenth century.

The traditional portraits of the seven-figured Deesis and the Golgotha Cross on the bowl of the chalice are framed by cartouches. The decoration shows an interesting combination of two of the most popular decorative techniques of the time – carving and niello. The carved images and ornaments are on a ground covered with delicate nielloed grasses, while the metal surrounding the nielloed floral motifs is carved. This, combined with the smooth gilded details on the surface of the chalice, gives the whole a rich stylistic effect.

PATEN AND COVER: DISKOS AND ZVEZDITSA

✜

MOSCOW, 1697

SILVER, NIELLO

DIAM. OF PATEN 27 CM,

H. OF COVER 14.5 CM

INV. NOS MR-4432, MR-4963

In a special part of the Orthodox service small pieces were broken off the Communion bread in honor of Christ, the Virgin, the heavenly powers, all the saints, the living, and the dead; these pieces were placed on the *diskos* or paten. The base of the bowl-shaped paten contains an image of the Christ Child as an infant, symbolizing the sacrificial lamb. The sides of the interior have figures of the archangels, with the Lord of Hosts and the Holy Spirit in the form of a dove above them. The twelve Apostles are portrayed around the outside of the bowl, and on the bottom are the symbols of the Evangelists, seraphim and cherubim.

The *zvezditsa*, symbolizing the star of Bethlehem (*zvezda* in Russian means star), was placed on the diskos, and, like the chalice, was covered with a special cloth. In the center of the *zvezditsa* is a portrayal of the Last Supper, and, instead of the traditional cherubim and seraphim, the arches contain portraits of the Moscow saints Alexei, Peter, John and Philip.

This *diskos* and *zvezditsa* come from the Church of the Exaltation of the Cross in Moscow.

PATEN COVER: VOZDUKH

✜

CLOTH: ITALY, 17TH CENTURY; EMBROIDERY: MOSCOW, 17TH CENTURY

DAMASK, BROCADE, BRAID, STONES, PEARLS, GLASS, LACE

54.5 X 50 CM

INV. NO. TK-1711

The *vozdukh* was the biggest of the three cloths used in the Orthodox Communion service. The two smaller cloths, one square, the other cross-shaped, were used to cover the chalice and the *diskos* and *zvezditsa*, while the largest, rectangular cloth was placed over both together. The name stems from the fact that the priest would wave it about as he recited the Creed, so that the air (*vozdukh* in Russian) would be stirred.

The *vozdukh* is made from two types of Italian patterned brocade *(aksamit)*. Cloth imported to Rus´ was used with extreme care, and its patterns were chosen to set off the design of the finished article. In this case the center of the *vozdukh* contains a small piece of stitched *aksamit* with fragments of cloth, positioned in such a way as to form a crown over the Cross of Golgotha, which is embroidered with pearls and precious stones.

✛

PATENS

✛

MOSCOW, END OF 17TH CENTURY

SILVER, NIELLO

DIAM. OF BOTH 23 CM

INV. NOS MR-4486, MR-4487

The number of patens used for the Communion bread ranged from one to three. In the sixteenth and seventeenth centuries two were generally used. One of the patens was decorated with the liturgical portrait of the Virgin with raised hands and the Child at her breast, known in ancient Rus´ as Our Lady of the Sign (*Znamenie*); the other bore an image of the Crucifixion.

On these patens, which come from the Chudov Monastery in the Kremlin, there are additions to the traditional subjects: on one, the twelve prophets, and on the other, the Lord of Hosts surrounded by archangels and the nine Apostles in sacred vestments.

The decoration of the patens consists of ornamental baroque motifs, given an individual interpretation; this was characteristic of seventeenth-century Russian art, which adopted elements of Western European culture.

✛

RIPIDA

✤

RUSSIA, 1656

SILVER-GILT, WOOD

L. WITH HANDLE 108 CM,

DIAM. OF DISK 34 CM

INV. NO. MR-5102

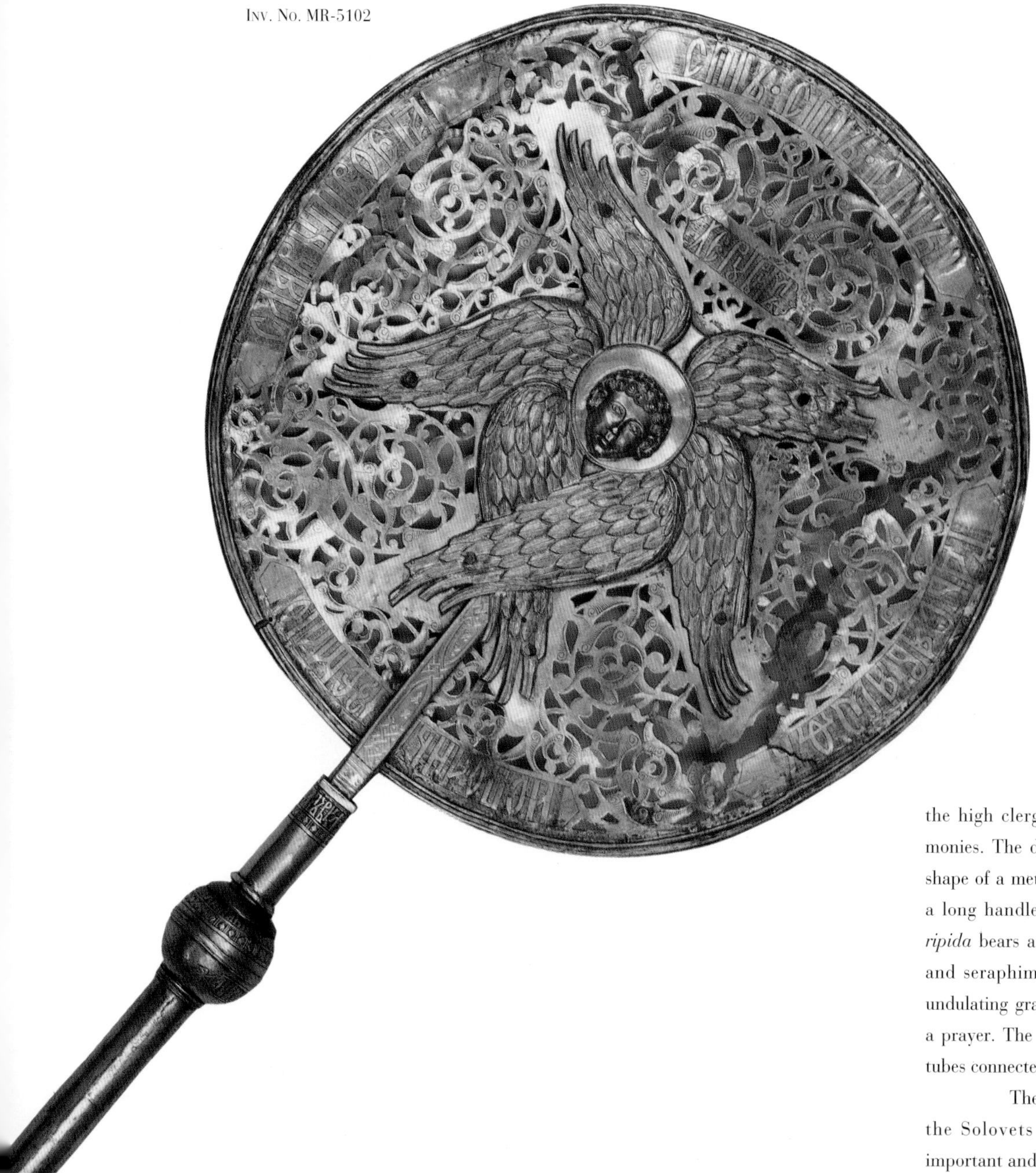

Ripidy were used by the high clergy during solemn church ceremonies. The device was a type of fan, in the shape of a metal disk carved on both sides, on a long handle. The center of this silver-gilt *ripida* bears a stamped depiction of cherubim and seraphim, on a background of stylized undulating grasses and a carved inscription of a prayer. The handle consists of three smooth tubes connected by joints in the form of apples.

The *ripida* comes from the vestry of the Solovets Monastery, one of the most important and richest monasteries of the north of Russia.

HOLY WATER VESSEL
✣

MOSCOW, KREMLIN WORKSHOPS, 1695

MASTER MATVEI AGEEV

SILVER, NIELLO

H. 39 CM, DIAM. 44 CM

INV. NO. MR-8987/1-2

Vessels of this type were used in the church ceremony of the sanctification of holy water. They were made in the shape of a large hemispherical bowl with two handles.

This holy water vessel is the only one in the Armory collection with a removable lid which could be turned over and used as a dish. On the underside of the base is an inscription which tells us that the goblet is made of "pure *efimki*," and is the work of one of the leading craftsmen of the Silver Chamber of the Moscow Kremlin, Matvei Ageev. *Efimok* was the Russian name for Western European sterling silver coins known as *thalers*, because they were made from silver mined at Joachimsthal in Germany. (This is the origin of the word '*dollar*'.) Silver coinage from abroad was used in Rus´ as raw material by silversmiths, since the metal was not mined there until the end of the seventeenth century.

The massive silver-gilt vessel weighs more than 24 lb (11 kg). It is made in the Russian baroque style, and decorated with carved oval roundels in lavish floral mounts.

The bottom of the interior contains a gilt plate with a stamped image of Our Lady of the Sign. The underside of the lid has an image of the Trinity.

The royal craftsman Matvei Ageev was one of Moscow's leading artists, a master of the technique of niello work. His surviving works contribute greatly to the Armory collection.

CANDLE HOLDER: KANDILO
✣

MOSCOW, 1694

SILVER-GILT

DIAM. OF CUP 32 CM

INV. NO. MR-9929

The *kandilo* was a vessel used to hold the candles which were placed in front of icons. According to its inscription, this example was made in 1694 by order of the boyar Lev Kirillovich Naryshkin, the brother of Czaritsa Natalia Kirillovna, who was the second wife of Alexei Mikhailovich and mother of Peter the Great.

The decoration of the silver-gilt *kandilo* shows the influence of the Western European baroque. This is visible in the rich relief of the stamped design, the motifs of the ornament in the form of acanthus leaves and bunches of grapes hanging on ribbons, and the combination of silver and gilt details. Some of the artistic principles of the baroque, as interpreted by Russian masters, formed the basis of the stylistic movement in Russian art of the late seventeenth century known as "Russian" or "Naryshkin Baroque." The second name comes from the Naryshkin boyars, relatives of the royal family, who commissioned many articles in this style.

TABERNACLE

❖

MOSCOW, KREMLIN WORKSHOPS,
SECOND HALF OF 17TH CENTURY
GOLD, SILVER, PRECIOUS STONES,
PEARLS, ENAMEL, NIELLO
H. 36 CM, W. 14 CM
INV. NO. MR-3390/1-6

This gold tabernacle,
from the vestry of the Cathedral of the
Annunciation in the Moscow Kremlin, is decorated with a large quantity of precious stones
and brightly colored enamel. It is characteristic
of the work of Russian jewelers of the second
half of the seventeenth century.

The drawers in the side of the
tabernacle were intended for the sacraments.
Niello portraits on these drawers show the
Evangelists. The sides of the tabernacle bear a
nielloed depiction of the Eucharist. These decorations are remarkable for the quality of their
execution, and the expressiveness and accuracy
of the drawing. The portraits show the influence of Western European engraving, which
was quite well known in Russia in the seventeenth century. The pink tourmaline which
crowns the tabernacle weighs 650 carats;
together with the four turrets, one at each corner, these symbolize the traditional five-domed
roof of Russian churches.

ICON CROWN

❖

RUSSIA, END OF 17TH CENTURY
GOLD, SILVER, PRECIOUS STONES,
PEARLS, ENAMEL
39 X 10 CM
INV. NO. MR-3708

This crown was part of
the *oklad* of a large icon which belonged to one
of the court churches of the Moscow Kremlin.
Its decoration shows all the richness of foliate
motifs in the Russian jeweler's art of the late
seventeenth century. These include the rhythmic flourishes of the undulating stems, the
large many-petaled rosettes, and the pointed
buds of the fantastic flowers. Amid the opulence and complexity of the ornament the artist
has retained the clarity and definition of the
relief design, which stands out against the matt
surface. As is traditional for the *oklad*, a
brightly colored strip in the center sets off
the golden crown with its painted enamel and
precious stones.

OVERSLEEVES: PORUCHI

✤

EMBROIDERY: MOSCOW,
SECOND HALF OF 17TH CENTURY
CLOTH: PERSIA, 17TH CENTURY
SATIN, SILVER, GOLD THREAD, PEARLS,
PRECIOUS STONES, GLASS
21.5 x 30 CM
INV. NO. TK-157/1-2

P*oruchi* were an essential part of the attire of Orthodox priests. They were armlets or oversleeves that were worn during services.

The foliate design of the embroidery on these *poruchi* is enriched with images of stylized flowerpots and cornucopias. Such a combination of traditional Russian ornamentation with motifs borrowed from Western European art became fairly widespread in Moscow art in the second half of the seventeenth century. Equally typical of the time is the variety of materials used by Russian embroiderers. Thus, for example, the embroi-

dery of these *poruchi* involves the use of pearls of various sizes, large and small precious stones, gold threads of intricate design, and gold sequins. The principal details of the design are executed in medium-sized pearls; smaller pearls are used for the secondary details, while the smallest pearls are applied to the gold sequins which make up the background of the embroidery. The center of each *poruch* bears an oval silver plate with a carved image of the Mother of God on one, and the Archangel Gabriel on the other; together they represent the Annunciation.

MITRE

✤

MOSCOW, KREMLIN WORKSHOPS,
SECOND HALF OF 17TH CENTURY
GOLD FIGURED STUDS: ISTANBUL, 17TH CENTURY
ENAMEL PLATES: ROSTOV (?), 18TH CENTURY
GOLD, PRECIOUS STONES, PEARLS, NIELLO
H. 22 CM, DIAM. 19 CM
INV. NO. TK-83

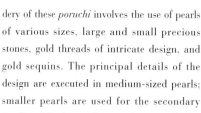

T*he mitre was the for-* mal headgear of high-ranking Orthodox clergy; its shape was modeled on that of the Imperial crown. The mitre was first worn by Orthodox bishops of the Byzantine Empire, symbolizing the unification of secular and ecclesiastical powers. In Russia, the high mitre with a circular crown was used from the beginning of the seventeenth century. Mitres of this type bore a cross above portraits of the saints. These were generally those belonging to the Deesis; but the particular saints portrayed would depend on the owner of the mitre, on who endowed it, or on the place of its endowment.

This mitre is notable for the abundance of precious stones and pearls, and for the use of Turkish gold figured studs with diamonds, rubies and emeralds. The State Treasury possessed a large number of such studs. The mitre was undoubtedly produced in the Kremlin workshops. The high quality of the execution is particularly evident in the gold plates with niello portraits. The upper part of the mitre carries a plate with a depiction of Our Lady of the Sign (*Znamenie*); beneath it, four plates in the form of icon cases bear images of the archangels Michael and Gabriel and the Apostles Peter and Paul.

The mitre was a royal endowment to the Spaso-Preobrazhenskii Monastery in Iaroslavl. This is why the central part contains images of the Fathers of the Church on oval enamel plates: St Basil the Great, St Gregory of Nazianzus, and St John Chrysostom. Also portrayed is the Russian St Leontii. Killed in the eleventh century by pagans, and one of the first saints to be canonized by the Russian church, Leontii was bishop of the Rostov diocese, in which the Iaroslavl monastery was situated in the seventeenth century. The style of the enamel plates suggest that they are of later, and probably local, Rostov origin. It is likely that they are part of an eighteenth-century restoration of the mitre, which was kept in the vestry of the Iaroslavl monastery.

MANTLE OF THE PATRIARCH ADRIAN

MOSCOW, KREMLIN WORKSHOPS, 1690s
VELVET: ITALY, FIRST HALF OF 17TH CENTURY
EMBROIDERY: RUSSIA, 1690s
VELVET, SATIN, BRAID, GOLD,
PRECIOUS STONES, GOLD THREAD
L. 147 CM
INV. NO. TK-2273

The mantle was the outer garment worn by Russian Patriarchs. It was in the form of a long cloak, fastened at the collar. Stripes, known as *istochniki* (sources), were sewn crosswise onto the mantle, while two pairs of quadrangular stripes, known as *skrizhali* (annals), were applied along the collar and the hem. The former symbolized the spirit of grace in the wearer, while the latter represented the Old and New Testaments, on the basis of which the clergy conducted the service. Documents show that Patriarch's mantles in seventeenth-century Rus´ were woven from velvet or dense silk cloth, pink, green, blue, or dark crimson in color.

The mantle of Adrian, the last Patriarch before the reign of Peter the Great, is made of Italian green pile-on-pile velvet, with a design of crowns and stylized roses. The *istochniki* are of gold braid; the *skrizhali* are of dark crimson velvet. The upper *skrizhali* are decorated with gold crosses with precious stones, while the lower ones are decorated with studs in the shape of rosettes. Analysis of the design of the velvet shows that it was produced in the first half of the seventeenth century. This suggests that the mantle for the Patriarch Adrian was remade from a garment of one of his predecessors. This was most likely the Patriarch Nikon, who at the reception of the Antioch Patriarch Makarios in 1655, wore a mantle "of green figured cut velvet, with *skrizhali* of red velvet, in the center of which were pictures of cherubim with gold and pearls."

THE KOLOMENSKII SAKKOS (DALMATIC)
OF THE PATRIARCH NIKON

EMBROIDERY: MOSCOW,
KREMLIN WORKSHOPS, 1653
FABRIC: TURKEY, FIRST HALF OF 17TH CENTURY
SATIN, VELVET, GOLD, PEARLS,
PRECIOUS STONES, GOLD THREAD
L. 139 CM
INV. NO. TK-14

The *sakkos*, or dalmatic, was the most ceremonial of the vestments of the highest-ranking Orthodox clergy. It was originally worn by the Byzantine Emperors, and in the eleventh or twelfth century became part of the Patriarch's dress; eventually, during the sixteenth and seventeenth centuries, the *sakkos* became part of the full vestments of all Greek bishops. In Russia the right to wear a *sakkos* was accorded the Patriarch and a few metropolitans, by special order of the Czar. The difference between the Patriarch's *sakkos* and the metropolitan's consisted in the stripe sewn onto the front, known as a *perednik*.

The pearl-embroidered inscription shows that the Kolomenskii *sakkos* was presented to the Patriarch Nikon by Czar Alexei Mikhailovich and Czaritsa Maria Il'ínishna, during a service at the palace in Kolomenskoe, a village outside Moscow. The vestment is woven from richly figured golden satin from Turkey. Strips of red velvet with a foliate design embroidered with pearls and gold thread are applied to the shoulders, the armlets, the sides, and the hem. The *perednik* is of red velvet with embroidered portraits of saints: St Basil the Great, St Gregory of Nazianzus, St John Chrysostom, and St Nicholas the Miracle Worker.

The presentation of the *sakkos* to the Patriarch was a mark of particular honor by the Czar. In so doing, Alexei Mikhailovich copied the Byzantine Emperor Constantine, who, according to an ecclesiastical document popular in Moscow in the seventeenth century, presented a precious vestment to Pope Sylvester

SHOULDERS OF A SURPLICE

✤

BROCADE, STUDS: ISTANBUL, 17TH CENTURY

EMBROIDERY: MOSCOW, KREMLIN WORKSHOPS,

END OF 17TH CENTURY

ALTABAS (BROCADE), PEARLS, PRECIOUS STONES,

GOLD, SILVER, ENAMEL, GOLD THREAD

W. 30 CM, L. 16 CM

INV. NO. TK-41

These surplice shoulders are a part of a church robe that was never completed. The preservation of fragments from outworn articles of clothing was widespread in Russia in the seventeenth century. This was due not only to the high value of the material –imported cloth (*altabas* - silk cloth interwoven with silver), gold and silk threads, stones and pearls– but also to a desire to preserve fine embroidery. Remnants of clothes belonging to members of the royal family, or commissioned by them from the Kremlin Workshops, were particularly popular keepsakes. So it is with these surplice shoulders, which are undoubtedly the work of the Kremlin Workshops.

The design is made up of large pearls embroidered onto a gold ground. Foliate flourishes are combined symmetrically with large gold studs of a stylized floral form, executed in diamonds, rubies, emeralds, and enamel. A thread of tiny pearls is applied to the outline of the embroidery.

There is no doubt that the material for the embroidery came from the Royal Treasury. This was the only place where a large quantity of gold studs was kept; these were brought from Turkey as diplomatic gifts. Studs of this kind were used in the preparation of royal parade attire, in articles of parade ceremonial, and in items presented to the vestries of Kremlin cathedrals and churches in the name of the Czar.

STOLE

CLOTH: WESTERN EUROPE, 17TH CENTURY

EMBROIDERY: MOSCOW,

SECOND HALF OF 17TH CENTURY

VELVET, SATIN, DAMASK, PEARLS,

SILVER, ENAMEL,

125 X 33 CM

INV. NO. TK-2723

The stole was an essential part of the dress worn by Orthodox priests for the ceremony of the Eucharist. It was in the form of a breastpiece, placed over the head and worn at the front on top of the cassock or beneath the *phelon* (mantle).

The design of this stole is typical of court art in the second half of the seventeenth century. The richness and intricacy of the design is achieved through the principal embroidered details being based on a background of fine gold sequins. The flowers, leaves, and stems are embroidered with a single thread of medium-sized pearls, while the crosses and other separate details of the design are executed throughout in tiny pearls. Small semiprecious stones are applied to the embroidery, either in settings, or through holes drilled in the stones. Further stones decorate the silver and enamel buttons. A row of gilt tassels with pearls running along the hem adds to the garment's refined intricacy.

COFFIN CLOTH: THE METROPOLITAN PETER

✠

CLOTH: ITALY, 17TH CENTURY
EMBROIDERY: MOSCOW,
KREMLIN WORKSHOPS, 1648-69
DAMASK, VELVET, GOLD AND SILVER THREAD,
SILK THREAD, PRECIOUS STONES,
PEARLS, ENAMEL
220 X 92 CM
INV. NO. TK-31

Coffin cloths with embroidered images of a saint were placed on the tomb or shrine of the saint during important services. This was one of the traditional forms of reverence for the saint. In the middle of the seventeenth century a set of large coffin cloths were made in the workshops of the Czaritsa's Chamber for the shrines containing the relics of the Moscow prelates —the Metropolitans Peter, Alexei, John and Philip. The dedication on each of the cloths shows that they were specially commissioned by Czar Alexei Mikhailovich and his wife Maria Il'inichna. This one has an embroidered portrayal of the Metropolitan Peter. Peter transferred the seat of the Metropolitan from Vladimir to Moscow, and was revered as a miracle worker and as the protector of Moscow.

The portrait of the metropolitan on the coffin cloth is full length and full face. He is dressed in a chasuble and *klobuk* (traditional monk's headgear); one hand holds the Gospels, while the other is in a gesture of prayer. Above the head of the prelate is an image of the Trinity. The face and hands of the saint are embroidered in white and blue silk. The rest of the cloth is of gold and silver thread, with colored ornamentation. The outline, details, and inscription are threaded with pearls. The halo of the saint consists of gold studs set with precious stones, two of which are in the shape of a bow and decorated with black enamel. The background is entirely embroidered with a design of gold threads, imitating fine imported cloth.

✛

Pall (pelena):
The Dormition of the Virgin

✛

Embroidery: Moscow,
Kremlin Workshops, 1640-42
Velvet, damask, gold and silk thread, pearls
210 x 140 cm
Inv. No. TK-2802

The model for this pall was an icon in the Dormition Cathedral, which researchers believe was painted in 1470. The pall was made during the time when the cathedral was under construction, around 1640. Documents relate that the royal icon painters Mark Matveev and Sidor Osipov made a copy of the icon and transferred it to taffeta for embroidery. The embroiderers of the Czaritsa's Chamber then worked on the pall for two years. In the center of the composition is a bed with the dead Virgin Mary. Behind this, surrounded by angels with candles, stands Christ, with a shrouded figure in his arms –the spirit of the Virgin. Above him the angels carry her to heaven, and alongside are angels bearing the Apostles to the skies. Apostles, prelates, angels, and crowds of people stand beside the bed. Beneath, an angel raises his sword against Avfonii, who is trying to overturn the bed of the deceased. The images are embroidered in silk and spun gold threads, the background is entirely embroidered with gold thread. The various applied designs are of colored silk. The border of the pall is of Turkish cut gold velvet. It is likely that the border was added some time after the pall was completed. The large dimensions of the pall indicate that it was ornamental and was used for services in the cathedral, particularly for the feast of the Dormition.

THE CORONATION
OF THE
RUSSIAN EMPERORS

✥

In 1721 Peter the Great adopted the title of Emperor of All Russia. In the later years of his life he was concerned about the fate of the Russian throne, since he had no direct heir, and was ill disposed towards his grandson, the son of the executed Czarevich Alexei. For this reason, shortly before his death he decided to crown his wife Catherine, intending to proclaim her as his rightful heir. The coronation took place on May 7 1724, in the Dormition Cathedral of the Kremlin. The new ceremony differed little from the rites of the consecration of the Czar; indeed, the order of events of the coronation largely retained that of the consecration.

Peter had, however, founded a new capital in St. Petersburg, where the royal court now resided. This inevitably led to significant changes in the preparations for the new ceremony. As the coronation festivities approached, the whole court set off from St. Petersburg to Moscow. As they waited to make their solemn entry into the ancient capital, the royal family was accustomed to halt in one of the villages nearby. This was normally the village of Vseviatskoe, where, at the end of the century, the famous Russian architect M. Kazakov was to build the Petrovskii Palace in neo-Gothic style.

The entry into Moscow was greeted with a gun salute, the ringing of bells from the Ivan the Great Bell Tower in the Kremlin, and the sound of trumpets and kettledrums. The arrival of the royal family was marked by a grand procession in which huge numbers took part, including representatives of all the peoples of the mighty Russian Empire. The procession was conducted according to a strictly defined order which was to remain almost unchanged until the end of the nineteenth century. For coronation ceremonies, triumphal gates were erected "with unparalleled decoration;" they were funded by the Church, Moscow merchants, the municipal government and other benefactors. People bearing gifts greeted the Czar at the gates, and choirs sang solemn hymns. Priests with crosses and other holy articles came from the many churches of Moscow to greet the royal family.

All along the route of the ceremonial procession platforms were erected for onlookers, the streets were strewn with fir twigs, and valuable carpets of silk and wool were hung from the open windows. Fine cloth was also often draped from the buildings on Red Square. So the magnificent procession made its colorful way to the Kremlin. Here the Emperor bowed down before ancient sacred objects, and in the Dormition Cathedral a solemn service of prayer was held for the Empress.

The ceremony of the coronation in the eighteenth and nineteenth centuries had certain differences from the ancient Russian consecration of the Czar. It is clear that the order of the ceremony was drawn up with the participation of Peter the Great himself, who included in it several elements adapted from Western European practice. Thus, for example, the rights of succession of the sovereign were affirmed not in speeches in the Dormition Cathedral, but in a preparatory manifesto. High-ranking officials and representatives of foreign embassies were informed of the day of the coronation by the Masters of Ceremonies, while the people were told the news on the squares of Moscow by heralds on horseback, to the accompaniment of trumpets and kettledrums.

Some new features were introduced into the outward form of the coronation cere-

Coronation procession on Cathedral Square

mony. The traditional journey from the Granovitaya Palace to the Dormition Cathedral was undertaken by the Emperor on a raised walkway, while onlookers sat on high platforms erected around the Cathedral Square. The decoration of the Dormition Cathedral became more complex and lavish. In the center a large dais was set up, surrounded by a balustrade. Above, a magnificent canopy was draped over the arch of the dais, decorated with an embroidered emblem of the Russian Empire, the two-headed eagle, surrounded by the emblems of the main provinces. The thrones of the Russian Czars of the sixteenth and seventeenth centuries were placed on the dais. Here, too, was a special table for the coronation regalia. Before the coronation the regalia were brought from the Winter Palace in St. Petersburg to the Moscow Armory, which from the beginning of the eighteenth century had become a state treasury. On the eve of the coronation the regalia, along with other ancient ceremonial articles, were carried to the Dormition Cathedral.

The coronation procession was preceded and followed by Horse Guards. The signal for all those involved in the procession to gather was given by the firing of cannon. The procession was made up of court figures, generals, representatives of the Russian gentry, Russian and foreign merchants, members of the governing Senate, senior clerics, and other high state officials. The regalia were carried on cushions of red or gold brocade. In the center of the procession, under a splendid red canopy, walked the Emperor.

The general procedure of the coronation largely followed the example of the consecration of the Czar, but had several new features. Following the abolition of the Patriarchate by Peter the Great, and the establishment of a Holy Synod – a collegiate body with control over the Church – the Emperor did not sit on his throne alongside a member of the church hierarchy, but alone or with the Empress. The coronation ceremony began with a proclamation by the Emperor of the basic doctrines of the Christian faith, which he read solemnly from a book.

The laying on of the regalia was accompanied by the recital of a prayer. Here, too, there were changes. Peter the Great, who so fervently desired the growth and prosperity of the Russian state, attempted to lend the coronation ceremony an identifiable state character. The life-giving cross was no longer placed on the Czar; the *barmy*, or ceremonial collar, also disappeared, to be replaced by a new coronation mantle. Likewise, the ancient crown of the Russian Czars, the Cap of Monomach, was replaced with a Western European-style crown, made of two hemispheres separated by an arc. At first new crowns were usually made for each coronation. In 1762, however, the famed St. Petersburg jeweler Ieremiia Poz´e created a magnificent diamond crown for Catherine the Great, which is now kept in the Diamond Fund of Russia. Thereafter, this masterpiece of the jeweler's art was used in all subsequent coronations, right up to that of the last member of the Romanov dynasty, Nicholas II.

Unlike the consecration of the Czar, when the Cap of Monomach was placed on the sovereign's head by elders of the Orthodox church, at the coronation of Catherine I it was her husband who crowned her, and in all subsequent coronations the Emperor himself placed the crown on his own head.

Starting with Paul I, son of Catherine the Great, both the Emperor and

Empress were crowned at the same time, according to the Byzantine tradition. The Empress knelt before the Emperor, who took the crown from his head, touched it lightly on the head of his wife, and placed it back on his own head. Then the Empress put on a small coronation crown, which was first made for Maria Feodorovna and seems to have been used at all subsequent coronations.

From 1742, with the coronation of the Empress Elizaveta Petrovna, daughter of Peter the Great, further items were added to the coronation regalia: these were the state banner, and the state sword, on one side of which was portrayed a two-headed eagle, with a slain dragon in its claws, and on the other a griffin with a drawn sword. In 1762, with the coronation of Catherine the Great, a further addition was made: a chain of diamond links. This was the chain of the Order of St Andrew the First Called, the highest of the Russian orders, established at the end of the seventeenth century by Peter the Great. Although Peter had proposed that the order be awarded for acts of the highest service to the state, his descendants decided that the heirs to the throne should become Knights of the Order of

St Andrew from birth. For this reason, the Emperor would enter the Dormition Cathedral for his coronation already bearing the insignia of the order on his breast, and during the ceremony would replace the normal chain with the diamond one.

From the eighteenth century the practice of showering the Czar with gold and silver coins was discontinued. During the procession to the Archangel and Annunciation Cathedrals gold and silver medals were thrown into the crowd. In addition, courtiers were awarded medals specially minted for the coronation. For several weeks after the coronation ceremony was over, audiences were held in the royal palace, where the Emperor received congratulations, and hosted banquets. Balls, masquerades and theatrical presentations followed one after the other. For a short time, lavish illuminations and fabulous fireworks turned the ancient capital into a fairy-tale city.

The rejoicing of the people at the accession to the throne of a new ruler was expressed in various ways: there were swings and carousels, jugglers and acrobats, and many different kinds of refreshments. Wheeled tables and platforms were set up on the squares of the

city, with roast sheep and oxen, stuffed birds, and pyramids of *kalach*, a traditional Russian loaf. Fountains of wine poured forth, and barrels of beer and wine were driven about the town. Commemorative gifts were also distributed among the people: kerchiefs and tankards with a portrait of the new Emperor, or of some symbol of the coronation.

M. V. Martynova

✥

EMBROIDERY: THE DORMITION CATHEDRAL

✥

RUSSIA, END OF 19TH CENTURY

SATIN, SILVER, SILK AND GOLD THREAD, GLASS

98 X 86 CM

INV. NO. TK-2841

The picture of the Dormition Cathedral of the Moscow Kremlin is embroidered in relief on a white satin background. The Dormition Cathedral was built in 1479 at the order of the Great Muscovy Prince, Ivan III, by the Italian architect and engineer, Aristotele Fioravanti. For many centuries the Dormition Cathedral was not only the principal ecclesiastical center of Russia, where the most solemn church services were held; it was also the country's most important state building. All the chief ceremonies of state were held here: the consecration of the Russian Czars, the coronation of Emperors and the ordination of metropolitans and patriarchs. The most important documents of state, including Emperors' declarations of their successors, were kept in the altar. The heads of the Russian church – metropolitans and patriarchs – were also buried in the Dormition Cathedral.

The south (central) and east (altar) façades of the cathedral are shown in the picture, embroidered in silver and gold thread. The decoration of the façades is embroidered with colored silks with gold thread added for some details. The cupolas of the cathedral are faced with silver-gilt plates and the roof is embroidered with various gold threads. In the foreground, stitched with silver and gilt threads, can be seen the railings which surrounded the cathedral square of the Kremlin in the nineteenth century, but which are no longer there.

✥

TAPESTRY PORTRAIT OF CATHERINE THE GREAT

RUSSIA, ST. PETERSBURG IMPERIAL TAPESTRY
MANUFACTORY, 1833
AFTER FEODOR STEPANOVICH ROKOTOV (?)
CANVAS, WOOL AND SILK THREAD
272 X 210 CM; INV. NO. TK-2943

This portrait of Catherine the Great is a rare example of formal portraiture in tapestry. The model for the tapestry was a portrait of Catherine the Great now believed to be by the eighteenth-century Russian artist, Feodor Stepanovich Rokotov, who painted one of the first formal portraits of the Empress. It was highly acclaimed and was copied more than once by the artist himself and by other masters.

Catherine the Great is portrayed in a brocade dress in "Russian" style which she wore for ceremonial processions at court. Particular attention is paid to the appurtenances of Imperial power. In her right hand, the Empress holds a gold sceptre set with the world-famous Orlov diamond. One of the most historic stones in the world, this diamond was presented to the Empress on her name day in 1773 by Count Grigorii Orlov. On a table beside her stand the orb and a large Imperial crown made for her coronation in 1762. The crown, the work of the court jeweler, Ieremiia Poz´e, occupies a unique place among European regalia. It is decorated with around 5000 cut diamonds and surmounted by a deep red spinel. This stone was bought in Beijing from the Chinese emperor Kangxi by the Russian ambassador Nikolai Spafarii, on the orders of Czar Alexei Mikhailovich.

The Empress is also wearing the cut diamond chain of the Order of St Andrew the First Called, another part of the regalia.

The regalia illustrated in the tapestry was used in all subsequent coronations. It is now kept in the Diamond Fund of Russia. The badges of two orders complete the parade dress of the Empress: the Order of St George and the Order of St Vladimir, of which Catherine was the founder. At the top, woven into the blue border of the tapestry with black threads, appears the inscription: "I.Sh.M. (Imperial Tapestry Manufactory) 1833" and a two-headed eagle.

✠

The Coronation of
Catherine the Great

✠

Russia, second half of 18th century
After Stefano Torelli
Oil on canvas
148 x 176 cm
Inv. No. ZH-1931

The original picture of which this is an anonymous copy was commissioned at the time of the coronation of the Empress Catherine the Great, which took place on September 22 1762 in the Dormition Cathedral of the Kremlin. The paintings of Stefano Torelli were popular during Catherine's reign. This is one of an allegorical series praising the Empress and her accomplishments. As in others of these pictures, the Empress is prominent in her favorite image of Minerva, the goddess of wisdom. She is surrounded by various characters who personify her good works. Unlike other compositions of this type, however, the present painting is sober and powerful; it portrays real events clearly and with historical accuracy.

The action takes place inside the Dormition Cathedral, whose arches, walls and columns are decorated with frescoes.

The principal characters in the action stand on a raised dais against the cathedral's west wall. They are the Empress Catherine, in full coronation dress, the highest state dignitaries, and the elders of the Russian church with the Metropolitan Platon at their head. The secondary participants in the coronation are divided into two symmetrical groups framing the protagonists as if in the wings of a theatre. These many masters of ceremonies, ladies, and grandees seated along the cathedral walls play only the modest role of extras. The figures in the foreground, however, are executed with great panache, as befits their role in the drama. Their wonderful dress is set off by their lively expressions and theatrical gestures, bringing an emotional quality to the otherwise formal record of the ceremony. The magnificent candelabra add to the solemnity of the scene.

The picture's purpose is to demonstrate the fundamental principle of Catherine's reign: the divine right of the sovereign. In the minds of the Russian people this idea found its clearest expression in the seats of honor in the Dormition Cathedral. Chief among these was the Throne of Monomach, used when Emperors and Empresses attended ceremonies in the cathedral. This carved wood throne was made in 1551 for Ivan the Terrible. It is partly visible at the left of the canvas. Alongside the throne are the carved white stone seats for the elders of the Russian church, made at the end of the sixteenth century. The right of the canvas shows the place of prayer for the Czarinas and Czarevnas, which was created in the cathedral during the seventeenth century.

COMMEMORATIVE MEDAL FOR THE CORONATION
OF EMPEROR ALEXANDER II

✤

RUSSIA, ST. PETERSBURG, 1856

VASILII ALEXEEV AND ROBERT HANNEMAN

GOLD; DIAM. 5.1 CM; INV. NO. OM-58

From the time of their introduction in Russia, commemorative medals were not only official memorials but also emblems of state ideology. They depict the most important events in the history of the Russian state. For coronation ceremonies, special medals of gold and silver were commissioned by the government from the St. Petersburg mint. These were worn during the ceremonies by members of the Imperial family, by Russia's chief dignitaries and by foreign ambassadors.

On August 26 1856, the coronation day of Alexander II, the Privy Councillor and Minister of Finance, P. F. Brok, brought a golden plate bearing two gold medals, minted for the occasion, to the mother and wife of the new Emperor, Alexandra Feodorovna and Maria Alexandrovna. One of them was this medal.

The obverse of the medal shows a half-length, right profile portrait of the Emperor Alexander II. Beneath the portrait is the inscription: "Crowned in Moscow 1856." Around the edge is the name of the medallist, V. Alexeev. On the reverse side is a portrayal of the Russian state emblem. Above it is the inscription: "God is with us." Beneath it, along the edge, is the name of the medallist, R. Hanneman. The two medallists who collaborated in this production were renowned artists at the St. Petersburg court mint. Alexeev created a whole gallery of medal portraits of leading figures of the day.

SEAL OF EMPEROR ALEXANDER II

✤

ST. PETERSBURG, BEFORE 1890

MASTER SAMUEL ARNDT

ONYX, GOLD, RUBIES, EMERALDS, PEARLS

H. 9.6 CM, FACE 3 X 2.6 CM

INV. NO. OM-2148

On the accession to the Russian throne of a new Czar, new state seals had to be produced. These included a large, medium, and small seal, the use of which was strictly regulated by law. The personal seal of the Emperor was used to confirm the authenticity of papers, letters and other correspondence originating from the sovereign's office, and to confer legal powers. It is possible that this elegant seal, along with others, came into use soon after Alexander II's coronation in 1856. It is cut in a stone of rare beauty; the case bears the name of the well-known St. Petersburg firm, Nicholls and Plinker.

The seal is made from a single piece of dark brown banded onyx set in a thin gold ornamental band with small rubies and emeralds. On the striking surface of the seal the name ALEXANDER is engraved in Cyrillic beneath an Imperial crown. Samuel Arndt (1812-90) was a master silver- and goldsmith from 1845. Between 1855 and 1860 his workshop was intensively and productively engaged in court commissions for the firm Nicholls and Plinker.

✤

PORTRAIT OF EMPEROR ALEXANDER II

✠

RUSSIA, SECOND HALF OF 19TH CENTURY

UNKNOWN ARTIST, OIL ON CANVAS

102.5 x 71 CM

INV. NO. ZH-1992

This portrayal of Emperor Alexander II is typical of official Imperial portraits of the middle of the nineteenth century. The brush strokes are professional, dry and impassive; the artist has captured the external features of the Emperor precisely without trying to penetrate the subject's inner feelings. Following the style of official portraits of the time, Alexander II is presented in the uniform of an Adjutant-General, with gold epaulettes and aiguillettes.

One of the most important duties of the monarch was the defence of the fatherland from internal and external foes. In this role

Alexander II was, by tradition, commander of the most important Russian regiments. These included the Preobrazhenskii Regiment of Life Guards, the Horse Guards, the Hussars, the Cuirassiers, the regiment of the Cossack Ataman, and others. The leadership and personal courage of the Emperor were essential to the state ideology of monarchical power. For this reason, the dominant themes in this portrait of Alexander are the military duties and merits of the Emperor. Alexander wears several decorations on his chest: the blue moiré ribbon and star of the Order of St Andrew the First Called, the Order of St Vladimir Equal

to the Apostles, the cross of the Order of St George, fourth class (awarded to officers for distinguished service), a gold sword with the ribbon of St George, and crosses of three foreign orders.

CORONATION ROBE OF EMPRESS
MARIA ALEXANDROVNA

✛

RUSSIA, 1856
BROCADE, SILK, FUR, GOLD THREAD, BRAID
L. 376 CM
INV. NO. TK-2597

Coronation robes in Russia were traditionally made of smooth gold brocade *(glazet)* and trimmed with ermine. New coronation robes were made for each coronation and, after 1856, not only for the Emperor and Empress but also for dowager Empresses.

Along with other articles of the regalia, robes were carried by courtiers on special cushions through the Cathedral Square into the Dormition Cathedral where they were placed on the Emperor and Empress. After the end of the coronation ceremony, the robes were placed in the Armory for eternal preservation. This robe, woven from delicate gold brocade and decorated with appliquéed two-headed eagles, was made for the coronation of the Empress Maria Alexandrovna, consort of Alexander II, in 1856.

Coronation Dress of
Empress Maria Feodorovna

Russia, St. Petersburg, 1883
Brocade, silk, silver thread, ribbon, gauze
L. of bodice 36 cm, L. of skirt 112 cm,
L. of train 420 cm
Inv. No. TK-2900/1-3

Throughout the eighteenth century and the first third of the nineteenth century, the coronation dresses of the Russian Empresses usually reflected European fashions. Attempts to introduce elements of traditional Russian dress into contemporary clothing had been made at court during the time of Catherine the Great, with her personal participation. Portraits have been preserved of Empresses and court ladies in "Russian" dresses with the long, turned-back sleeves which were one of the distinctive features of Russian parade dress. From 1834, it was ordered that all parade dresses for court ladies were to be made in "Russian" styles. The dress for court ladies consisted of a velvet bodice with a low, horizontal décolletage and long, loose-fitting sleeves with turned-back cuffs, an outer skirt with a train and an underskirt of white satin. Female members of the royal family wore dresses of a similar cut but made of smooth, silver brocade woven with silver thread.

The coronation dress of the Empress Maria Feodorovna, consort of Alexander III, consists of three parts: a bodice, a skirt and a train. The maker's mark, woven into the bodice, shows that the dress was the work of the St. Petersburg firm, Isanbard Chanseu. On either side of this name is a badge with a heraldic shield bearing the initials MF. It is most likely that these are the initials of the Empress Maria Feodorovna herself, who was either a patron of the workshop or a regular customer.

CORONATION UNIFORM, BELT AND HELMET OF EMPEROR ALEXANDER II

RUSSIA, 1856
HELMET: ST. PETERSBURG, COURT FACTORY OF
OFFICERS' ARTICLES, 1856
E. D. BITTNER
UNIFORM: BROADCLOTH, BROCADE, GOLD
THREAD, GOLD; BELT: BROCADE, SILK THREAD;
HELMET: LEATHER, BRONZE, FEATHERS
UNIFORM L. 84 CM; BELT 18.5 X 4.5 CM;
HELMET H. 17.5 CM
INV. NOS TK-1988, TK-1918, TK-1558

The eighteenth century in Russia was an epoch of female rule. The only Emperor to be crowned during that period was Peter II, grandson of Peter the Great. He was crowned in civilian dress, but Paul I and all subsequent Russian Emperors were crowned in the uniform of the Preobrazhenskii Regiment, one of the two oldest regiments of the Russian Imperial Guard.

The uniform of Alexander II is in the form of a half caftan, woven from dark green, almost black, broadcloth; the red broadcloth collar and cuffs are decorated with oak leaves woven with gold thread. The monogram of Nicholas I, father of Alexander II, is applied to the epaulettes, which are made of smooth brocade and trimmed with a gold fringe.

The aiguillettes on the uniform have gold tips and two stars, the first of the Order of St Andrew the First Called, the highest Russian order, and the second of the Order of St Vladimir, first class – the second most important order.

The belt is of silver brocade decorated with woven strips of gold- and sand-colored silk, the colors of the Imperial household. The helmet, which completes the uniform, is made of dark, lacquered leather with two peaks, a plume of white, black and red feathers and a two-headed eagle in gilt bronze.

COSTUME OF A CORONATION HERALD

✛

RUSSIA, ST. PETERSBURG, 1896

BROCADE, MOIRÉ, GOLD THREAD, GALLOON,

FEATHERS

DALMATIC 93 x 89 CM; BESHMET L. 102 CM;

TROUSERS L. 105 CM; BOOTS L. 61 CM;

SLEEVES L. 16 CM; GLOVES L. 28.5 CM; HAT H. 12 CM

INV. NOS TK-1629, TK-1630, TK-1631,

TK-1632/1-2, TK-245/1-2,

TK 246/1-2, TK-1562

Heralds first appeared in Russia in 1724 with the introduction of Western European coronation ritual by Peter the Great. Their role was to announce the day of the coronation, to head the coronation procession and to stand in columns of honor by the Imperial throne.

The herald's costume consisted of a dalmatic, a buttoned knee-length tunic with short sleeves; a *beshmet*, a coat with long, narrow sleeves; trousers; boots; gloves and a hat. At his side the herald wore a dress sword with a gilt hilt on a gold baldric. He carried a silver staff.

Heralds' costumes were traditionally made in the workshops of the St. Petersburg Imperial Theaters. The theatrical influence in these extremely sumptuous and decorative garments is quite evident. Considerable sums were spent on their preparation. They were never used twice, and after the coronation ceremony they were placed in the Armory for safekeeping. They were sometimes given out as models for the weaving of new costumes for further coronations.

This costume was worn by a herald at the coronation of Nicholas II in 1896. Two state councillors were appointed heralds for this coronation. Judging by their uniforms, they were of a similar size. As was traditional, the dalmatic is made of smooth golden brocade with woven emblems of the Russian empire. This so-called "heraldic" brocade was specially commissioned from the brocade house of A. and V. Sapozhnikov in Moscow. The *beshmet* and wide trousers are made in the colors of the Imperial household. The dalmatic is also trimmed with black, yellow and white moiré. The hessian boots are decorated with gold embroidery and the cuffs of the gloves bear the monogram of the Emperor. The magnificent hat, in the traditional crimson color, is trimmed with ostrich plumes and feathers.

COMMEMORATIVE KERCHIEF
✥
RUSSIA, MOSCOW, 1896
CLOTH; 78 x 80 CM
INV. NO. TK-1453

COMMEMORATIVE KERCHIEF
✥
RUSSIA, MOSCOW, AFTER 1896
CLOTH
78 x 80 CM
INV. NO. TK-1452

In 1896, on the occasion of the coronation of Nicholas II and Alexandra Feodorovna, Russian manufactories produced a large number of commemorative, printed kerchiefs.

This example, with portraits of the Imperial couple framed by laurel and oak leaves, was produced at the well-known Trechgornaia manufactory in Moscow.

The tradition of producing commemorative kerchiefs with printed images celebrating important historical events probably began in Russia in the first quarter of the nineteenth century. This kerchief celebrates the coronation of Emperor Nicholas II.

In the center of the kerchief is the emblem of Moscow. Above it is a view of the Kremlin from the Moscow River, and on either side is a two-headed eagle with the inscription "THE FAMILY EMBLEM OF THE EMPEROR". The illustration at the bottom shows the ceremony of the Solemn Proclamation of the Day of the Holy Coronation, as it was conducted on the morning of May 11 1896, on the Kremlin's Senate Square, in front of representatives of foreign embassies and other guests.

COMMEMORATIVE DISH

✣

MOSCOW, SECOND HALF OF 18TH CENTURY

SILVER

77.5 x 50.1 CM

INV. NO. MR-156

Dishes with figurative decoration were intended for use in parade halls at court. They were first made by Russian craftsmen in the eighteenth century. Usually these articles were decorated with scenes of a biblical or allegorical nature, and illustrations on historical themes were extremely rare. All the more interesting, then, is this dish with a complex composition celebrating the coronation of the Empress Catherine I, which took place in the Dormition Cathedral of the Kremlin. The dish portrays the climax of the ceremony, when Peter placed the crown on his wife's head with his own hands. Beside them stands the Metropolitan, who officiated in the service. On either side of the central group are representatives of the nobility and foreign emissaries. The composition is executed in high relief. Russian craftsmen of the eighteenth century were masters of this technique: they could execute complex many-planed compositions enriched with varied textures and parcel gilding of the details of the portrait and the ornamentation. Here the jeweler portrays the costumes of all the characters in great detail, although not always with fashions appropriate to the first quarter of the eighteenth century. The interior of the cathedral is not represented with any great accuracy. The rows of columns supporting lancet arches, and the abundance of carved decoration, are no more than a stylization of early Russian architecture.

CEREMONIAL SCARF
✤
RUSSIA, 1896
SATIN, BROCADE
290 x 29 CM
INV. No. TK-1225

The ceremony of the Solemn Proclamation of the Day of the Holy Coronation preceded each coronation. In the eighteenth century, two heralds on horseback took part in the ceremony. They rode through Moscow separately, reading out the royal proclamation to the people. From 1896, each herald was accompanied by a ceremonial procession consisting of seven men – masters of ceremonies and assistant masters of ceremonies at court. The text of the proclamation was read out by an official while the heralds distributed printed copies. Members of the ceremonial procession wore a scarf made from a strip of satin in the colors of the Imperial household. This example was made for the coronation of Nicholas II in 1896 in the workshops of the Imperial Theaters in St. Petersburg. It is made of cloth bought from the Moscow firm of A. and V. Sapozhnikov.

PROCLAMATION BAG
✤
RUSSIA, 1883
VELVET, LEATHER, GALLOON, COPPER
74 x 47 CM
INV. No. TK-1285

The Solemn Proclamation of the Day of the Holy Coronation began in the Kremlin. After a trumpet salute, an official read out the text of the proclamation while the herald distributed printed copies from a special bag. The procession then continued to Red Square. Over the next three days the proclamation ceremony was repeated in various parts of Moscow. The text of the proclamation was reproduced from a handwritten original by the artist V. M. Vasnetsov. In all, around 50,000 copies were distributed.

This bag was made for the coronation of the Emperor Alexander III in 1883. It was probably also used in 1896 for the coronation of the last Russian Czar, Nicholas II. The bag is made of red velvet; it is rectangular in shape and has a long strap. A gilt bronze two-headed eagle is attached to the front.

Embroidered Map of the Russian Empire

Russia, 1872

Canvas, wool

175 x 318 см

Inv. No. TK-3158

This map of the Russian Empire shows the borders and the principal provinces and *oblasts* as they were in 1872. It was made by students of the Moscow Institute of the Order of St Catherine. The map is embroidered in cross stitch with colored wools. In a semicircle at the top is a portrayal of a two-headed eagle with heraldic shields on its wings.

The Institute of the Order of St Catherine was founded in 1797 at the decree of Emperor Paul I for the education of orphaned daughters of the gentry. It was under the special patronage of the Imperial family and was run by Dames of the Order of St Catherine; these included all princesses of royal blood, and their head, or *ordenmeister* was the Empress herself. In 1841, by order of Emperor Nicholas I, entrance to the institute was opened to the daughters of knights of all the Russian orders. The institute was maintained by money given by the Dames to the Chapter of Orders through contributions by their order. The size of the contribution was fixed by Imperial decree. It is possible that the map was a gift for the Empress Maria Alexandrovna who, in 1872, was head of the Order of St Catherine; or for the Emperor Alexander II himself who, in 1860, significantly increased the financial contributions for the maintenance of the institute.

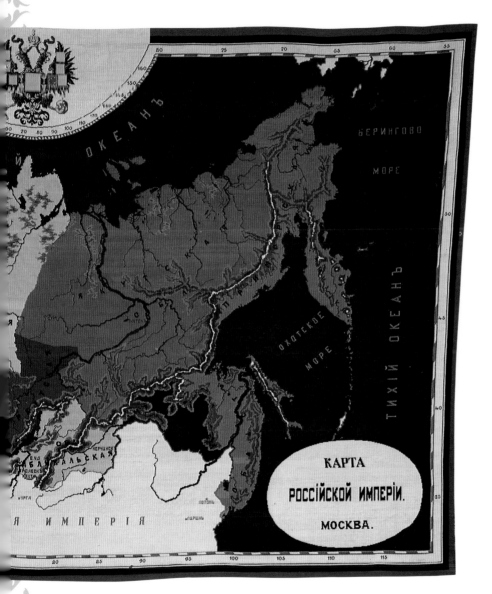

COURT LIFE IN THE EIGHTEENTH CENTURY

✛

The eighteenth century marked a new stage in the history of the Russian state and its ruling dynasty, bringing significant changes in the ceremonial of the royal court.

The rituals of Russian life had been built up over many centuries. There were some reforms in the second half of the seventeenth century in the reign of Czar Alexei Mikhailovich and his son Feodor Alexeevich. Yet it was not until the time of Peter the Great that changes were made that were seen by contemporaries as crucial in the development of the Russian state. This was a time of ambitious and fundamental reforms, even of the destruction of old foundations. Peter's irrepressible energy and zeal for reform were the driving force behind these processes, which led to the birth of a new society and a new secular culture.

The symbol of Peter's reforms was the new capital, St. Petersburg. The city was founded on uninhabited land at the mouth of the Neva, which had only just been recaptured from the Swedes. A nineteenth-century historian wrote: "It was the embodiment of all that Peter loved and the rejection of all that he hated; his love of the sea and the fleet, his need for open spaces, his regard for the outward expression of culture, his hatred of antiquity, and his fear of the mute, hostile old capital."

By the end of his reign St. Petersburg was a fair-sized town, spread out on both shores of the Neva. Unlike Moscow, the buildings were all of stone. Under Peter's descendants the new capital, known as the "Palmyra of the North," became a place of elegant architectural ensembles with magnificent palaces enclosing opulent interiors, and surrounded by stately parks and gardens.

The court nobles soon moved to St. Petersburg, where life quickly began to follow the European model. Even in Moscow significant new trends had already appeared by the beginning of the eighteenth century, although here the influence of old habits and traditions was still in evidence.

The eighteenth century also saw changes in the outward appearance of the Russian people. In 1698 the Czar issued a special decree forcing all his subjects to shave off their beards. Beards had for centuries been the pride of the men of Rus´, a sign of strength and virility. Those who disobeyed the royal decree were heavily fined; this fine was also imposed on those who merely trimmed their beards rather than shaved them. Next, Peter forbade all members of the population, apart from peasants and clergy, to wear the traditional long Russian dress. His decree´ (ukaz) of 1700 ordered that men "in Moscow and in other towns should wear foreign dress in the Hungarian manner." This meant loose-fitting clothing of a type already seen in old Rus´. Later decrees introduced German and French forms of dress, and costumes of European design were also prescribed for women. The new fashion was, in the words of the Czar, intended "to make Russian citizens look like Europeans," and he introduced it with his characteristic energy and resolve. Corporal punishment was inflicted on those who appeared in forbidden dress; this applied not only to ordinary citizens but also to members of the gentry. Offenders were beaten with cudgels, but, by order of the Czar, "with their honor intact," in other words, without having to remove their shirts. In contrast, those who refused to shave off their beards were forced to wear the ancient form of dress as a sign of dishonor.

✛

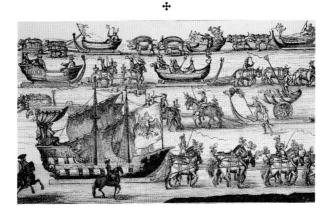

Masquerade in Moscow, 1722

The new forms of clothing were quite soon assimilated at court. Particular attention was paid to parade costumes for use during festivals and ceremonies. Russian society became familiar with European fashions. The wardrobes of the rich, men and women alike, came to include hundreds, even thousands, of articles of clothing. According to one contemporary writer, "women, hitherto unaware of their beauty, began to recognize its power. They began to emphasize it with fine clothes and, more than their mothers and grandmothers before them, to adorn themselves with luxurious ornaments."

A significant role in the change in women's appearance was played by new hairstyles. In Rus´, before the time of Peter, married women never appeared bareheaded; now, European dress demanded a variety of coiffures. That such styling was a new custom for Russian society is revealed by the fact that, at the beginning of the eighteenth century, there were only three hairdressers in Moscow who know how to style hair in the European manner. For this reason, ladies' hair was sometimes dressed as much as three days before a festival, and they were forced to sleep sitting up.

When Peter visited France he was particularly impressed with the informal gatherings of French noblemen. In 1718, the year after his return, he established "gatherings" — ceremonial public meetings of courtiers. In ancient Rus´, nobles had led enclosed lives, playing host only to those close to them — usually relatives — at festival times. Guests were received according to an established ritual whereby the host's wife greeted guests at the door, kissed them, and raised a glass of wine to them. Thereafter, women and men dined separately in their own parts of the house.

Up to the end of the seventeenth century the Czaritsa and the Czarevnas were shielded from public gaze, engaging in handicrafts in their rooms. They hardly ever took part in court life and had to observe court ceremonies through secret windows. Now, however, they began to appear openly at court. Peter ordered that gatherings of nobles should include their wives and daughters. He also decreed that courtiers should take turns to hold gatherings, three times a week, in their own houses.

Here, too, European fashion began to dominate. Walls were decorated with car-

pets, and there were mirrors with carved frames and elegant lamps. Sets of furniture were commissioned for parade halls, dining rooms, offices, and bedrooms. Special rules drawn up by the Czar himself specified that the host in whose house the gathering took place was to give over several rooms to his guests. The biggest of these was for dancing; the second for playing chess, a game which Peter loved; the third for conversations and smoking; and the fourth for ladies to play at forfeits and other diversions.

Before this time, meetings of nobles had been constrained by the etiquette of the Middle Ages. Now, however, men and women had to master the entirely new art of social interaction and informal conversation. For this reason, the Czar established rules which recommended that all participants in gatherings should not be stiff or formal but should conduct themselves freely, "sitting, walking, and playing in a relaxed way." Teachers of "German etiquette", and also of the dances which courtiers now had to master, began to appear in the houses of Russian nobles. These teachers were usually foreigners. In former times the nobility had avoided "the sinful dances" performed by the Russian people; as one foreigner wrote, "they considered it damaging to their dignity." But now dances became the most important of all entertainments at gatherings, and every nobleman employed his own orchestra. Often with Peter the Great and his consort leading off, they stepped out in the minuet, the anglaise and other fashionable dances.

Gatherings soon turned into balls with strictly defined rituals for the reception of guests, the order of dances and so on. A ball became an integral element of all official ceremonies — coronations, weddings, and diplomatic receptions. At the ball which the St. Petersburg grandee P. I. Shuvalov gave in honor of the Empress Elizaveta Petrovna, "the whole hall was decorated with trees so that it took on the appearance of a delightful arbor. A buffet was laid with antique vessels of gold, silver, and porcelain. All the other rooms were so richly decorated with jewels, Chinese curios, and other artistic objects that it seemed as though each room was trying to outdo the next in its magnificence. The grotto, with walls hung with ripe bunches of grapes, particularly amazed those who saw it."

Artists took part in the design of balls. They were not restricted to interior decoration, but encouraged to give their imagination free rein. Thus, at Shuvalov's ball, "the palace contained a ten-foot-high gallery with Ionic columns in the form of an amphitheater, made entirely of ice. As night fell, so delightful was the illumination that it seemed to be made of transparent stone and crystal. Beneath its arches stood tropical trees of colored ice, their branches laden with lifelike fruits."

Parties at court were rounded off by ceremonial banquets, also remarkable for their extreme opulence. The rituals surrounding these banquets were clothed in the most magnificent and refined fantasy. At one of the banquets of the Empress Elizaveta Petrovna the courtiers sat at an intricately laid table which, "after several dishes had been served seemed, as if by magic, to turn around, and suddenly presented a magnificent dessert with all manner of moving figures, fountains, floating vessels, and other curiosities."

Tables laid for banquets would usually have in their center an elegant cascading fountain surrounded by candles. The light of the candles would be reflected in the tumbling

water, creating a wonderful spectacle.

Parade banquets would often involve several hundred, sometimes more than a thousand, courtiers. The meal would be accompanied by instrumental and vocal music. Dishes from the cuisines of all Europe would be served by Russian and foreign waiters.

Receptions, balls and masquerades, their rituals and the clothes of the guests, all were admired — even by the French, who were so proud of their own court at Versailles. One Frenchman wrote:

"Almost unwillingly we were struck by the beauty and richness of these apartments. Our surprise, however, soon gave way to delight at the sight of so many ladies — more than four hundred, and almost all beauties, in magnificent diamond-studded costumes. But then a new spectacle greeted our eyes: the blinds were half drawn and the daylight without gave way to the sparkle of twelve hundred candles which were reflected on all sides in countless mirrors ... As the orchestra of eighty musicians struck up a thunderous noise, the Grand Duke and his Duchess [future Emperor Peter III and his wife Ekaterina Alexeevna] led the dances."

✠

Masquerade in the wooden Winter Palace, St. Petersburg

The jeweler Ieremiia Poz´e, who made Catherine the Great's magnificent imperial crown, was one of the many contemporaries who left delightful descriptions of court life. He describes one particular party held in the stupendous Hall of Mirrors: "A multitude of bodies wandered around in masks and rich costumes; they gathered in groups or danced quadrilles. All the rooms were lavishly illuminated: at any one time, no fewer than one thousand candles burned, and the whole effect was as magnificent and opulent as could be."

Like all other ceremonies and festivities at court, masked balls were carefully ritualized. Peter the Great issued decrees defining the exact sequence of events at a party. Each participant in the masquerade was informed in advance of his costume, and was given a number according to which he played a specific role in the masked spectacle. Under the Empress Elizaveta Petrovna masked balls were held on Tuesdays, and attendance was compulsory; those who failed to turn up were fined 50 roubles. This duty began at an early age. court journals from the middle of the eighteenth century show that only children under the age of thirteen were excluded from masked balls.

The programs for masked balls varied enormously. In planning them, the monarch often revealed remarkable inventiveness and humor. In 1744, for example, the Empress Elizaveta Petrovna hosted a number of court masked balls where all the men had to appear without masks but wearing enormous skirts and sporting ladies' hairstyles, while the ladies were dressed in men's court outfits. One contemporary described the scene: "The metamorphosis did not please the men, who were in low spirits, and the ladies looked rather like poor little boys. But the male costume suited Elizaveta very well indeed: with her considerable height and slightly plump build, the Empress cut an excellent figure."

The program for the magnificent masked ball held by Catherine the Great in Moscow soon after her coronation was particularly interesting and unusual. It was entitled "The Festival of Minerva," since the Empress liked to identify herself with the ancient goddess of wisdom and considered herself a patroness of the arts.

According to the printed order of ceremony, the ball was to represent "the infamy of the vices and the glory of good

works." The masquerade, which lasted for three days, took place on the streets of Moscow. A vast costumed procession was composed of groups each of which represented, in symbolic and theatrical form, the various human vices, such as stupidity, greed, and rudeness. The procession was completed by a marvelous train of chariots bearing figures dressed as the ancient gods, with Minerva at their head. They were surrounded by muses, poets, musicians, philosophers, and allegorical figures representing science and the arts. They were accompanied by shepherds and shepherdesses, merry ploughmen, and other attendants. More than 4,000 people and 200 ox-drawn chariots took part in the procession. This fantastic spectacle required an enormous amount of stage machinery. It was directed by F. G. Volkov, the founder of the first professional theater in Russia.

Masked balls and other festivals were also held to celebrate events such as military victories and the launching of ships. In 1721 the signing of a peace treaty with Sweden was marked by a seven-day masked ball. In 1774 many fabulous balls were held in honor of Russia's victory over Turkey. The principal

✠

festival took place on the vast green Khodynskoe Field, just outside Moscow. Here numerous temporary structures had been erected under the direction of the renowned Russian architect, V. I. Bazhenov: fantastic Eastern towns with minarets and watchtowers; fortresses, ballrooms, and dining rooms; theaters, cathedrals, gazebos; and other pavilions of all kinds. Onlookers watched from a platform in the form of a ship with masts and sails. All around this delightful scene was a large garden with tree-lined avenues.

The festival included all possible entertainments, with theatrical spectacles and a masked ball at which courtiers danced a quadrille dressed in Turkish costumes. The ball ended with brilliant fireworks portraying the Battle of Chesme. From the time of Peter the Great, "fire games", as fireworks were originally known, were a favorite diversion at the Russian court, accompanying all types of festivals — coronation ceremonies, carnivals, masked balls, and peace declarations, among others.

In the eighteenth century several masquerades were held at court for all levels of society. On these occasions, one hall in the palace would be designated for the court aristocracy, another for the landed gentry, and the remaining halls for merchants, the middle class, and others.

The Russian court of the eighteenth century attempted to outshine the French court in wealth and magnificence. Enormous sums were spent on ladies' costumes and other luxurious items — snuff boxes, watches, jewels, precious weapons and the like. The jeweler Ieremiia Poz´e wrote: "The ladies' dress was particularly lavish, as were their gold accoutrements. They would wear an extraordinary number of diamonds; even in private life, ladies never went out without wearing precious jewelry." The foremost exponent of this extravagance was the Empress Elizaveta Petrovna. During the fire of 1753 in Moscow 4,000 of her dresses were burnt; yet after her death her wardrobe was found to contain more than 15,000 dresses, two trunks full of silk stockings and ribbons, several thousand pairs of boots and slippers, and a vast number of other articles of clothing.

When Catherine the Great hosted a celebration in honor of the birth of her first grandson Alexander, the palace halls were decorated with enormous monograms of the letter A made of diamonds and pearls. The Empress played at cards, gambling with diamonds and precious stones. "How pleasant it is to play for diamonds," she wrote to her Parisian correspondent, the writer Friedrich Melchior Grimm. "It is like the Thousand and One Nights."

During the eighteenth century court etiquette, like much else, took on a largely European character. It defined not only the conduct of courtiers but also their appearance. A stream of decrees illustrates how strictly and in what detail court dress was regulated. A decree of the Empress Anna Ivanovna, for example, with an extravagance typical of the century, forbade people from appearing at court in the same dress on more than one occasion. According to the Empress Elizaveta Petrovna's decree of 1743, court ladies were not permitted to attend balls in dresses of the same color as that of the sovereign. Decrees from the beginning of the reign of Catherine the Great ordered that all should appear at court in "Russian" costume; later, ladies were forbidden to wear anything other than "Greek" costume. A decree from the last years of

Catherine the Great's reign banned waltzes and the hairstyle known as a toupee, where the hair was combed flat at the back and curled round into a top knot at the front.

Vast sums would often be spent in complying with these royal orders. When Peter III was to marry Catherine the Great, the Empress Elizaveta Petrovna ordered that courtiers should be given a donation a year in advance, to enable them to have new dresses made and to commission carriages "according to the decency of each;" that is, according to their rank.

The constant issue of decrees, rules, and orders concerning all aspects of court life established a new court etiquette in the eighteenth century. This etiquette achieved its final form towards the end of that century and, to a large extent, continued to define court life in the nineteenth century.

M. V. Martynova

CAFTAN AND CAMISOLE OF EMPEROR PETER II

✠

FRANCE (?), 1727-30

VELVET, BROCADE, SILK, GOLD THREAD

L. 105 CM

INV. NOS TK-2909, TK-2910

The Emperor Peter II, grandson of Peter the Great, came to the throne in 1727 at the age of twelve. He ruled until his death in Moscow from smallpox in 1730. His wardrobe was kept in the Kremlin storerooms until 1766, when it was transferred to the Armory. It is quite unique in its variety, but there is no certainty about where it was made. Probably it was entirely commissioned in France, but it is also possible that some of the items were made in Russia.

Documents record the names of two men who created Peter II's wardrobe, both of them foreigners: the tailor Andries Appelgrim and the wardrobe master Peter Bem. The latter served under Peter the Great, and was given a portrait of the Emperor in a diamond mount.

The wardrobe consists of a caftan of coarse cut velvet, and a camisole of patterned brocade. In addition to the caftan and camisole, male dress of the first third of the eighteenth century consisted of breeches and a shirt trimmed with lace, as well as stockings, shoes, hat, and other accessories. The caftan was worn open but drawn in at the waist, and the buttons and buttonholes that ran from the neck to the ornamented hem were purely decorative. Three slits, in the side seams and at the back, enabled the wearer to ride a horse, and to carry a sword beneath the caftan. Neither caftan nor camisole had collars, owing to the fashion of wearing full-bottomed wigs. The form and size of the cuffs and flaps on the caftan varied.

The camisole was made from the same cloth as the caftan, or from the material of the caftan's cuffs. In the most formal costumes the back and sleeves of the camisole were made of white silk, so that it could not be

worn without the caftan. Buttons were also sewn onto the camisole from neck to hem; in some examples they were functional, and in others purely decorative.

Parade versions of these costumes were made of patterned brocade or velvet, and also from plain cloth with a trimming of galloon or gold thread.

TAPESTRY PORTRAIT OF PETER THE GREAT

✠

RUSSIA, ST. PETERSBURG TAPESTRY

MANUFACTORY, SECOND HALF OF 18TH CENTURY

WOOL, SILK

81 X 64 CM

INV. NO. TK-3263

This tapestry was made after a painting by Andrei Matveev, one of the most important Russian artists of Peter's reign. His work reflects the Russia of the time, with its enthusiasm for reform, the new world view so characteristic of the age, and a new attitude to the human personality. The tapestry copy was transferred to the Armory in 1840 from the St. Petersburg Tapestry Manufactory.

The original portrait was one of Matveev's early works, undertaken during his time as one of "Peter's scholars," when he was a student at the Antwerp Academy of Arts in the workshops of A. Boonenn. The portrait was probably drawn not from life, but from memories of meetings with the Czar and from other well known portraits, in particular one by Carl de Moor. The portrait by this Dutch artist was painted in 1717 in the Hague. It was drawn from life while Peter was on his travels around Europe, and received his approval.

Peter the warrior king is portrayed wearing a caftan, with a cuirass visible underneath. He wears the blue ribbon of the order of St Andrew the First Called, which he was awarded in 1703 after he had successfully led the campaign to seize Swedish warships at the mouth of the Neva.

The second half of the eighteenth century saw the flourishing of Russian tapestry weaving. In the St. Petersburg Manufactory several portraits of Peter the Great were produced, from originals by well-known artists of the first half of the century: I. G. Tanauer, J.-M. Nattier, and Matveev himself.

MASQUERADE COSTUME OF THE FUTURE
EMPRESS CATHERINE I

✣

RUSSIA, FIRST QUARTER OF 18TH CENTURY
CAFTAN: VELVET, TAFFETA, LACE;
CAMISOLE: SILK, COTTON, GOLD
AND SILK THREAD, BRAID;
SKIRT: VELVET, SILK, BRAID
L. OF CAFTAN 117 CM,
L. OF CAMISOLE 115 CM,
L. OF SKIRT 105.5 CM
INV. NOS TK-2886, TK-2887, TK-2888

Masquerades were very popular at the Russian court in the eighteenth century, and many costumes were made for them. Of all the masquerade dresses of this time only one has been preserved, this Amazon costume of Catherine, at this time the consort of Peter the Great but later Empress in her own right as Catherine I.

The costume consists of a greenish-blue velvet caftan, a skirt of the same material, and a white satin camisole with a stylized flower design, embroidered with gold thread and colored silks. It was accompanied by a black felt hat with white plumes, and kid gloves cut to allow the wearing of rings.

Judging by the date on which the costume came to the Armory – March 5 1723 – it is likely that this is the dress that Catherine wore to the celebrations of the Treaty of Nystadt in Moscow at the beginning of 1722. On August 30 1721, after twenty-one years of bloody war between Russia and Sweden, a long awaited peace treaty was signed by which Russia gained the ancient lands of Livonia, Estonia, and Ingria, and part of Karelia.

According to the memoirs of the German emissary, F.V. Bercholtz, January 28 saw the beginning of celebrations in Moscow to mark the treaty. In honor of the occasion, a great parade of sleighs made up to look like boats passed through the Kremlin and Red Square. "Her Highness the Empress sat comfortably and quietly in a barge, as if in a room at home . . . she wore the costume of an Amazon . . . She changed her dress several times, appearing in red velvet, richly faced with silver, then in blue, with a variety of camisoles and other accessories."

✛

GARDEN CARRIAGE OF EMPRESS
ANNA IVANOVNA

✛

MOSCOW, 1725-30
OAK, VELVET, COPPER, IRON, OIL PAINTING
L. 3.1 M, H. 1.5 M, W. 1.4 M
INV. NO. K-3

This two-seated carriage with a box for the driver was intended for drives around the garden. This is evident from its construction. It is small, and the wheels are set close together but with wide felloes, so as not to damage the paths of the palace gardens. It is a very rare example of a vehicle of this kind.

In both shape and decoration the carriage shows features of the baroque style. It is decorated with gilt brackets, and relief carving in the form of shells and foliate scrolls. The panels of the body bear portrayals of the Russian emblem and a female figure on a green background. Judging by the iconography, this represents the Empress Anna Ivanovna. The portrait has clearly been painted from memory; nevertheless, there is a clear resemblance. The interior of the carriage was originally lined with green broadcloth, which was later replaced with velvet.

✛

TANKARD: STOPA

Moscow, 1735
SILVER
H. 24.3 CM, DIAM. 15 CM
INV. NO. MR-10544

In the second quarter of the eighteenth century, articles made of precious materials quite often carried portraits. As well as the traditional portrait of Peter the Great, this large silver *stopa* also bears images of his comrades in arms: Franz Lefort, Prince Pëtr Prozorovskii, Count Grigorii Chernyshev, Prince Vasilii Dolgorukov, and Count Andrei Osterman. Stamped relief portraits of this kind were normally based on engravings or drawings. The *stopa* was produced after the death of Peter the Great, during the reign of the Empress Anna Ivanovna. It was most likely commissioned by one of Peter's comrades in arms who outlived him.

The initials on the hall mark are NT, which may stand for Nikita Timofeev. Eighteenth-century documents often refer to Nikita Timofeev Beliakovskii, a member of a family of Moscow silversmiths.

✤

ARTICLES FROM A CHILD'S TEA SERVICE:
TEAPOT OF ALEXANDRA PAVLOVNA,
STRAINER OF NIKOLAI PAVLOVICH,
SUGAR BOWL AND COFFEE POT OF MARIA PAVLOVNA,
MILK JUG AND TRAY OF EKATERINA PAVLOVNA

✤

ST. PETERSBURG, 1780-96
MASTER JOHANN HEINRICH BLOM
SILVER, WOOD
H. OF TEAPOT 8 CM; L. OF STRAINER 14.5 CM;
H. OF SUGAR BOWL, 8 CM; H. OF COFFEE POT 13 CM;
H. OF MILK JUG 12 CM; DIAMETER OF TRAY 28.5 CM
INV. NOS. MR-4668/1-2, MR-4671, MR-4673/1-2,
MR-4674, MR-4678, MR-4677

On the birth of each of her grandchildren the Empress Catherine the Great ordered miniature tea and coffee services from the well known St. Petersburg silversmith I. Blom. All these services, of which there were ten, were made in the classical style. They are remarkable for their strong shapes, the symmetrical placement of ornaments on a smooth polished surface, and the predominance in the decoration of garlands, wreaths, and relief beading reminiscent of a pearl necklace.

These articles come from different services. Their ownership is indicated by the engraved monograms with the initials of the Czareviches and Czarevnas.

✤

Powder flask of Empress
Elizaveta Petrovna

✢

Russia (?), 1742-62
Gold, precious stones
l. 10.5 cm, w. 7 cm
Inv. No. MR-2244

This gold powder flask decorated with cut diamonds is unique. It was made either for a particularly ceremonial hunt, or as part of a fancy-dress hunting costume.

The flask was used to hold fine-grained gunpowder which was poured onto the priming pan of a pistol or other flintlock firearm. It was carried at the right side of the body on cross straps, known as a *bandel'er* (bandolier).

The flask has a traditional pear shape. The front bears an image of the Russian emblem in cut diamonds, between engraved flowers. It is interesting to note that the eagle is portrayed in Western European, rather than Russian, heraldic style, which suggests that the craftsman was foreign. On the reverse side is the monogram of Elizaveta Petrovna, made of cut diamonds. The engraving is in the rococo style.

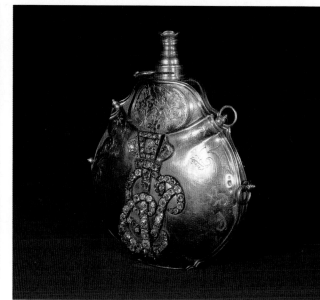

SNUFF BOX

✛

St. Petersburg, 1784 (?)

Master Jean-Pierre Ador

Gold, silver, precious stones,

glass, bone, watercolor on enamel

2.5 x 8.7 x 6.3 cm

Inv. No. MR-632

This snuff box is executed in the classical style; it is attractive for the delicate strength of its shape and design. The jeweler has achieved an impressive effect by combining the polished gold surface of the box with the gentle matt finish of the medallion containing a sparkling diamond monogram of the Empress Elizaveta Petrovna. A miniature with her portrait in enamel is mounted on the interior of the lid. Enamel miniatures in Russia were the result of developments in the technique of enamel painting by Russian craftsmen in the seventeenth century. The art of the miniature reached its high point in the eighteenth century. The most significant achievements were in miniature portraits, following the establishment of a national school of portrait painting. The portrayal of Elizaveta Petrovna inside the lid of the snuff box is the work of one of the finest craftsmen. He has employed the technique of *punktir*, in which color is applied by light touches of the brush. This conveys extremely delicate shading and chiaroscuro. The range of colors in the miniature is remarkably beautiful, based on a combination of pearl gray and blue tones with light touches of red. The painstaking detail creates an impression of cloth and lace.

The snuff box was made after the death of the Empress Elizaveta Petrovna. This is revealed by a hallmark of Jean-Pierre Ador, one of St. Petersburg's finest jewelers, who came to Russia from Switzerland in 1770 and undertook many commissions from the royal court until 1785. The date stamp on the snuff box has lost its third figure, but it appears

✣

SNUFF BOX

✣

ST. PETERSBURG, 1826
MASTER JOHANN WILHELM KEIBEL;
CAMEO: GIUSEPPE GIROMETTI
GOLD, AGATE, ENAMEL
3 X 9 X 6 CM
INV. NO. MR-642

Mounted on the lid of this gold snuff box is an oval cameo of white and pink agate with profile portraits of the Emperor Alexander I and his wife Elizaveta Alexeevna. Beneath the cameo is the inscription "GIROMETTI". Around the cameo in black enamel on a camphor ground are "November 19 1825" and "May 4 1826." These are the dates of death of Alexander I and Elizaveta Alexeevna.

The snuff box was made by Johann Wilhelm Keibel (1788-1862), a member of a family of court goldsmiths. In 1826 the craftsman made a small Imperial crown for the wife of Nicholas I and a number of order decorations and medals. Keibel's workshop continued in existence until 1910.

The cameo is the work of the well known Italian stone engraver and medallist Giuseppe Girometti (1780-1851), probably influenced by Gonzago's famous cameo *Ptolemy and Arsinoë*, given to Alexander I by Josephina Bogarna in 1814.

✣

✣

SNUFF BOX

✣

RUSSIA (?), LAST QUARTER OF 18TH CENTURY
MOTHER-OF-PEARL, PAINTING
9 x 6.5 x 3 CM
INV. NO. DK-1439

The outside of the lid of this mother-of-pearl snuff box is decorated with a miniature containing a portrait of Emperor Paul I. Inside the lid is a portrait of a young man in uniform who is clearly the Czarevich Alexander Pavlovich.

The snuff box is part of a set of mother-of-pearl articles. Other items include a lorgnette with carved portraits of Paul I and his wife Maria Feodorovna in mother-of-pearl, and twenty mother-of-pearl buttons with paste jewels and painted portraits of peasant men and women. Judging by their size, the buttons were part of a male costume. The set was kept in a case faced with green velvet and with a lid decorated with an embroidered Imperial crown.

It is likely that the mother-of-pearl set was a gift from the Empress Maria Feodorovna to her husband. This is confirmed by the inscription on the snuff box, which reads in Italian: "With your name can only be compared the sun." The case and its contents came to the Armory in 1835 and are registered among the articles from Tsarskoe Selo.

✣

SHOTGUN, RIFLE, AND CARBINE

RUSSIA, ST. PETERSBURG, 1780S

MASTER GAVRILA PERMIAKOV

IRON, STEEL, SILVER, WOOD

L. OF SHOTGUN 119.6 CM, BORE 18 MM;

L. OF RIFLE 105.2 CM, BORE 6 MM;

L. OF CARBINE 97 CM, BORE 14.4 MM

INV. NOS OR-2152/1-2,

OR-2171/1-2, OR-5007/1-2

In the eighteenth century, the parade hunt was an integral part of life at the Russian Imperial court. Essentially, this was a magnificent and solemn ceremony, but it often turned into a joyful and courtly occasion. Practically all Russian rulers of the eighteenth century – not only emperors but also empresses – were hunters; they placed a high value on good hunting weapons, equipment, and horses, and also on hounds and hawks.

Catherine the Great was a fine hunter and a skilled horsewoman and this hunting garniture was specially made for her. The set consists of weapons of varying calibre and size for different types of hunting. These are a flintlock shotgun, a rifle, and a carbine – a wide-bore weapon used for hunting large animals. The set was made by the Russian armorer Gavrila Permiakov, one of the finest craftsmen working in St. Petersburg in the second half of the eighteenth century, and a member of a family of armorers. His works are remarkable for the clarity of their execution, their precision as weapons, and the quality of their finish.

All the details of the weapons are richly ornamented. The deep blued steel of the barrel is decorated to great effect with gold embossing, the details of the lock are covered with carving in relief on a gilt ground, the silver work is finished with light engraving and the stock is delicately decorated with an intricate carved ornament. The style is the predominant classicism of Russian art at that time.

HORSE CLOTH

✢

RUSSIA, ST. PETERSBURG TAPESTRY
MANUFACTORY, END OF 18TH CENTURY

SILK THREAD, CANVAS

193 X 150 CM

INV. NO. TK-1473

PAIR OF PISTOLS (DETAIL)

✢

RUSSIA, TULA, 1750

STEEL, WOOD, SILVER

L. 46 CM

INV. NOS OR-2772, OR-2773

These superb pistols were made in Tula in the middle of the eighteenth century, the high point in the manufacture of Russian decorative weapons. The Tula craftsmen of that time often found their inspiration in richly decorated French and German hunting weapons. They gave their works extraordinary decorative qualities, achieved through the liberal use of gilding on the barrels and other metal details, and magnificent relief carvings including ornamental compositions of foliate designs, military accoutrements, wild beasts, birds, shells, and scrolls.

The monogram of Elizaveta Petrovna is visible on the barrels of the pistols; on the breech is the inscription "TULA 1750."

The monograms of Emperor Paul I and the Russian national emblem with a Maltese cross are embroidered on this horse cloth. This representation of the emblem, introduced on the personal order of Paul I on August 10 1799, was current for less than two years. In April 1801 Paul's successor, Alexander I, resurrected the former state emblem without the Maltese cross.

The formal nature of the horse cloth suggests that it was used for Imperial ceremonial parades. It is entirely possible that it was used for the ceremonial meeting between the nephew of Paul I and Prince Eugene of Württemberg, who came to Russia at the beginning of 1800.

Production at the St. Petersburg Tapestry Manufactory, where this horse cloth was made, was at its height in the second half of the eighteenth century. At that time more than 150 craftsmen worked there. They had a wonderful command of all aspects of tapestry weaving, as well as techniques of embroidery to imitate weaving. Thus, for example, the decoration around the border of the horse cloth imitates the border design of a tapestry rug. All the decorations on the cloth are embroidered in silk thread, using cross stitch, satin stitch and Gobelin stitch.

DRESS SWORD

✣

RUSSIA, ST. PETERSBURG, MID-18TH CENTURY

BLADE: SESTRORETSK, 1752

SILVER, STEEL, WOOD, AGATE, LEATHER,

MARCASITES

L. OVERALL 89 CM, L. OF BLADE 75.1 CM

INV. NO. OR-3999/1-2

This sword is an example of the richly decorated cold steels which were an essential part of male parade costume in the eighteenth century. Until 1797 it was in the diamond workshop in St. Petersburg, where, evidently, its agate hilt had been made. This is decorated with engravings and a row of faceted marcasites in silver mounts.

The blade of the weapon is of forged steel, decorated with engraved gilt ornament which includes the inscriptions "TO GOD AND THE FATHERLAND" and "VIVAT ELISAVET´ THE GREAT." At the top of the blade, near the silver guard of the hilt, is an engraved hallmark with the letters SB (standing for Susterbäck, the Swedish name for Sestroretsk) and the date 1752.

It is quite possible that this sword was made for the Empress Elizaveta Petrovna herself, or for Grand Duke Peter Feodorovich, the future Czar Peter III.

SABER AND SCABBARD

✢

RUSSIA, ST. PETERSBURG, END OF 18TH CENTU-
RY

BLADE: TURKEY, MASTER HADJI SANFAR,
16TH CENTURY (?)

STEEL, WOOD, SILVER, GOLD, SNAKESKIN,
CORNELIAN

L. OVERALL 100.5 CM,

L. OF BLADE 83.5 CM

INV. No. OR-4458/1-2

This saber is a unique example of the Russian weaponry and decorative art of the second half of the eighteenth century. It was presented by Catherine the Great as a gift to her favorite grandson Grand Duke Alexander Pavlovich, the future Emperor Alexander I.

The following Arab inscriptions are damascened in gold on the blade: "THE YEAR OF SULTAN SULEIMAN 957 [1540 1541]", "THERE IS NO GOD BUT ALLAH"; "GOD THE ALMIGHTY"; "ALLAH SAVES THE SUPPLICANT". The word "PROSPERITY" is repeated three times along the blunt edge of the saber. On the sharp edge, using the same damascening technique, the following inscription appears in Greek: "GOD SAVE AND PROTECT ME IN MY HUMBLE STRUGGLE; TAKE THIS WEAPON AND SHIELD AND SUCCOUR HERACLES". A large number of sabers with similar Turkish blades are to be found in museum collections in Russia, Turkey, and Hungary. They often bear Christian inscriptions and symbols, and have been identified by specialists as dating from the end of the seventeenth century.

The decoration of the hilt and scabbard of the saber is executed in the classical style and is full of symbolism. The handle of the hilt shows two male figures bound in chains inside a frame of military trophies. Rising above them is a female figure carved from cornelian. It is likely that this composition represents Russia's victory over Turkey and Poland. The crossguard is in the form of fascines surrounded by serpents, symbolizing justice. In the center of the crossguard, on one side is a portrayal of the goddess of victory, Nike, with a wreath in her hand, and on the other a figure of a lamenting woman.

The scabbard is faced with green snakeskin and in its construction is reminiscent of the scabbards of ancient Roman swords. The silver mouth, sling hoops and chape are decorated with chased depictions of military accoutrements. A silver-gilt band of laurels runs along both edges of the scabbard. The most remarkable feature of the saber's decoration is the use of engraved gems, possibly taken from the famous collection of Catherine the Great, which was kept in the Hermitage. The front of the handle of the hilt contains a gem with a portrayal of the Emperor Augustus and on the reverse Alexander the Great; these symbolize the future role of Grand Duke Alexander Pavlovich as Emperor of Russia. It is known that Catherine the Great saw him as her successor, rather than her son the future Emperor Paul I. The mouth and sling hoop of the scabbard also bear embossed silver medallions with the profiles of Greek heroes personifying military might and statesmanship.

ORDERS OF KNIGHTS AND THEIR FEAST DAYS

✛

Among the new ceremonies which appeared in Russia in the eighteenth century were the feast days of knights' orders. The orders themselves, special marks of excellence and the highest state award, were hitherto unknown in Rus´. In 1698 Peter the Great founded the first and highest order of the Russian Empire, that of St Andrew the First Called. The draft statute of the order, drawn up in 1720 with Peter's participation, included specifications for the dress of the order and for the celebration of its feast days. The Czar adopted the idea of special feast days for an order from Western Europe where, to this day, feast days of some of the oldest and most illustrious orders are celebrated annually.

Knights of the Order of St Andrew the First Called gathered in wintertime on St Andrew's Day and in summer on St Peter's Day, and processed to the Church of St Andrew. They wore solemn parade dress with the cloak (*epancha*) of the order, the color of which was not at first fixed by decree. In the church they took part in a solemn service of prayer. At the end of the service the knights held a feast which was paid for from the order's funds. The knights of the order also wore their parade uniforms when taking part in other important ceremonies on the invitation of the sovereign, such as weddings and christenings of members of the Imperial family.

In 1714 Peter the Great founded the highest female order, that of St Catherine. In the eighteenth century this order was awarded very rarely. Catherine I made the first awards after the death of her husband, honoring seven courtiers as Dames of the order. During the reign of Elizaveta Petrovna the award was made to thirteen more, and only during the reign of Catherine the Great did it come to be distributed more liberally. The rarity of the award may be the reason that official instructions concerning the forms of dress for Dames of the Order have been preserved. At first the holders gathered at court for their feast day on St Catherine's Day in parade court dresses; by the 1750s, however, they were already appearing at the court of Elizaveta Petrovna in opulent dresses specially designed for such a solemn ceremony. Order dresses were made of silver brocade with gold thread and velvet decorations in the shape of falbalas and broad ribbons, trimmed with gold braid. On their heads the Dames wore delicate velvet hats with a semicircle of precious stones representing the top half of the wheel, and with an exuberant red ostrich feather at the side. In a portrait by A. P. Antropov, the Countess Anna Karlovna Vorontsova, who had a high position at court, is wearing just such a dress with the insignia of the Order of St Catherine.

The design of dresses for Dames of the Order, their cut and the color, trimmings, and decorations, were still being established during the second half of the eighteenth century by Catherine the Great.

Knights of the Order of St Alexander Nevsky celebrated their feast day on the date of the order's foundation, August 30. This was the anniversary of the arrival in St. Petersburg's Alexandrovskii Monastery of the relics of the holy prince Alexander Nevsky, which had previously been housed in the Rozhdestvenskii Monastery in Vladimir. On this day in 1725 Catherine I awarded herself the insignia of the Order of St Alexander Nevsky, and also conferred the order on foreign sovereigns. The order received official approval and was accorded the status of a high state award. One year later a special ceremony was established for the celebration of the day

✛

Entry of the Roman envoy into Moscow, 1661

of the prince and saint. On August 30 the Empress, accompanied by noblemen and knights of the order, arrived at the Alexander Nevsky Monastery. Her arrival was marked by a cannon salute and illuminations. The celebration was crowned by a dinner in the house of the Archbishop. Every year from 1743 for nearly two centuries the same day saw a religious procession from the Kazan Cathedral along Nevsky Prospekt to the Alexander Nevsky Monastery. Paul I decreed that junior knights of the order were to take part in this procession.

On her accession to the Russian throne in 1762 the Empress Catherine the Great founded two new orders. The more prestigious of these was the highest officers' Order of St George, awarded for noble deeds and established in 1769; the second was the Order of St Vladimir, established in 1782. The Order of St George was celebrated in St. Petersburg on November 26 with a magnificent ceremony. At 11 o'clock "Russian nobles of both sexes, dignitaries and overseas ministers" arrived at court. They gathered in the state rooms where they were joined at 12 o'clock by the Empress, who emerged from her private apartments in

the dress of the order and accompanied by the heir to the throne. The whole party processed solemnly to the court church for a service. In the aisle stood a table, on which the insignia of the order lay on a gold dish. At the end of the liturgy the ceremony of conferral of the order took place, accompanied by a special prayer and the pouring of holy water on the insignia. To the sound of a 101-gun salute from the cannon of the St Peter and St Paul Fortress and the Admiralty, the Empress took the cross, star, and ribbon from the dish and put them on.

Once the Empress had received congratulations from the clergy, dignitaries, diplomats, and military men, a dinner for 18 people was served in the palace dining room, accompanied by musicians, singers, and drummers. That evening a grand ball was held, attended by court ladies in parade dresses, knights in colorful robes, and soldiers in scarves and uniforms covered with gold and medals of enamel and precious stones. Later that evening a magnificent banquet was organized for 76 people, which Catherine herself attended. The fortress and all the houses in the town were magically illuminated.

Catherine the Great constantly demonstrated her respect for this order: she often took part in sittings of the Council of the knights of St George, which met in the Chesme Palace. On the order's feast days she received the knights at court. On one famous occasion, on the eve of one such a feast day, the Empress felt unwell. When it was suggested to her that she cancel the knights' reception, Catherine replied, "I would rather be carried to the reception on a bed than allow myself to incur the displeasure of these people who have dedicated their lives to receive this honor." For the annual reception of knights of the order in 1777 and 1778 she commissioned several table services from the Gardner porcelain factory. The first of these to be completed was the St George service. It produced a great impression on all who saw it and delighted the Empress. The pieces are painted in black, yellow, and green with gilt on a white background, and decorated with the crosses, stars and ribbons of the order and laurel garlands. In 1780 the St Andrew and St Alexander services were produced, and in 1785 the biggest of them all, the St Vladimir for 140 people.

On the day of his coronation, April

5 1797, Paul I, son of Catherine the Great, included in the Statute of Russian Orders the Order of St Anne. This order had originally been founded in 1735 by his grandfather, Karl Friedrich, Duke of Holstein-Gottorb, in memory of Anna Petrovna, daughter of Peter the Great, but it was Paul who "established it by royal appointment." This meant that it became part of the Single Office of Orders, later renamed the Chapter of Russian Orders. Officials of the order were appointed: a chancellor, a master and deputy master of ceremonies, a treasurer, a secretary, and heralds of the order, who received special awards and wore official uniforms.

Members of the Orders of St Andrew the First Called, St Catherine, St Alexander Nevsky and St Anne were also granted the right to wear special ceremonial order dress, woven from silk, brocade, and velvet and embroidered in gold and silver with the insignia of the order.

The costume of a knight of the Order of St Andrew the First Called at the end of the eighteenth century consisted of a long green velvet cloak lined with white silk, hung with silver tassels and cord and bearing a large embroidered star on the left side. Over this the knight wore a tabard of white brocade with a gold galloon fringe and a cross embroidered on the breast. The costume of the order was completed with a black velvet hat decorated with a red feather and the saltire of St Andrew on a narrow blue ribbon.

Dress for Dames of the Order of St Catherine was also legally fixed by royal decree, although half a century later a new design for the dress appeared. This was modelled on an ancient Russian style with a *sarafan* (cloak) and a *kokoshnik* (headdress). The new costume was, in fact, never made, but sketches for it still exist.

Paul I, although he did not include the Order of St George in the general statute and never awarded the honor, did specify the costume for its knights in December 1797. It consisted of an orange velvet tabard trimmed with a gold and silver thread border, with black velvet crosses on the back and front.

Knights of the Order of St Vladimir, and of the two Polish orders — those of the White Eagle and St Stanislav — which became Russian orders in 1831, did not have official dress.

Knights had to appear at court in their order dress on solemn feast days, on the dates of the foundation of each order. These were November 30 for the Order of St Andrew the First Called; November 24 for St Catherine; August 30 for St Alexander Nevsky; November 26 for St George; September 22 for St Vladimir; February 3 for St Anne; November 17 for the Order of the White Eagle; and April 25 for St Stanislav.

In addition, one general feast day was designated for all knights: November 8, the day of the Archangel Michael. Masters of ceremonies and heralds of the orders made arrangements to ensure that the ceremonial was properly observed. On this feast day, the knights processed solemnly to the church appointed for their order where, after prayers, they listened to a sermon on the duties of Christian knights.

This general feast day saw a wonderful procession of knights in formal dress, headed by the Emperor and Empress themselves. Under Paul I precedence was given to knights of the Order of St Anne; they were followed by knights of the Order of St Alexander Nevsky, behind whom came knights of the

✣

Order of St Andrew the First Called; each class of each order was led by its officials. Next came the head of the Order of St Catherine and Dames of the Grand and Minor Crosses, accompanied by their officials. On the day of receptions and banquets in the palace, the knights of the Order of St Andrew sat on the right of the Emperor; next to them came the knights of the Orders of St Alexander Nevsky and St Anne. Dames of the Order of St Catherine sat to the left of the Empress. The evening was rounded off with illuminations and fireworks.

As time went by, knights and officials wore their order dress increasingly rarely. In the nineteenth century its significance was almost entirely lost and it became a picturesque costume for fancy-dress balls. The order ceremonies, however, continued to be preserved by statute.

V.M. Nikitina

CROSS, CHAIN, AND STAR OF THE ORDER OF ST ANDREW THE FIRST CALLED

✛

ST. PETERSBURG, FIRM OF KEIBEL,
1850s-60s

CROSS: H. 8.9 CM, W.6.4 CM;

STAR: DIAM. 9.2 CM;

CHAIN: L. 107.5 CM

INV. NOS OM-2419, OM-2420, OM-2421

The Order of St Andrew the First Called (*Andrei Pervozvannyi*) was named in honor of the Apostle who, from the time of the Kiev princes, had been the patron saint of the Russian lands. The highest Russian order of St Andrew was awarded very rarely. It was conferred principally on members of the royal family, heads of foreign states, and "exceptional servants" of the state – dignitaries, diplomats, or successful military commanders such as Count Alexander Suvorov and Prince Mikhail Kutuzov. The heir to the Russian throne was awarded the order at his christening.

The order had one class. Its symbol was a saltire, or X-shaped cross, with the letters SAPR (St Andrew Patron of Russia) on the ends of the arms, and an enamel image of the crucified saint. The cross is attached to the breast of a black two-headed eagle wearing three crowns with ribbons. The cross was worn on a broad blue sash stretching from the right shoulder to the waist.

The star is silver with eight points interspersed with rays. In the center of the star is a two-headed eagle, holding a blue cross of St Andrew in its beak and claws, and surrounded by the motto of the order: "FOR FAITH AND FAITHFULNESS."

On the feast day of the order, and on other particularly solemn occasions, the knights of the order wore a gold chain instead of a ribbon. The chain is made up of three alternating links decorated with brightly colored enamels. These three links bear the state emblem of the two-headed eagle, rosettes with the cross of St Andrew, and a cartouche bearing the monogram of Peter the Great.

The order was redesigned for the Emperor Nicholas I during the 1850s, and the new design was ratified and adopted by the Chapter of Orders from December 1856.

The example seen here was originally issued from the Chapter of Imperial Orders with a decree that it was the property of the Czarevich Nikolai Alexandrovich, who died in 1865 at the age of twenty-two. It carries the hallmark of Master Alexander Kordes and of the most famous St. Petersburg firm of medallists, Keibel. This firm produced insignia of all the orders throughout the nineteenth century for the Chapter of Orders and the Cabinet of His Imperial Highness.

HERALD'S COSTUME OF THE ORDER OF ST ANDREW THE FIRST CALLED

✤

RUSSIA, 1797
EMBROIDERY: RUSSIA, 1809 (?)
DALMATIC: VELVET, SILK, GALLOON,
BROCADE, FOIL, SEQUINS
SHIRT: BROCADE, SILK, GALLOON;
BOOTS: VELVET, LEATHER, GALLOON, CORD;
GLOVES: KID-SKIN, GALLOON
L. OF DALMATIC 80 CM;
SHIRT 97 X 70.5 CM;
L. OF BOOTS 28 CM;
L. OF GLOVES 33 CM
INV. NOS TK-1692, TK-1694, TK-1693,
TK-256/1-2

At the general meeting of the knights of the Order of St Andrew, two heralds of the order were elected by a majority vote and were confirmed by the head of the order; that is, by the Emperor himself. The main role of the heralds was to act as marshals of the order's ceremonies, although they also undertook various official duties of the order.

In accordance with the statute of 1797, the herald's costume consisted of a silver brocade shirt, a green velvet dalmatic with stars of the order sewn on to the front and back, trousers of silver brocade or white broadcloth, white silk stockings and boots with lacings, and other decorations in the form of embroidered lions' heads and silver rosettes. The costume also included a black velvet hat trimmed with silver galloon and a white plume, a saltire badge, and white kid gloves with silver galloon trim. The herald carried a silver staff bearing the symbol of the order.

This herald's costume was made in 1797. As a result of the Emperor's decree in 1809, the design of the star of the Order of St Andrew was changed. The old stars on the heralds' dalmatics were removed and were replaced with new stars incorporating a two-headed eagle with a cross on its breast and a laurel wreath and heavy-pointed arrows in its talons.

CLOAK AND HAT OF A MASTER OF CEREMONIES OF THE ORDER OF ST ANDREW THE FIRST CALLED

RUSSIA, 1797
CLOAK: VELVET, BROCADE, SILK, LACE;
HAT: VELVET, TAFFETA, REP, FEATHERS
L. OF CLOAK 124 CM, H. OF HAT 19 CM
INV. NOS TK-1691, TK-1573

In 1720 the state created new official appointments for the Order of St Andrew the First Called, among which was the Master of Ceremonies. His role was to officiate at ceremonies and to ensure that on ceremonial occasions the Imperial throne, the knights' seats, and the orders, insignia, and costumes were present and correct. The details of the Master of Ceremonies' costume were first decreed in the statute of 1797. On feast days, according to the statute, the Master of Ceremonies, like the cavaliers of the order, had to wear a silver dalmatic with gold galloon trim, a green velvet cloak with a silver brocade collar and tassels, a black velvet hat with three upright plumes, and a saltire badge fixed to his lapel by a blue ribbon. These articles of clothing were worn over a parade court costume of the Master of Ceremonies' own choice.

The Master of Ceremonies' clothing differed from that of the knights in the shorter length of the cloak, the absence of an embroidered star of the order on the left side of the cloak, the presence of a gold Greek cross on the dalmatic, and his staff with a badge of the order on the knop.

The costume was kept in the wardrobe of the Office of the Order and was issued on feast days. It was used until the end of the reign of Nicholas I, when such dress ceased to be worn.

✤

STAR OF THE ORDER OF ST CATHERINE, FIRST CLASS

✣

ST. PETERSBURG, SECOND HALF OF
18TH CENTURY

SILVER, DIAMONDS, ENAMEL

DIAM.11 CM

INV. NO. OM-1264

In the center of the eight-pointed star is a round medallion, bordered with a fillet of diamonds, with an image of a cross on a semicircle – part of the wheel which symbolized the martyrdom of St Catherine. In a ring of red enamel surrounding the medallion is the motto of the order, "FOR LOVE AND THE FATHERLAND", and an Imperial crown.

According to legend, this star belonged to Catherine the Great. She was awarded the order when she became a Grand Duchess, as the wife of the heir to the throne Peter Feodorovich, later to become Emperor Peter III.

✣

DOLL IN THE DRESS OF THE
ORDER OF ST CATHERINE

RUSSIA (?), LAST QUARTER OF 18TH CENTURY

WOOD, PAINT, BROCADE, VELVET, TAFFETA

H. 57 CM

INV. NO. TK-3113

This mannequin doll is from the wardrobe of the Office of Orders; it is an extremely rare example of a so-called Large Pandora (*bol'shaia pandora*). Before the appearance of fashion magazines, in the 1770s dolls of this type were the only source of information for customers and dressmakers in the preparation of formal wear.

This doll wears the dress in which Dames of the Order of St Catherine were to appear on the feast day of the order, November 24. Dress for Dames of the Order was probably established during the reign of Elizaveta Petrovna. During Catherine the Great's reign several changes were made to the dress, and these were confirmed in the statute of 1798, which contained pictures of dresses for the Dames of the Grand Cross and the Minor Cross. The dresses were made of smooth silver brocade with a green velvet trim and train; in addition the costumes included a velvet hat, decorated with a semicircular Catherine wheel badge in silver braid, and red and gold feathers. Dress for Dames of the Grand and Minor Crosses differed only in terms of the character and richness of their finish. In contrast, the Head of the Order (a role always filled by the Empress), wore the dress with the longest train, and the semicircle badge on her hat was decorated with diamonds and rubies. The statute, however, contains no illustration of the dress itself.

The statute also contains no illustration or description of the dress of the Deputy of the Order (usually the wife of the heir to the throne). It is likely, however, that this doll is dressed in the Deputy's costume. It is identical to the order dress of Grand Duchess Maria Feodorovna, which survives to this day. She was wife of the heir to the throne, the future Emperor Paul I.

STAR OF THE ORDER OF
ST ALEXANDER NEVSKY

✣

ST. PETERSBURG,
FIRST QUARTER OF 19TH CENTURY
SILVER, ENAMEL
DIAM.10.6 CM
INV. NO. OM-2324

This eight-pointed star of the Order of St Alexander Nevsky is of openworked silver. On the white ground of the central medallion is a monogram with the letters SA (St Alexander) beneath a prince's crown. Around the edge of the medallion is a ring of red enamel with the motto of the order, "FOR WORK AND THE FATHERLAND".

The star was worn on the left side of the chest. The reverse side of the star is gilt, and the ends of the arms are secured to plates. The rays of the star have small holes to fasten it to the uniform. This star belonged to Emperor Alexander I.

CROSS AND RIBBON OF THE
ORDER OF ST ALEXANDER NEVSKY

✣

ST. PETERSBURG, END OF 18TH-BEGINNING OF
19TH CENTURY
CROSS: GOLD, GLASS, SILVER, ENAMEL;
RIBBON: SILK MOIRÉ
H. 19.6 CM, W. 7.1 CM
INV. NOS OM-2311, OM-2312

This order was named in honor of Prince Alexander Nevsky, victor over the Swedes in 1240 and the Teutonic Knights in 1242. Peter the Great intended that the award should be strictly a military honor. However, when the order was actually instituted on May 21 1725 by Empress Catherine I it was awarded for both military and civil service. The first twelve knights of the Order of St Alexander Nevsky were invested on the day of the marriage of Peter the Great's daughter Anna to Karl Friedrich, Duke of Holstein-Gottorb. Among these knights were dignitaries, foreign sovereigns, and military and civil figures.

The order had one class, and its insignia were a gold cross, a red moiré ribbon, and a star. The ends of the arms of the cross were of ruby-colored glass, and between these were two-headed eagles flanking a medallion with a portrait of Alexander Nevsky on a horse with a spear in his hand. The reverse side of the medallion shows a monogram with the letters SA (St Alexander) beneath a prince's crown. After 1816 the glass on the cross was replaced by red enamel. The cross was worn on a sash from the left shoulder.

This insignia of the order belonged to Elizaveta Alexeevna, wife of Emperor Alexander I, who ruled between 1801 and 1825. During the coronation she was invested with the insignia of both this order and the Order of St Andrew the First Called.

THE IMPERIAL COURT
IN THE
NINETEENTH CENTURY

❖

In the nineteenth century the Russian court was one of the grandest in Europe, and St. Petersburg was one of Europe's most elegant capital cities. Court ceremonies of the time, combining "Eastern luxury" with the "refined taste of the West," fittingly upheld the prestige of the Russian monarch.

The magnificence of the "Palmyra of the North" impressed foreign diplomats and travelers alike. The Marquis de Custin, for example, could not recall a single ceremonial reception in all Europe which could compare with "the celebration held by Emperor Nicholas I on his daughter's wedding day in the Winter Palace: how rich its jeweled dress, how varied and opulent the uniforms, what magnificence and harmony in the whole ensemble." The refinement and lavishness of the ladies' dresses made a particularly strong impression.

Imagine, then, the expensive attire of the society figures, worn for the spectacular production staged at the Bolshoi Theater to mark the marriage of Grand Duke Vladimir Alexandrovich and Grand Duchess Maria Pavlovna in 1874. The bride wore a white satin dress decorated with diamonds. On her head she had a *kokoshnik* (head-dress) embellished with immense diamonds, beneath which could be seen a wreath with several white camellias. She wore a necklace of three strings of diamonds with magnificent solitaires attached, a large clasp on her breast made of three ruby medallions framed with round diamonds, diamond bracelets, and a bouquet of fresh flowers. The sovereign Czarevna (the future Empress Maria Feodorovna) wore a blue satin dress, richly embroidered with brocade and stunning diamonds. Her headdress was a jeweled diadem, but the guests who gathered at the theater were particularly struck by her three necklaces: a black velvet ribbon studded with large diamonds, a string of pearls, and a chain of large diamonds supporting diamond pendants. Such opulent accoutrements sparkled not only on the members of the royal family, but also on the *grandes dames* of St. Petersburg society. The wives of the *nouveaux riches*, the new financial and industrial class, were almost equally richly adorned, in testimony to the success of their husbands. They reflected the creation of a new class in nineteenth century Russian life, the bourgeoisie, who valued possessions highly, and wanted to play a more active role in the secular life of the Russian capital.

The dress of Russian noblemen was also rich and varied. All the colors of the rainbow shone in the parade uniforms of courtiers, soldiers, and civilians. Indeed sometimes, as Théophile Gautier observed, the fairer sex "with their light and delicate adornment could not compete with such finery."

The uniforms of the cavalry were particularly striking: the Guards in white and silver, the Hussars all in red and gold with dolmans richly lined with fur slung over their shoulders, and Uhlans with bright stripes and revers. Notable, too, was "the romantic finery of the Caucasian uniforms." Parade uniforms worn by courtiers and senior officials were remarkable for the profusion of gold embroidery: the more senior the rank, the more striking the decoration.

The dresses of court ladies were also richly embroidered. At the coronation of Nicholas I the cut, color, decoration, and material of the dresses worn by court ladies was strictly regulated. Such dresses were consequently known as "Russian" or, unofficially, as "Frenchified *sarafans*", since they contained

❖

From "The Holy Coronation of Alexander III"

some of the details of national female costume: long folded sleeves, for example, not attached to the armholes. The color of loose-fitting court dresses, and their decoration — either silver or gold embroidery — would depend on the particular calling of the ladies, and to which court they belonged; whether it was the royal court or the court of a Grand Duchess. Court ladies wore *kokoshniki* on their heads, with white veils, glistening with precious stones, pearls, and brilliant-cut diamonds, while the young maids of honor would wear red or blue velvet hair bands. This was how ladies at court would appear on the most ceremonial feast days and, in particular, during "parades of the highest-born," which took place after the arrival of the royal family in St. Petersburg from one of their country residences.

During this ceremony the Emperor and Empress left the inner apartments of the Winter Palace and processed solemnly to the court church. Before the service the halls were filled with nobles of both sexes: courtiers, the military, and those "with access to the court." The royal family gathered in the Malachite Hall, while the highest-ranking court figures assembled in the Concert Hall, where a guard

of honor from the Horse Guards regiment dressed in white parade uniforms and red tunics stood at the entrance. Not everyone was allowed into the inner area; courtiers were divided into two categories: those who were allowed to "pass beyond the Horse Guards" and those who were not. Military generals and other senior officers and staff gathered in the St Nicholas Hall. Members of the merchant class and other invited guests waited in other state rooms, while newspaper correspondents stood in the galleries.

The Imperial procession was a magnificent sight. Like a glittering, multicolored ribbon it wove its way through each opulent hall between two walls of people draped in gold, silver, jewels, ribbons, and medals. The senior courtiers processed in front of their Highnesses: Palace Furriers in red and gold caftans, white silk stockings and white velvet pantaloons: Gentlemen of the Bedchamber;

Chamberlains; and Masters of the Hunt — all "wearing every medal, star and cross imaginable on their gold embroidered chests." The Chief Steward went before the Imperial couple with his tall rod.

The New Year saw the return of the royal family to the capital, and heralded the opening of the winter season in high society. The season included Italian and Russian opera, performances in theaters and amateur theatricals, concerts, receptions, parties, and balls. The St Nicholas Ball was the first event in a series of similar celebrations, and was considered a ceremony more important even than the "Parade of the Highest-born." It took place in the St Nicholas Hall of the Winter Palace — a "temple of magnificence," more suitable for such ceremonies than any other palace in Europe. "Its vast halls had room for thousands of people, and even then there was room for more."

About 3,000 guests were invited to the St Nicholas Ball (in 1890 the figure reached 4,000), representing the cream of high society. The guests gathered in a sea of gold and diamonds — ministers, senators, members of the State Council, heads of the St. Petersburg city council, leaders of the provinces, and senior representatives of the gentry. On this evening the whole of St. Petersburg *beau monde* could be presented to their Highnesses; different sections of society would be invited separately to subsequent events.

The rules governing invitations to the royal court in Russia were different to those for other European courts. There a noble name was enough, while in Russia noble parentage was considered secondary, and did not ensure presentation at court. The right of presentation was accorded to all officials and officers, starting with the members of the sitting state council, and their wives and daughters. Members of the diplomatic corps were also present at the St Nicholas Ball, along with representatives of Russian and foreign officials. Others who were invited were courtiers, knights and dames, serving officers and guardsmen, other officers of the military and the navy, and the wives and daughters of all of these.

A portrait of Nicholas I hung in the hall, above a display of colored lilies. Groups of delicate trees were placed about the room, so that the whole hall was filled with their scent. Opposite Nicholas's portrait, in the center of

the hall, a stage was erected for the orchestra, decked with exotic plants and crowned with a canopy of enormous flowers. While the streets outside were thick with frost and snow (for the St Nicholas Ball was held in January), in the halls of the palace it seemed that a whole forest of exotic plants had grown by magic.

The Emperor and Empress entered the Concert Hall from the Malachite Hall, where the Chief Steward of the Royal Household, the Steward of the Royal Household, and page boys awaited them. At half past nine, two black footmen in fantastic Mauritian costumes threw open the doors and their Highnesses entered the St Nicholas Hall to the strains of the polka from Glinka's opera *A Life for the Czar*.

Other, less grand balls were also held in the smaller Anichkov Palace on the banks of the river Fontanka. From 1816 this was the usual residence of heirs to the throne after their marriage. This palace was particularly liked by Nicholas I; balls were held here later in the year, when the guests "danced all week in the white drawing room." It was also a favorite place of Alexander III, who lived here for more than a quarter of a century while he

was heir to throne, and built up a magnificent collection of works of art. Here, too, he would host amateur theatricals, concerts, and balls.

A number of changes were introduced into court life under Alexander III. For example, all the court staff, including the chefs and the maitre d'hôtel's assistant, had to be Russian. A national orchestra and choir were formed; the musicians played at balls in new red parade caftans of a Russian cut, and performed from a stage covered in red broadcloth. The Czar himself had a bushy beard, and wore his trousers tucked into his boots. All around saw "something magnificent" in his appearance; in the words of the artist V. Surikov he was "a true representative of the people."

At the St Nicholas Ball of January 23 1885, for the first time some of the halls of the Winter Palace were lit with electricity. The Emperor Alexander III attended the ball in the red parade uniform of the Royal Cavalry Regiment, with the star and ribbon of the Order of St Andrew the First Called. The Empress Maria Feodorovna wore a diamond tiara and necklace, and a dress of silver gauze decorated with garlands of white roses and ivy leaves, on which brilliant-cut diamonds sparkled like morning dew. That evening the Empress danced the quadrille with the English ambassador, the Grand Duchess Elizaveta Feodorovna, and the Prussian envoy.

The St Nicholas Balls of the reign of Nicholas II were graced by the Empress Alexandra Feodorovna. She was tall, with a magnificent bearing. The Czaritsa was extremely fond of large pearls and, according to one contemporary, had one necklace which hung down almost to her knees. The sister of the Czaritsa, the Grand Duchess Elizaveta Feodorovna, decorated her golden hair with a diadem containing a cabochon emerald of 35 carats.

Court receptions and other festivities were especially glittering during the reigns of the last two Romanovs, but they were not held as often as before. In the first place, this was the result of the never ending sequence of balls held in many other high society homes in St. Petersburg; secondly, both Alexander III and Nicholas II valued their privacy and intimate family life. The illness of Nicholas's heir, Alexei Nikolaevich, and the constant indisposition of the Empress Alexandra Feodorovna meant that the life of the royal family became ever more solitary and confined. Nicholas II, like his father before him, was quite "indifferent to matters of ceremonial life" and, as the historian S. S. Oldenburg testifies, "had no love for ceremonies or grand speeches, while etiquette was a burden to him." The Empress Alexandra Feodorovna "fulfilled numerous ceremonial and dynastic duties, but all the time looked on the court around her with cool detachment".

St. Petersburg society also had ready access to the palace on the Moika of the brother of Alexander III, Grand Duke Alexei Alexandrovich, a lover of the "Muses and Graces." Grand Duke Vladimir Alexandrovich and Grand Duchess Maria Pavlovna also hosted spectacular balls and masquerades; their palace was considered the most magnificent in St. Petersburg at the turn of the twentieth century.

And what of the ancient Russian capital, Moscow? Here, too, the city had its own unique style. Muscovites were not used to the refined opulence of St. Petersburg, and here festivities were notable for the grand, limitless hospitality of true Russians. When balls were held in honor of the arrival of the heir to the throne or some other member of the royal family, Muscovites would try to outdo the splendour of stuffy St. Petersburg. When Moscow hosted a ball in honor of the marriage of the Duke of Edinburgh and the Grand Duchess Maria Alexandrovna, the daughter of Alexander II, two fountains illuminated by multicolored flames were set up at the entrance to the grand hall of the noble assembly. One of these, situated opposite the royal box and set between columns in front of a mirror, was in the form of an enormous goblet. The royal box itself, a luxurious marquee of purple velvet with a lining of white satin, was decorated with flowers and Sèvres vases. Here was a steel armchair made in Tula for the Empress Elizaveta Petrovna, while the royal dressing room contained an eighteenth-century silver toilette set from the house of the Stroganov family. Forty servants in plush liveries lined the stairway, and the ballroom was filled with wreaths of fresh hyacinths.

In the nineteenth century the critical attitudes towards the nation's past that had been prevalent in the previous century began to be reappraised. People began to appreciate that the Russians were an "ancient, distinctive, and original" race, and interest in the history and culture of the country began to grow. These tendencies were supported by Nicholas I in his state policy, and found expression in the three tenets "orthodoxy, autocracy, and nationality," which defined the official ideology of the state.

The increase in national self-awareness may be traced back to the war of 1812, when the whole nation rose up against Napoleon and defeated him. The celebration of antiquity, and of an idyllic past, also found expression in the works of the Romantics. The reforms of Alexander II further increased interest in all that was "Russian, national, autochthonous." Alexander III, too, based his policies on the principle of the "supremacy of Russian elements in the country." Finally, Nicholas II, like his father, strove to develop Russian traditions, and "uphold all that was specifically Russian."

Costume balls became an opportunity for the aristocracy to wear the clothes of their forebears, and the finest of such balls were held in the ancient capital, Moscow. It was here in 1849, in the palace of the Governor-General A. A. Zakrevskii, that a magnificent celebration was held for 1,000 guests. Members of high society wore costumes which portrayed first England, and then Russia, since these were considered the only states in Europe that "can understand each other with their unwavering national independence."

On this occasion the Russian procession represented the history and geography of the nation, "the centuries-long burgeoning of a great people and a great state." The procession was led by two *ryndy* in tall fur hats, and a Varangian knight, followed by guests in pairs, representing the towns, regions and tribes of the Russian empire. Moscow was evoked by a "bright-eyed" princess and a bearded boyar with a leisurely gait and a "contemplative and impressive expression." The personification of St. Petersburg was young, like the capital he represented, but dressed in an ancient Russian brocade and fur coat with silk roses, as if to symbolize "those roses with which the opulent life of our northern Palmyra is strewn." The procession ended with Ermak and the Tungus, Iakut and Samoyed tribes of Siberia. The masquerade was awash with sparkling *sarafans*, *dushegrei* (sleeveless jackets), *panevy* (woolen skirts), *kokoshniki*, and *kiki* (headdresses) studded with pearls, brilliant-cut diamonds and semiprecious stones.

The historian and writer M. Pogodin observed that all the European costumes seemed to turn to dust before such magnificence, and that the French language which poured forth from peoples' mouths was "hateful," comparing it to impure blood sullying the milk of a delicate noblewoman or of a simple Russian maid with plaited hair.

The nobility in St. Petersburg, following Moscow's lead, also wanted to display their roots in "ancient Russian times." St. Petersburg ladies began to talk about *sarafans*, and in 1855 a plan for new uniforms was discussed at court. Courtiers wanted to wear caftans and beaver-fur hats, and, according to I. Aksakov, the leader of the Slavophile movement, there was even a plan to rename chamberlains *stol'niki* (old Russian nobles), and gentlemen of the bedchamber *kliuchniki* (old Russian stewards).

Such plans, however, were never implemented. The nobles continued to deck themselves with caftans, *feryazy* (loose tunics), and *sarafans* at masquerades, where they were able to give free rein to their nationalistic feelings. And the most splendid of such masquerades were those held to celebrate the coronations of the last two Russian Emperors.

A ball, which had long been the subject of lively gossip and rumors in high society, was held on January 25 1883, the year of the coronation of Alexander III, in the palace of the Grand Duke Vladimir Alexandrovich. 250 people were invited to the ball: ministers, courtiers, officers of the guards, and also some of the professors from the Imperial Academy of Arts. In addition to the host, three other brothers of the Czar were present at the ball: the Grand Dukes Alexei, Pavel, and Sergei Alexandrovich. The guests began to gather towards ten o'clock in the evening. They were greeted by servants lining the ornamental staircase and guarding the doors to the dining room, dressed in picturesque costumes from various eras "connected with Russian history:" Varangians, Scythians, Novgorod and Moscow *strel'tsy*. The halls of the palace were filled with boyars and boyarinas, falconers, carvers, bakers, *ryndy*. Varangians and Zaporozhian Cossacks. A scribe of the Boyar's Duma appeared, with an inkwell and quill attached to his belt, then came a musician with his psaltery. The weapons and other accou-

trements for the costumes were genuine antiques. For example, Grand Duke Georgii Mikhailovich, dressed in the costume of a huntsman, had a silver hunting horn on his baldric, while Count Leuchtenburg was attired as a knight in an ancient hauberk with a saber from the sixteenth century.

The year 1904-05 cost Russia dear: the mighty effort of the war with Japan, which ended in catastrophe, was followed by the bloody events of the first Russian revolution. These circumstances brought a halt to the splendid string of balls and other entertainments. Contemporaries noted "a certain drop in the standards of secular life." In 1910, however, there was a return to the old customs and habits. The famous Russian ballerina Matilda Kshesinskaya wrote in her memoirs that "the 1910-11 season was exceptionally joyful: many banquets, dinners and masquerades." But the end of the mighty empire was drawing near. Only a few years would pass, and the world of magnificent palaces and glittering balls — so enchanting, but so remote from the rest of Russia — would be destroyed.

T. N. Muntian

THRONE OF EMPEROR PAUL I

ST. PETERSBURG, 1799-1801
MASTER C. MEIER
BIRCH, VELVET, GOLD THREAD
H. 182 CM, W. 86 CM
INV. NO. R-36

Thrones played an important role in palace ceremonial in the eighteenth and nineteenth centuries. They were used in state rooms in the Imperial palaces, where various official ceremonies took place in the presence of heads of state. The throne stood on a high stepped dais beneath a canopy, and was often the only piece of furniture in an enormous state room.

Particular attention was paid to the construction and decoration of thrones. They were often made to the design of the most important architects of the time. It is known, for example, that the eminent court architects

G. Quarenghi and V. Brenner took part in work on the thrones commissioned by Paul I. Brenner's name is connected with the manufacture of six identical thrones for Paul I, which were almost exact copies of the one made in England for the Empress Anna Ivanovna, for use in the Winter Palace in St. Petersburg. Unlike the original, which is silver, these six thrones were made of gilded wood, by the court furnisher Christian Meier. Documents show that they were commissioned in 1797.

Two of the six thrones have survived to this day. One is kept in the Hermitage, and the other in the Moscow Armory. The velvet backs of the thrones are decorated with embroidered images of two-headed eagles, and on the throne from the Armory the emblem contains a Maltese cross. The Maltese cross became part of the state emblem by order of Paul I in 1799. Here it enables us to date the Armory throne as being from an earlier period than that in the Hermitage.

PORTRAIT OF EMPEROR PAUL I

RUSSIA, 1844
AFTER V. L. BOROVIKOVSKII
OIL ON CANVAS
311 x 201 CM
INV. NO. ZH-1971

This portrait is a copy of the original painted in 1800 as a decoration for the conference hall of the St. Petersburg Academy of Arts. The original painting was commissioned from Borovikovskii to commemorate the investiture of Paul I as Grand Master of the Order of the Hospital of St John of Jerusalem (also known as the Knights of Malta) in 1798, and the proclamation of this order's establishment in Russia. The painting is essentially a coronation portrait: the official representation of the Emperor therefore includes symbols of kingship in Russia, as well as those relevant to Western Europe.

Paul I is presented in the full glory of his power and majesty. He wears a diamond crown, and is dressed in Imperial purple with a dalmatic, the ancient costume of the Byzantine emperors. He stands beside a throne. The traditional set of ceremonial articles include the orb on a velvet cushion, and the sceptre held in the Emperor's right hand. Paul I was, in real life, an unprepossessing man; here, however, skilled idealization suffuses his features with an expression of proud majesty. The interior is conventional: the Emperor stands on a stepped dais, covered with a velvet carpet. The surrounding décor and the coronation regalia glorify the good works of the monarch, and symbolize his majesty and royalty. The columns supporting the building represent the strength and steadfastness of his power; the Maltese crosses embody his knightly status; the artistic accessories show the Emperor to be a patron of the arts; the architectural plans, along with compasses, hammer and bevel, show the Masonic sympathies of the sovereign, and represent him as "architect" of his own kingdom.

MALTESE CROWN

✤

RUSSIA (?), END OF 18TH CENTURY

SILVER, GOLD, ENAMEL, VELVET, SILK

H. 29.4 CM,

BASE 20.3 CM X 19.1 CM

INV. NO. MR-9792

The Maltese crown is one of the rarest of the historic artefacts in the Armory. The introduction of this regalia into Russia links the political history of Russia with that of the Order of the Hospital of St John of Jerusalem during the short reign of Emperor Paul I.

This famous order of knighthood was founded in Palestine in the eleventh century, after the first Crusade. In 1113 the statutes of the order were ratified by the Pope. After the loss of Acre in 1291 the Order left Jerusalem, and in 1530 established itself in Malta, from where it acquired its name.

The first diplomatic links between Russia and the order were established at the end of the seventeenth century. In 1697 Peter the Great's ambassador, B. P. Sheremetev, was received in Valetta; links were maintained under Catherine the Great, and took on a new character under Paul I.

At that time the order was in need of a strong protector as never before. The French Revolution had dealt it a heavy blow, almost bringing financial ruin. The order lost all its privileges and rich lands in France. In the Russian Emperor, therefore, the order saw a powerful protector. In January 1797 Count Litta, the order's ambassador, concluded an accord with Russia, and in November of that year Paul I became Protector of the order. With the seizure of Malta by Napoleon in June 1798, the surviving members of the order placed even greater hope in the patronage of the Russian Emperor, and consequently, on November 29 1798, in a solemn ceremony in the Winter Palace, Paul was adopted as Grand Master of the Order of Malta. By his decree the Maltese cross was introduced into Russia's state emblem and seal. After Paul's death in 1801, however, the insignia of the order was removed from the emblem. In 1803 Alexander I returned the relics of the order to its new Grand Master, Jean-Baptiste Tommasi, and in 1817 its activities ceased in Russia.

INSIGNIA OF THE ORDER OF MALTA

✤

RUSSIA (?), END OF 18TH CENTURY

GOLD, ENAMEL

H. 10 CM, W. 4.4 CM

INV. NO. OM-2570

This insignia of the Order of Malta belonged to the Empress Maria Feodorovna, the wife of Paul I. She would have worn it on a bow of black ribbon on her left shoulder. At the beginning of the nineteenth century, when the Order of Malta ceased its activities in Russia, the insignias of Maria Feodorovna and Alexander I were transferred to the Chapter of Imperial and Royal orders.

FLASK

✛

LONDON, 1891-2
JAMES MORTIMER GARRARD
SILVER
H. 77.5 CM
INV. NO. MZ-720

The silver body of this flask is decorated with a band of ovoli in relief around the lower part, and bacchanal *mascaron* on each side. The latter are connected to the large cap of the flask by chains. Engraved on the front of the body is the emblem of the Russian Empire – the two-headed eagle – with an inscription in French: "TO EMPEROR ALEXANDER III AND EMPRESS MARIA FEODOROVNA ON THE OCCASION OF THEIR SILVER WEDDING, 1866-1891". On the other side is another engraved inscription with the names of the members of the Danish and English royal families.

It was traditional in European silverwork of the turn of the twentieth century to reflect earlier forms. This flask is a copy of a vessel from the beginning of the eighteenth century, which in turn has its roots in the leather water canteens used by pilgrims in the Middle Ages.

TWO-HANDLED CUP

✣

LONDON, 1902
CHARLES STUART HARRIS LTD.
MASTER SEBASTIAN HENRY GARRARD
SILVER
H. 38.5 CM
INV. NO. 3984/1-2

The smooth body of this two handled cup is decorated with applied matted scroll cartouches, flower festoons, masks of lions and satyrs, and vine flourishes. The emblem of Great Britain is engraved on one side beneath a crown, and the emblem of the Russian Empire on the side shown here. Engraved on the lower part of the body is the inscription: "To His IMPERIAL HIGHNESS THE CZAREVICH, HEREDITARY GRAND DUKE ALEXEI NIKOLAEVICH, ON THE OCCASION OF HIS CHRISTENING 24/11 AUGUST 1904. FROM HIS AFFECTIONATE GREAT UNCLE AND GODFATHER, KING EDWARD VII".

The cover is crowned with a stylized pineapple finial, and is decorated with *mascaron, flowers and vine fruits*; around the base of the cover are cartouches containing an eagle, salamander, serpent and fish, which symbolise the four elements — air, fire, earth and water.

The cup has its roots in English silverwork of the eighteenth century, with its characteristic bell shape, tall cover with finial, and the combination of engraving and cast decoration in relief on a smooth polished ground.

TABLECLOTH: NASTOL'NIK

✣

MOSCOW, END OF 18TH CENTURY
BROCADE, GOLD AND SILK THREAD
175 X 160 CM
INV. NO. TK-1764

The *nastol'nik* was a tablecloth for use in court ceremonies of the eighteenth and nineteenth centuries, such as the long coronation festivities and ambassadorial receptions. *Nastol'niki* were usually made of fine decorated brocade; examples also exist, however, made from smooth velvet or silk with decorations in embroidery or appliqué work.

This *nastol'nik* is woven from three panels of decorated brocade with a bullion trim. The decoration is in colored silks on a gold ground, and consists of ribbons in the form of undulating stems, surrounding festoons. The brocade is of Russian origin, probably from Moscow.

✣

MASQUERADE COSTUME OF
EMPEROR NICHOLAS II
✛

CAFTAN: ST. PETERSBURG,
IMPERIAL THEATRICAL COSTUMIER I I KAFFI,
BEGINNING OF 1903; STUDS AND BUTTONS:
WESTERN EUROPE, RUSSIA, TURKEY,
17TH CENTURY; CHEVRONS: RUSSIA, TURKEY,
16TH-17TH CENTURIES;
HAT: ST. PETERSBURG, MILLINERY WORKSHOP
OF THE BROTHERS BRIUNO, 1903
UPPER CAFTAN: DAMASK, BROCADE, GOLD,
ENAMEL, PRECIOUS STONES; LOWER CAFTAN:
VELVET, SILK, LACE, GOLD, PRECIOUS STONES,
PEARLS; BELT: BROCADE, SILK, GOLD, PRECIOUS
STONES; HAT: BROCADE, SABLE, SILK, GOLD,
ENAMEL, PRECIOUS STONES
L. OF UPPER CAFTAN 142 CM;
L. OF LOWER CAFTAN 130 CM;
BELT 91.5 X 7 CM,
H. OF HAT 17.7 CM
INV. NOS TK-2921, TK-2922, TK-2923, TK-2924

On February 11 1903
a spectacle was staged in the Imperial Theater
of the Hermitage. All those invited, apart from
foreign diplomats, were dressed in costumes
from the time of Czar Alexei Mikhailovich. On
February 13 a costume ball was held in the
Concert Hall of the Winter Palace for the
Dowager Empress Maria Feodorovna and
Grand Duke Mikhail, who had not been able to
attend the earlier occasion.

Nicholas II was dressed in a cos-
tume copying the "Parade Dress" of Czar
Alexei Mikhailovich; the dress of Empress
Alexandra Feodorovna copied the dress of
Czarina Maria Ilinichna (born Miloslavskaya,
the first wife of Alexei Mikhailovich).

It is very probable that the designer of
the costumes of the Imperial couple for this "last
court ball in the history of the empire" was the
wonderful stylist and dress designer
I. A. Vsevolzhskii, who was the Steward of the
Royal Household and Director of the Hermitage
(and previously Director of the Imperial Theaters).

Two historians and archaeologists also took part in the creation of these costumes: V. I. Sizov in Moscow, and K. D. Chicagov in St. Petersburg. All the costumes for this ball, including those of the Imperial couple, were made in the Office of the Imperial Theaters in St. Petersburg. Velvet and satin, in the style of seventeenth-century Italian textiles, were specially commissioned from the factory of A. and V. Sapozhnikov in Moscow.

Decorations from ancient royal attire were brought from the Armory. Nicholas II personally chose the decorations for his costume, including pearl bracelets which had belonged to Czar Feodor Ivanovich.

On April 2 1903 the Armory was presented with that part of the Emperor's costume which had been decorated with authentic and valuable adornments from royal clothing of the sixteenth and seventeenth centuries. These were an outer open-necked caftan with a figured turned-down collar and long sleeves with turned-back cuffs, decorated with gold lace, gold adornments and buttons with enamel and precious stones; an inner caftan with a stand-up collar and long narrow sleeves, decorated with jeweled studs and buttons; pearl bracelets; a belt with gold decoration; and a hat with a band of sable fur lined with openwork gold decoration.

Apart from these articles, Nicholas II's costume consisted of loose-fitting silk trousers, a silk shirt with an embroidered collar and a silk belt with tassels.

✣

DISH

✣

MOSCOW, 1882

SILVER, ENAMEL

DIAM. 45 CM; INV. NO. MR-11480

This dish is the work of a Moscow silversmith of the end of the nineteenth century. It is remarkable for its pictorial qualities, enhanced by the contrast between the silver-gilt and bright enamel. The decoration commemorates important events in Russian history at the end of the sixteenth century. The bowl of the dish is decorated with an enamel portrayal of the Archangel Michael – the symbol of the Cossack Ataman Ermak Timofeevich. He was instrumental in the assimilation of Siberia into Russia during the reign of Ivan the Terrible. Four enamel badges are positioned to each side of the Archangel Michael. One of these shows a pyramid with military attributes, the emblem of the town of Tobolsk, founded in 1587 as the center of the Russian colonization of Siberia; two other badges show a fish and a sheaf of corn, representing the occupations of inhabitants of the region; the fourth badge bears the monogram of Emperor Alexander III. Clearly the dish was commissioned by the local authorities in Tobolsk as a gift for Alexander at his coronation.

✛

Dish

✛

Moscow, 1903

Workshop of K Shol´ts

Wood

DIAM. 56 CM; INV. No. DK-352

The workshop of K. Shol´ts often undertook commissions from social organizations and distinguished citizens for carved articles to be presented to members of the Imperial family. A number of such commissions were undertaken in 1903, when the ancient capital ceremoniously received the Imperial family for the festival of Easter. March 30, Palm Sunday, which had long been celebrated in the Kremlin, saw a magnificent procession of the Imperial family into the Dormition Cathedral. The procession began in the Great Kremlin Palace, where the Imperial family lived during their stays in Moscow. The state rooms of the palace were filled with representatives of the nobility and important dignitaries. In the St George Hall, the first to welcome the royal guests with the ancient Russian custom of bread and salt was the governor of the city, Prince V. M. Golitsyn. Thereafter the procession moved to the St Vladimir Hall, where gifts were presented from various guilds. Among these was the Moscow Guild of Merchants, which played an important role in the life of the city, and was celebrating its fortieth anniversary that year.

A representative of the guild presented the sovereign with bread and salt on this wonderful wooden dish, which is still kept in the Armory. The dish's carved decoration tells its history: the bowl is decorated with the monogram of Nicholas II and the inscription "FROM THE MOSCOW GUILD OF MERCHANTS"; along the rim are medallions with the state emblem of Russia and the date, and on the underside of the dish the inscription reads "K Shol´ts. Moscow".

✛

PLATES AND VASE FROM THE KREMLIN SERVICE

✛

ST. PETERSBURG, 1843-61, 1901, 1903
DESIGNER F.G. SOLNTSEV
PLATES: KORNILOV BROTHERS, 1843-61;
IMPERIAL PORCELAIN FACTORY, 1903
VASE: IMPERIAL PORCELAIN FACTORY, 1901
PORCELAIN
DIAM. OF PLATES 28 CM, 24.2 CM;
VASE H. 18.1 CM, W. 23.5 CM
INV. NOS F-434, F-760, F-916

The Kremlin Service was commissioned by Emperor Nicholas I for the Great Kremlin Palace, and manufacture was commenced by the Imperial Porcelain Factory in 1839.

Intended for use at parade banquets, the service is extraordinary for the number of pieces it contains (nearly 1,000 articles). It was designed, at the behest of the Emperor, by F. G. Solntsev, a gifted decorative artist, archaeologist, researcher and expert in old Russian art.

The Kremlin Service represents the first attempt to apply the Russian Historical style to porcelain. Well versed in the Armory collection, Solntsev took as the basis for his design some of the finest examples of the decorative arts of the seventeenth century. For instance, the model for the decoration of the dinner service was that on the ewer of the washbasin set belonging to Czarina Natalia Kirillovna, which was made of gold, and decorated with colored enamel and precious stones. For this reason the pieces in the dinner service are richly gilded, painted in bright colors and decorated in a way that imitates the chasing of the gold, and the sparkle of the stones and enamel in the original. The task before the artist was not simply to bring out the beauty of the porcelain, but also to create an impression that the work was made from precious materials.

The Kremlin Service was in use from the moment it was fired. For this reason, it was sometimes necessary to add to the service. For much of the second half of the nineteenth century, work on the service was undertaken by the famous private firm of the Kornilov Brothers, whose works were famed for the high quality of their materials and the skill of their finish. The Kornilov Brothers added large plate stands to the dinner service.

In creating the service in the Historical style, Solntsev did not confine himself to the use of antiquarian ornamentation. In the various vases and salad bowls, Solntsev used traditional shapes of old metalware alongside more typical shapes for porcelain. Here, for example, the small vase is based on a *rassol'nik* vase from the seventeenth century, a shallow cup on a graceful stem. The painted decoration of the vase – palm branches and roses – matches the decorative elements of the table and dessert services.

**CUP AND SAUCER, SWEETMEAT STAND AND
DESREST PLATE FROM THE KREMLIN SERVICE**

✣

ST. PETERSBURG, IMPERIAL PORCELAIN
FACTORY, 1839, 1892
DESIGNER F. G. SOLNTSEV
CUP AND SAUCER, 1892;
STAND AND PLATE, 1839
PORCELAIN, BRONZE
CUP H. 6 CM, DIAM. 9 CM; SAUCER DIAM. 15.5 CM, STAND
H. 50 CM, PLATE DIAM. 21.5 CM
INV. NOS F-856, F-879, F-996, F-752

Of all the articles that
constitute the Kremlin Service, the dessert
plates are most remarkable for their elegance
and brilliance. Their ornamentation was based
on that of one of the masterpieces of the seventeenth century, the plate of Czar Alexei
Mikhailovich made in 1667. The enamelwork
of the original is here reproduced in small
details on the porcelain, and the rich variety of
the enamel colors is beautifully conveyed. The
inscription around the medallion contains the
name of the man who commissioned the
Kremlin Service: "EMPEROR AND SOVEREIGN OF
ALL RUSSIA NICHOLAS".

The articles which make up the
dessert part of the service vary considerably:
there are deep bowls for fruit, shallow bowls on
tall stems and so on. The tall serving stands for
sweetmeats are notable for their refinement.
They consist of three plates of different sizes
attached to a gilt bronze stem and crowned
with a cast representation of the Russian
emblem. A detail of the ornament on the plate
– stylized roses in gilt lozenge-shaped cartouches – is used to decorate the stand with
great success.

The cups and saucers repeat the
ornamentation of the dinner service. But in
these frail, delicate articles covered with gold
both outside and inside, the sense of a valuable
piece of jewelry is particularly vivid.

✣

SALT CELLAR

✣

MOSCOW (?), 1898

WOOD, METAL, ENAMEL

H. 12 CM; INV. NO. DK-481

Thishis wooden salt cellar is decorated with ornamental carving and the Russian state emblem. It was presented to Nicholas II and Alexandra Feodorovna in Moscow in 1898 by the religious sect of the Old Believers, after the Imperial couple had been presented with bread and salt.

From ancient times salt cellars had been highly valued; this was originally connected with the scarcity and high cost of salt. The traditions surrounding salt cellars were continued in the nineteenth and early twentieth centuries, when particularly beautiful examples were produced. From the second half of the nineteenth century wooden and silver salt cellars were produced in the shape of lavishly decorated thrones, with lids representing the seat of the throne. These were particularly popular in Moscow art, which, in comparison with that of St. Petersburg, was notable for its adherence to folk and old Russian traditions. This example from the Kremlin combines the shape of traditional Russian salt cellars with ornamentation based on ancient Russian motifs, a combination which is typical of the Russian Historical movement. Also characteristic is the use of wood, a material much favored in Russian folk art. The richly expressive qualities of wood were rediscovered by carvers of the Historical movement, and continued to be used by the Modernists. At the Universal Exhibition in Paris in 1900, Russia was represented as a fairy-tale land of neat wooden huts with carved decorations and pointed towers, from designs by K. Korovin.

Designs for wooden articles were produced by other well known Russian artists at the turn of the twentieth century; these sketches were then employed by a large number of workshops.

GLASSES FROM THE BAKHMETEVSKII SERVICE

✣

RUSSIA, NIKOL'SKO-BAKHMETEVSKII FACTORY, 1806-07

CRYSTAL GLASS

GOBLET H. 12.6 CM;

WINE GLASSES H. 16.8 CM, 7.5 CM;

TUMBLER H. 8.2 CM

INV. NOS F-1879, F-1631, F-1890, F-1882

Thehe Bakhmetevskii Service is an extremely interesting example of Russian glassware of the beginning of the nineteenth century. The history of its production is linked with the struggle of Russian manufacturers for supremacy in the Russian market. The Nikol'sko-Bakhmetevskii factory was one of the oldest and most celebrated glassworks in Russia, renowned for the quality of its materials and its high standards of design. In 1806 a collection of articles from the factory was presented to Emperor Alexander I. With this gift the owner of the factory, N. S. Bakhmetev, hoped to demonstrate that Russian glassworks could successfully compete with more expensive imported crystal. Alexander I then commissioned a large service from the factory. So strong was the impression created by the service that Russia imposed a ban (albeit only for a short time) on imported crystal, in particular the celebrated English lead crystalware.

The service includes a wide range of different articles: decanters, *bokaly* (goblets), *riumki* (wine glasses) and *stakany* (tumblers) in various shapes and sizes. They are remarkable for the quality of the crystal and their elegant and refined shape, typical of glasswork of the beginning of the nineteenth century. The decoration is simple but effective, combining smooth fluted friezes, friezes with a diamond border, and narrow gilt bands. The engraved gilt eagles show that the service was the property of a royal customer.

CORONATION TOWEL

✛

POLTAVA, 1883

LINEN, SILK, SILK THREAD

260 x 56 CM

INV. NO. TK-693

This towel is made of white linen decorated with cross-stitch embroidery, appliqué work and bobbin lace. In the center is the emblem of Poltava province under a crown, executed in appliqué, with the date 1883. The ground around the emblem is embroidered with a geometrical pattern. Along the sides of the towel are monograms of Alexander III under a crown, framed in laurel branches; beside the monograms are two-headed eagles under crowns. Strips of ornamental embroidery and lace run along the ends of the towel.

Two embroidered inscriptions show that the towel was presented to Emperor Alexander III on his coronation in 1883, by members of the gentry from Poltava province.

For coronations, the most noble representatives of the Russian provinces were invited to Moscow. They took part in the coronation ceremony, joining the Emperor's retinue. During the days of celebrations and audiences that followed the coronation, they would bring the Emperor bread and salt on silver or carved wooden dishes. These would be carried on beautifully designed towels such as this one, the work of local provincial seamstresses and lacemakers.

THE RUSSIAN ORTHODOX CHURCH FROM THE EIGHTEENTH TO THE TWENTIETH CENTURY

✣

The eighteenth century, which began with the reforms of Peter the Great, marked a new period in Russian history. The primacy of the sovereign in all spheres of secular and religious life, the predominance of secular culture over ecclesiastical, and finally the establishment in the second half of the eighteenth century of the idea of "enlightened absolutism" all led to a significant change in the relations between the Czar and the Church.

The most significant stage of this transformation was Peter's abolition of the Patriarchate and the introduction of a collegiate form of church rule in 1721. The Ecclesiastical College, or Synod, was made up of eleven religious figures of various ranks, and was directly subordinate to the Czar. State supervision over the Synod was exercised by the Chief Procurator, a person from a military or civilian background.

The first sitting of the Synod was held after a ceremonial church service on February 14 1721. Its members took oath and swore to be "serving vassals and subjects" to the sovereign, and to recognize him as the "supreme judge of this Ecclesiastical College." Soon afterwards a three-storeyed stone build-

ing was erected for the Synod in St. Petersburg, its design based on that of existing colleges. The interior decoration of the building underlined the secular nature of the new supreme body of Church rule. The central meeting hall contained a portrait of Peter the Great. In 1723 all overseas patriarchates recognized the new body as their equal colleague.

The Russian Orthodox Church became part of the apparatus of state, and lost its nominal independence from the secular powers. Local bishops were now essentially state servants, differing from other ranks only in their clothing. The secularization of all church and monastery property carried out by Empress Catherine the Great in 1762 made the clergy materially dependent on the Treasury.

At the beginning of the nineteenth century the secular powers continued their interference in the affairs of the Church, which began more and more to be turned into an apparatus of state. A Ministry of Religious Affairs and National Enlightenment was established in 1817 (only to be abolished in 1824). The principal idea behind its creation was that "Christian piety should always be the basis of a true education." At this time the preparation of

priests was becoming increasingly close to the state system of education for the civil service. Teachers in religious institutions effectively became civil servants, employed to prepare Church personnel.

During the reign of Nicholas I, who was a committed advocate of the influence of the state in Church life, legislation was introduced which affected all aspects of the Orthodox Church. A system of control over the Church was gradually established, which in all its principal features remained unchanged until 1917. The Czar was head of the Orthodox Church; directly subordinate to him were the Chief Procurator, his assistants, and the plenum of the Church Synod. A special link in the organization of the Church and clergy was formed by priests who served the royal court, the army and the navy. The Emperor chose his own confessor, who in the Church hierarchy occupied "first place after the bishops" and was head of the clergy serving in the court and palace churches.

The Church naturally resented its subordinate position to the state, and its disaffection was aggravated by the social and political crisis that gripped Russia at the beginning

✣

Archangel Cathedral of the Moscow Kremlin

of the twentieth century. A campaign was started to convoke a local council and re-establish the Patriarchate. This council was eventually set up under the interim government on August 15 1917, by which time the government had abolished the duties of the Chief Procurator and had established a Ministry of the Creed. The Moscow Metropolitan Tikhon was elected chair of the council, and soon after was appointed Patriarch.

Despite the changes to the organization and legal status of the Russian church since the beginning of the eighteenth century, the role of Orthodoxy as the ideological foundation of the state remained unchanged. Peter the Great's first reforming decrees declared religion "the basis of the prosperity of the state, and the strongest support of the throne of the monarch." Events decreed by royal proclamations and government edicts were understood by the people to be primarily of a religious character. This was no accident. Throughout Russian history, from the time of the adoption of Christianity, religion had pervaded society. Russian Emperors, from the time of Nicholas I, conducted their policy on the basis of "Orthodoxy, Autocracy,

Nationality," in that order. This theory was a natural outcome of the traditional religiosity of the Russian people, in particular on their conception of the monarch as a *"Czar-batiushka,"* or paternalistic Czar. To the people the Czar was always the "Sovereign anointed by God," head of both state and Church.

Russian Emperors traditionally demonstrated their faith in Orthodoxy to the people during solemn church services and ceremonies. For example, on Christmas Eve 1722 Peter the Great sang in the choir in the Cross Chamber, part of the former Palace of the Patriarch in Moscow. Contemporaries observed that Peter was well versed in Church doctrine and considered the Bible "a book exceeding all others in wisdom." Peter's daughter, the Empress Elizaveta Petrovna, was particularly noted for her piety. From Catherine the Great onwards, all the Empresses of the eighteenth and nineteenth centuries were particularly strict in their observance of the laws of the Russian Church. This included those who, like Catherine, had been born as Western European princesses and had converted to the Orthodox faith in Russia. The Russian Emperors were no less committed believers.

Church ritual in the eighteenth and nineteenth centuries maintained the forms of previous centuries. Feast day services and traditional ceremonies such as christenings, marriages, and funerals all followed the ecclesiastical canon. At the same time, from the beginning of the eighteenth century new decrees were issued regulating Church activities. One of these introduced an obligatory annual confession. Another new element in Church life was the inclusion in the calendar of "Czar's days." These commemorated the coronation, the name days of the Czar and Czaritsa, the birth of an heir, and other events. Printed tables listing such dates were distributed to all the cathedrals of the country, where they were kept on the altar or in the vestry. On these days services would begin with a prayer for the health of the Czar, and the traditional pealing of the church bells was now accompanied by cannon and rifle salutes. The façades of houses were decorated with state flags and royal monograms, and the evenings were marked with illuminations and promenades.

Ceremonial church services were held to mark the conclusion of military campaigns, or to celebrate the anniversaries of past victories. After the conclusion of peace with Turkey in 1775 a solemn prayer service was held in the Kazan Cathedral in St. Petersburg, attended by all the city nobility. The street from the Winter Palace to the cathedral was lined on both sides by two ranks of guards and artillery regiments. At the moment when the prayer for long life to the sovereign was intoned three volleys rang out, accompanied by a cannon salute from the St Peter and St Paul Fortress and the ringing of the church bells. All evening until after midnight great crowds of people promenaded about the brightly lit streets. At this time the Empress Catherine the Great was in Moscow. Here the main thanksgiving services were held in the Dormition Cathedral in the Kremlin, which remained the principal holy place in the land. This notable event was also marked by the richest of royal donations to the Kremlin cathedrals. These included the magnificent collection of liturgical plate, made of gold with brilliant-cut diamonds and rubies, which the Empress herself placed on the credence table at the altar of the Dormition Cathedral. For this thanksgiving service Prince Potemkin ordered some 2,000 icons to be distributed from the Armory, which

were placed on newly constructed iconostases on the south and west walls of the cathedral.

In 1812, during the invasion of the Napoleonic forces, a special service of prayer was held in the Dormition Cathedral to bless the Moscow militia, about to be sent to the battlefield, and the standard which had been specially made for the Russian troops. After Russia's victory the standard, torn by grapeshot and bullets, was returned to the cathedral and treasured as a sacred object. A hundred years later, when the anniversary of the Patriotic War of 1812 was celebrated, a royal manifesto was read out at the service in the cathedral, declaring that "the Orthodox clergy underwent great deprivation and adversity, along with all the Russian people, and showed themselves true servants of the Fatherland."

The last service of thanksgiving in Russia held in connection with military events took place in the Dormition Cathedral in August 1914. It was attended in person by Nicholas II, who had come to Moscow specially. Pierre Gillard, the former tutor to the Czarevich Alexei, wrote that Nicholas "wanted to follow the example of his forebears in times

of trouble, and ask God's blessing on himself and his people." The whole council of the Orthodox Church conducted the service: the Metropolitans of Moscow, St. Petersburg and Kiev, along with other senior members of the clergy. At the end of the service members of the royal family paid their respects to the relics of the prelates buried in the cathedral, and to the shrine of Alexei, one of the first Moscow Metropolitans, in the Chudov Monastery of the Kremlin. When the Czar made his way to the station an enormous crowd filled the streets and squares of the city, and as the bells rang out unceasingly they sang the anthem "God Save the Czar." Priests held icons lit by lamps as they stood in full dress at the open doors of the churches, and blessed the royal procession as it passed.

All ceremonies connected with the private life of the royal family, such as weddings and christenings, took place in the private chapel of the Winter Palace in St. Petersburg. The famous French traveler and man of letters, the Marquis de Custin, wrote a wonderful description of the wedding ceremony in 1839 of Count Leuchtenberg and the daughter of Nicholas I, the Grand Duchess Maria.

"The marriage ceremony was prolonged and magnificent. Every aspect of the Eastern Church served as a symbol, and the magnificence of the church was enhanced by the glitter of the ceremony. The jewelry and precious stones worn by the ladies sparkled magically among the treasures adorning the walls of the cathedral, and it seemed almost as if royal opulence was competing with the greatness of God. The congregation respected the might of heaven but did not forget earthly powers. When the clergy and choir sang "We praise thee, O God," cannon fire rang out, telling the city of the conclusion of the wedding ceremony. The chorus of music, artillery, church bells, and the shouts of the people defies description. All musical instruments have been banished from the Orthodox Church, and male voices alone give praise to the Lord. During the prayers, as one choir answered another, the royal door was thrown open to reveal priests in gold vestments and headdresses studded with sparkling precious stones."

All court church services were preceded by a solemn royal procession conducted according to strict rules which reached their final form at the beginning of the nineteenth century. The members of the royal family gathered in the Malachite Hall of the Winter Palace, from where they emerged in pairs according to the line of succession. The royal couple were followed by their pages, serving generals and aides-de-camp; the other pairs were followed by their own pages. The column processed slowly through all the halls of the Winter Palace to the royal chapel.

Church festivals were also celebrated in the royal chapel and attended by the monarch. Chief among these were the Sanctification of the Water at Epiphany and the Easter Matins. During the first half of the eighteenth century, several new additions had been made to the seventeenth-century ceremony of the Sanctification of the Water. Court chronicles of 1740 and 1741 describe how, at the end of the service in the royal chapel, the Sanctification of the Water took place on the Neva opposite the Winter Palace. The ceremony was accompanied by gun salutes from the St Peter and St Paul Fortress and the Admiralty. A special canopy was erected above a hole in the ice, and nearby troops in full parade uniform answered the artillery with a volley of fire. The Empress Anna Ivanovna observed the events from the windows of the Winter Palace.

Easter was the principal festival of Russian Orthodoxy. It was preceded by a forty-day Lenten fast, culminating in Holy Week which was marked by particularly stringent abstinence, constant prayer and charitable works. In 1900, after a break of more than half a century, Moscow again became the center of the grandiose Easter celebrations attended by the royal family, who once more observed the Orthodox "Festival of Festivals" in the ancient capital of the Russian state. The arrival of Nicholas II in Moscow was in itself a ceremonial event. When the Imperial train arrived from St. Petersburg the first peal from the great Kremlin Bell Tower rang out, followed by the ringing of the bells of all Moscow's churches. As the bells rang out, a mass of people flocked to the square in front of the station, bared their heads and shouted, "Hurrah!" in a mighty symphony with the clanging of the church bells. The first service of Holy Week attended by the royal family in the Dormition Cathedral was the Feast of the Entry into Jerusalem . Although the ceremonial of the holiday no longer included the famous "Journey on The Ass", many details of the ancient Russian ritual were retained. In a revival of the ritual of two centuries earlier, the Czar emerged from the Palace to be met by a court priest with a cross and holy water, accompanied by singing from the court choir. After the ceremony of the Kissing of the Cross, the Czar took "bread and salt" on a carved wooden dish carried by the senior standard-bearer of the Dormition Cathedral. The Czar and Czaritsa emerged from the Palace onto the square to the accompaniment of ringing from all the Kremlin bells. At the same time, the south doors of the cathedral were thrown open and members of the clergy came out onto a dais. They carried *dikiri* and *trikiri* (two- and three-branched candlesticks), censers, ancient crosses, the altar icon of the Mother of God, a gold cross on a dish and a vessel containing holy water, all of which articles were kept in the cathedral. Priests were followed by senior representatives of the clergy who were to conduct the service, led by the Moscow Metropolitan Vladimir; all the priests wore robes of smooth gold brocade. After the Metropolitan's welcoming speech and the kissing of the cross by the Emperor, the partici-

pants processed into the cathedral where a solemn service took place.

On Monday of Holy Week, the royal couple went to the Mirovarennaia Chamber of the former Palace of the Patriarch in the Kremlin. Here, once every few years, the *Mirovarenie* (Boiling of the Chrism, or anointing oil) took place — one of the oldest rituals in the Orthodox church. Members of the clergy were specially nominated to conduct this ceremony. Metropolitan Vladimir, and other clerics wore black velvet chasubles decorated with silver galloon crosses. Immediately before the service, lighted candles were brought to the royal couple. The Metropolitan sprinkled holy water over the hearth, cauldrons and scented oil. He poured the holy water into the cauldrons and then, having taken the vessels containing wine, butter and scented oil, he blessed each of them and poured them into the cauldrons. He then added a hard fragrant balm kept on silver plates. A synodal clergyman presented the Metropolitan with a bunch of spills which he lit from a candle and placed in a furnace. Nine deacons stood by the cauldrons and with special little spades began to stir the wine, butter and scented oil and balm. Readings from the

Gospel continued for the three days of the *Mirovarenie*. On the Thursday of Holy Week the ritual ended with the solemn ceremony of the Consecration of the Holy Chrism in the Dormition Cathedral.

During Holy Week, the royal couple attended all the most important services in the Kremlin churches, and in the Cathedral of Christ the Saviour, which had served as the Cathedral of Moscow from the time of its consecration in 1889. The Easter Matins service was held in the Dormition Cathedral. In accordance with ancient custom, two censers were placed by the royal door in the church. From nine o'clock in the evening passages from the holy scriptures were read out. At midnight the Metropolitan entered the church to conduct the principal service, after which a Procession of the Cross set forth from the church. The procession was headed by the standard bearers, who were dressed in parade caftans and carried the nine standards of the cathedral. They were followed by the choristers of the Synod, then by priests carrying the icon of the Mother of God, ancient crosses, the icon of the Resurrection of Christ, and the Gospels. The Metropolitan followed the priests, carrying a gold cross and a three-branched candlestick. His mitre was decorated with a precious cross of brilliant-cut diamonds, which had been presented to him by the Emperor specifically for this service. All the members of the clergy were dressed in rich robes of crimson velvet. The Procession of the Cross wound its way round the church until it arrived at the West doors, where a solemn hymn to the Resurrection was sung. At the end of the service, the Metropolitan exchanged triple Easter kisses with the congregation in the cathedral. The service ended at two o'clock in the morning. The Emperor Nicholas II and Empress Alexandra Feodorovna took part in both the service and the Procession of the Cross.

Later on, the ceremony continued in the palace. From nine o'clock onwards processions of gaily dressed people entered the Kremlin. By half past eleven, all the Moscow nobility that had been invited to participate were already in their places in the palace, in different halls, according to rank. At that time the first celebratory cannonade rang out: half an hour later, the chimes of the Saviour Tower heralded the dawn of a new day. They were answered by more cannon fire, along with the peals of the Ivan the Great Bell Tower, and the bells of all the "forty times forty" churches of Moscow. Above the Kremlin and the Zamoskvoreche region the sky was lit up with cannon fire: Bengal lights flared, illuminations glowed, and flickering candles appeared in the hands of the people. At the first peal of the Kremlin bells, the most magnificent royal procession began. The cortege made its way through all the halls of the Great Kremlin Palace towards the Upper Cathedral of the Saviour. The Emperor wore the uniform of a Life Guard of the Preobrazhenskii regiment, with a chain of the Order of St Andrew the First Called, and a ribbon of the Order of St Alexander Nevsky, while the Empress was dressed in a white dress embroidered with gold, with the ribbon of the Order of St Catherine and the chain of the Order of St Andrew the First Called. The Easter Matins service finished at half past three in the morning. In the days that followed, according to tradition, the Empress gave each guest her best wishes of the season, and presented them all with an Easter egg. Throughout the whole Easter festival, which lasted a week, Moscow was decorated with flags, flowers and illuminations.

The main Easter services attended by the Emperor in 1900 were held in the Dormition Cathedral, which was still considered by the faithful to be the most important church in Orthodox Russia. It was here that one of the defining events of the Russian Church took place on November 21 1917, when the Metropolitan Tikhon was ceremonially enthroned, marking the re-establishment of the Patriarchate in Russia.

I. I. Vishnevskaya

✠

ALTAR CROSS

✠

RUSSIA, ST. PETERSBURG, 1759

MASTER ZAKHARII DEIKHMAN

SILVER, PAINTING ON ENAMEL

53 x 33 CM

INV. NO. MR-4691

This massive altar cross in the rococo style is the work of one of the finest engravers of the eighteenth century, Zakharii Deikhman. His silver works were extremely varied, ranging from delicate vessels for medicaments to luxurious palace dinner services. The wonderful stamped ornament on this cross reveals his extraordinary talent. Miniatures painted in enamel are mounted in the cross, showing the Lord of Hosts, the Virgin, and the Apostle John. In the center is a Crucifixion in relief, and the bottom of the cross has a scene of the Deposition. The miniatures are the work of an unknown artist.

The second half of the eighteenth century was the heyday of religious enamel miniatures. At this time brilliant miniaturists were at work in St. Petersburg, Moscow, and Rostov, of whom many received special training at the St. Petersburg Academy of Arts. Their works were used in the decoration of chalices, gospel covers, mitres, tabernacles, and other articles. The miniatures mounted in this cross are striking in their dynamic composition and rich range of colors.

✠

Icon: The Kazan Mother of God

✛

MOSCOW, BEGINNING OF 18TH CENTURY

OKLAD: MOSCOW, 1804

WOOD, TEMPERA, SILVER

32.3 x 27.3 CM

INV. NO. ZH-2614/1-2

The icon The Kazan Mother of God, which, according to tradition, first appeared in Kazan in 1579, was believed to work miracles. During the Time of Troubles, when Moscow was driving out the Polish invaders, Prince D.M. Pozharskii, who led the national militia, owned a copy of the icon. It was believed that the Russian forces overcame the enemy thanks to the protection of the Virgin. In memory of this event Czar Mikhail Feodorovich Romanov established a cult of the icon in Moscow, and during the reign of his son Alexei Mikhailovich this spread across the entire state.

The icon was one of the most revered in all Rus´. Rare indeed was the Russian family that did not have a *kazanskaia* icon – as it was popularly known – in its icon case. And it may be said with certainty that there was not a single Russian church that did not have a similar icon. Parents used the image to bless their children on their marriage. In people's homes, lamps stood in front of the icon, and children from their earliest years knew and loved the image of the Mother of God, bathed in gentle light.

This icon was probably painted at the beginning of the eighteenth century, during the reign of Peter the Great; many of its features, however, are reminiscent of the style of the end of the previous century. The deep blue background, the festive pink and light blue clothing decorated with gold and silver ornament, and the gentle expressions of the Virgin and Child are all reminiscent of the work of the "royal icon painters" – the artists who worked at the court of the Moscow Czars in the middle of the seventeenth century. Although the provenance of the icon is not known, it is thought that it is the work of Moscow artists connected with the royal workshops.

PANAGIA WITH CHAIN

✣

RUSSIA, 1787-92

GOLD, SILVER, DIAMONDS, PEARLS,

ENAMEL

14.8 X 6.8 CM

INV. NO. MR-568/1-2

A panagia – Greek for "all holy" – was a pectoral icon with an image of the Virgin or Christ. Only the highest ranks of the clergy – metropolitans and patriarchs – had the right to wear one. Early examples were in the form of a locket, sometimes containing a holy relic; later, however, panagiae ceased to be used as reliquaries, and became a mark of dignity among the high orders of the clergy, taking the form of a round or oval icon.

In the second half of the eighteenth century panagiae were particularly opulent and magnificent: with their abundance of brilliant-cut diamonds, pearls, and other gems, they were similar to the decorations of the secular nobility. To some extent this is true of the panagia in the Kremlin collection.

It is an expressive example of the classical style in Russian applied art. Particularly noteworthy are the cool, restrained range of colors, consisting mainly of blue and gray enamel, the strength and delicacy of the composition, and the refinement and precision of the detail.

In the center of the panagia is a small half-length enamel portrayal of Christ the Good Shepherd. A plaque in a sumptuous diamond frame is decorated with intertwined ribbons, rosettes, ovals, and crosses. Diamonds are combined with a large and splendid pear-shaped pearl pendant.

The panagia came to the Armory collection in 1918 from the Troitskii (Trinity) residence in the Kremlin. This was the place where monks from the Troitse-Sergiev Monastery stayed during their visits to Moscow. It is of a commemorative nature, and was probably made for the fifth anniversary of some event: the reverse side contains a carved monogram with the letters PRMAM under a crown, and the inscriptions "1787, JUNE 29" "GLORY TO GOD IN ALL THINGS" and "1792".

PECTORAL CROSS

✣

RUSSIA, END OF 19TH CENTURY

GOLD, SILVER, DIAMONDS, AMETHYSTS,

ROSE QUARTZ

15 X 8 CM

INV. NO. MR-9413

P ectoral crosses were worn by the highest ranks of the clergy. They were often the work of first-class craftsmen, and attained the highest level of the jeweler's art.

The design of this cross relies on its combination of precious stones. The contrast between the icy glitter of the diamonds and the deep violet of the amethysts lends it an unusually ceremonious and splendid character.

✣

TEXT: MOSCOW, 1681
COVER: MOSCOW, 1772
MASTER PETR AFINOGENOV
SILVER, PAINTING ON ENAMEL
47 X 31 X 9 CM
INV. NO. KN-81

The creation of these gospels combined the mastery of the engraver and the enamelist. Five oval medallions are applied to the cover of the book, each with miniatures in painted enamel. The central medallion portrays the Harrowing of Hell, with the four Evangelists inset at the corners. In the 1770s the rococo style was still popular in the work of Russian jewelers, and this is reflected in the cover. The bright colors of the enamel, the restless drawing of large numbers of folds and pleats in the clothes and curtains, and the high relief of the stamped design with its characteristic shells and flourishes all combine to create a highly festive impression. The text, printed in Moscow in 1681, contains four engravings of the Evangelists.

ALTAR CROSS

✠

MOSCOW, 1835
MASTER WITH MONOGRAM NP
SILVER, AMETHYST, GLASS, ENAMEL
42 X 22 CM
INV. NO. MR-6564

This silver-gilt cross, decorated with enamel and large amethysts surrounded with paste jewels, is a worthy example of the silverware of Moscow smiths of the nineteenth century. Their works preserved and continued the best traditions of the Russian jeweler's art and satisfied the demand of a wide range of Russian society, from members of the royal court to inhabitants of provincial towns.

As the carved inscription shows, this cross was commissioned from a city jeweler by the inhabitant of the small and ancient town of Bogorodsk. It was then presented to one of the town's churches at Easter.

CHALICE
✠

RUSSIA, ST. PETERSBURG, 1795
MASTER IVAN VENFELD BUKH
GOLD, SILVER, PRECIOUS STONES
H. 01.5 CM, DIAM. 17.6 CM
INV. NO. MR-842

This gold chalice belonged to one of the splendid sets of church plate that Catherine the Great donated to the most important cathedrals and monasteries in Russia. Unfortunately none of them has come to us in its entirety. To judge by what has been preserved, however, these sets were very similar in terms of form and artistic decoration. Made in the 1780s and '90s, they were the work of the famous St. Petersburg master Ivan Venfeld Bukh, and were brilliant examples of the classical style. Their finish combines precious stones with engraved gems; this is a reflection of the contemporary interest in classical antiquity and the ancient art of gem carving.

It was at this time that a collection of carved stones began to be built up in the Hermitage, with the active participation of the Empress. She personally ordered that Bukh be given stones from the collection for the decoration of chalices. An example from the set ordered by Catherine for the Troitse-Sergiev Monastery, for example, contains cameos and intaglios of Western European origin from the fifteenth to the seventeenth centuries; each is surrounded by brilliant-cut diamonds. A similar combination of gold, carved stones, and diamonds may be seen in the chalice made by Bukh for the Alexander Nevsky Monastery in St. Petersburg, now in the Hillwood Museum in Washington.

MITRE OF THE ARCHBISHOP ARSENII

✤

RUSSIA, ST. PETERSBURG, 1744

BROCADE, SILK, GOLD, SILVER, PRECIOUS STONES,

PEARLS, GLASS, GOLD THREAD

H. 22 CM

INV. NO. TK-95

A gold band runs along the lower edge of this mitre, with a stamped inscription showing that it was presented to Arsenii, Archimandrite of the Troitse-Sergiev Monastery, by Empress Elizaveta Petrovna on November 25 1744.

The mitre is decorated with enamel panels containing portraits of the three-figured Deesis, the guardian angel, St Zachary and St Elizabeth, St Sergei of Radonezh, and the Patriarch Nikon. St Elizabeth was the patron saint of the Empress, while Sergei and Nikon were the founders of the Troitse-Sergiev Monastery. The Trinity is portrayed on a lozenge-shaped panel in the center of the mitre.

The mitre is made of gold brocade; it is decorated with sparkling brilliant-cut diamonds and rubies, and smooth, carefully selected pearls. It was clearly a royal endowment, the work of the finest court craftsmen. It is therefore not surprising that the mitre includes pearl-embroidered images of the two-headed eagle under a crown with an orb and sceptre in its claws – the state emblem of Russia.

✣

MITRE

✣

RUSSIA, AFTER 1832

BROCADE, ENAMEL, PRECIOUS STONES,

GOLD THREAD

H. 24.5 CM

INV. NO. TK-89

This mitre is remarkable for the delicacy of its range of colors. Vine leaves, embroidered in gold thread, and bunches of grapes made of large amethysts are depicted on a background of silver brocade. Nine enamel panels decorate the mitre. The highest panel depicts the Transfiguration; the four middle panels show the Evangelists, while the four lower panels depict the three-figured Deesis and St Mitrofan.

This last portrait suggests that the mitre was made after 1832; this was the year of the canonization of Mitrofan, the first bishop of Voronezh, who lived in the seventeenth century. It was Mitrofan who presented the Cap of Monomach to Peter Alexeevich, the future Emperor Peter the Great, at his consecration as Czar in 1682. The Emperor had a particular respect for Mitrofan: he played a direct part in the bishop's funeral, helping to bear his coffin to the burial place in the Annunciation Cathedral in Voronezh.

✣

OVERSLEEVES: PORUCHI

✤

MOSCOW, 1896
BROCADE: SAPOZHNIKOV FACTORY
BROCADE, SILK, SERGE, GALLOON
14.5 x 20 CM
INV. NO. TK-391/1-2

Poruchi were part of the parade dress of the clergy of the Dormition Cathedral at the time of the coronation of Nicholas II.

The Sapozhnikov firm, at whose factory the brocade and galloon for these *poruchi* were manufactured, had two offices – one in Moscow, the other in Kurakin outside the city. The firm not only produced parade brocade and furniture cloth, but also made simpler materials for everyday use. The founder of the firm was V.G. Sapozhnikov; for his successful development of the Russian textile industry he was awarded five Russian orders. A co-owner of the firm and one of his relatives was the reformer of the Russian theater, S.K. Stanislavskii.

PALITSA

✣

MOSCOW, 1896
BROCADE: SAPOZHNIKOV FACTORY
BROCADE, BRAID
38 x 38 CM
INV. NO. TK-168

The *palitsa* was part of the dress of the Orthodox clergy. It was worn on the right side, and symbolized the sword of the Lord. In Russian church ritual, the *palitsa* was a mark of excellence, and could be awarded to ordinary priests, who were entitled to wear it at ceremonial church services.

This *palitsa* was made for a priest from the Dormition Cathedral who took part in the coronation of Nicholas II in 1896. It is made of brocade from the Sapozhnikov firm, which also wove the brocade for the vestments of the rest of the Kremlin clergy for these ceremonies, as well as special braid and gold galloon for the finish of these garments.

MANTLE: PHELON

✣

RUSSIA, 1890s-1900s

BROCADE, SATIN, GOLD THREAD, GALLOON

L. 150 CM

INV. NO. TK-887

The *phelon* (from the Greek *phailonion*) is an ancient ecclestiastical garment in the form of a long, broad mantle without sleeves. This *phelon* is of blue velvet with gold embroidery applied to the shoulders and hem. It was a gift from the Grand Duchess Elizaveta Feodorovna to the church of the Apostles Peter and Paul in the St Nicholas Palace of the Moscow Kremlin.

The St Nicholas Palace, pulled down in 1929, was situated on Ivanov Square in the Kremlin. Originally a two-storeyed house for senior members of the clergy, designed by the architect M. Kazakov in 1775-76, it was given an extra storey and rebuilt several times during the nineteenth century. The domestic church of the Apostles Peter and Paul was consecrated in 1787. It was from the porch of the St Nicholas Palace that a carriage set forth at 2.40 pm on February 4 1905 carrying Grand Duke Sergei Alexandrovich, Governor-General of Moscow and uncle of Nicholas II. A few minutes later he was killed on Ivanov Square by the terrorist Ivan Kaliaev. It is likely that this gift from Grand Duchess Elizaveta Feodorovna, widow of Sergei Alexandrovich, was connected with this sad event.

It is probable that the *phelon* was reworked from the parade dress of a court lady, or from the pattern for such a dress. This theory is supported by the nature of the applied gold embroidery, which resembles the embroidery on court dresses and parade uniforms of the turn of the twentieth century. Also, traces of an outline for the cut of a dress are clearly visible on the blue background of the body of the *phelon*.

✛

Mantle: phelon

✛

Russia, 1768

Studs: Moscow, 15th-18th centuries

Brocade, galloon, gold, silver,

precious stones, pearls, glass

l. 160 cm

Inv, No, TK-2137

The *phelon* was modeled on an outer garment worn in the East before Christianity. "Crossed *pheloni*", made of cloth with embroidered or woven crosses, were worn by members of the high clergy, before the introduction of the *sakkos*. As a result, the *phelon* became a particularly sacred vestment.

to be worn during church services over other ecclesiastical garments. The oldest *pheloni* were in the shape of a bell tower and covered the body from head to foot. From the seventeenth century, Russian *pheloni* became narrower, with a large slit in the front, revealing a stole beneath. This garment is an example of this type

of *phelon*. It was made in 1768 by order of the Empress Catherine the Great, for the Dormition Cathedral. The inscription embroidered in small pearls and black chenille along the edge of the shoulders and the hem of the *phelon* shows that it was made of "church brocade" – a magnificent gold and silver brocade.

✛

SURPLICE

✤

RUSSIA, 1890s-1900s

BROCADE, SATIN, GOLD THREAD, GALLOON, COPPER

141 x 100 CM

INV. NO. TK-888

The surplice was a traditional article of clothing for all ranks of clergy in the Russian Orthodox Church.

This example, made of blue velvet with applied gold embroidery, was part of a set of vestments commissioned by Grand Duchess Elizaveta Feodorovna for the church of the Apostles Peter and Paul in the St Nicholas Palace of the Moscow Kremlin.

DALMATIC: SAKKOS

✛

MOSCOW, 1896

BROCADE: SAPOZHNIKOV FACTORY

GOLD BROCADE, GOLD THREAD,

GALLOON, SILVER, SEQUINS, BRAID

137 x 121 CM

INV. NO. TK-669

For the coronation ceremonies of Nicholas II in 1896 all the priests of the Kremlin cathedrals were dressed in garments of figured brocade specially made in the Sapozhnikov textile factory. The model for this cloth was the famous gold velvet commissioned by the Moscow court from Venice in the seventeenth century. Documents show that this velvet was used at the end of the seventeenth century to create a range of parade garments for male and female members of the royal family. Among the owners of these garments were the Czars Feodor and Ivan Alexeevich, and the Czaritsas Agaf´ia Semeonovna and Martha Matveevna, wife of Feodor Alexeevich. In 1696 the caftan of Czar Ivan Alexeevich was remade into a *sakkos* for the last Russian Patriarch, Adrian; alone among the garments described above, this *sakkos* has been preserved in the Armory collection. The "Venetian gold velvet with eagles" from which the *sakkos* was made was faithfully recreated by Russian textile makers of the end of the nineteenth century: they not only reproduced the design in full, but also imitated the original methods of manufacture of the cloth.

The Sapozhnikov factory was one of the most famous firms of the turn of the twentieth century. It supplied the court, specializing in imitations of fabrics from the Royal Treasury, and, in particular, those that had historically belonged to the Armory. In addition to the fabric for the *sakkos*, a unique woven image of the Russian emblem was chosen from the Armory for the coronation ceremonies of 1896.

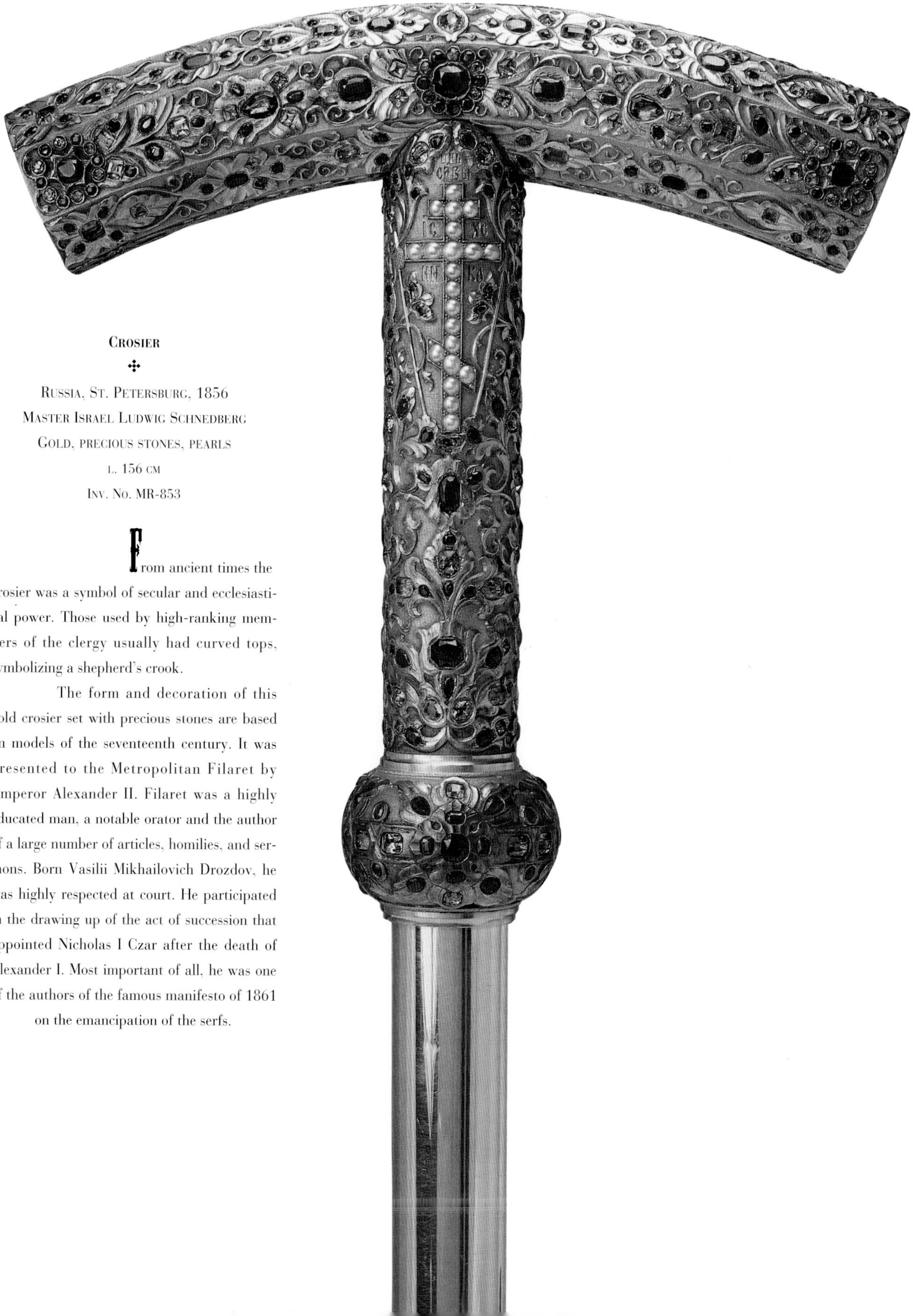

CROSIER

✠

RUSSIA, ST. PETERSBURG, 1856

MASTER ISRAEL LUDWIG SCHNEDBERG

GOLD, PRECIOUS STONES, PEARLS

L. 156 CM

INV. NO. MR-853

From ancient times the crosier was a symbol of secular and ecclesiastical power. Those used by high-ranking members of the clergy usually had curved tops, symbolizing a shepherd's crook.

The form and decoration of this gold crosier set with precious stones are based on models of the seventeenth century. It was presented to the Metropolitan Filaret by Emperor Alexander II. Filaret was a highly educated man, a notable orator and the author of a large number of articles, homilies, and sermons. Born Vasilii Mikhailovich Drozdov, he was highly respected at court. He participated in the drawing up of the act of succession that appointed Nicholas I Czar after the death of Alexander I. Most important of all, he was one of the authors of the famous manifesto of 1861 on the emancipation of the serfs.

✤

MEMORIAL PALL: PELENA

✤

MOSCOW, 1908

DESIGN: V. M. VASNETSOV

FABRIC: SAPOZHNIKOV FACTORY; EMBROIDERY: WORKSHOP

OF THE ASCENSION MONASTERY OF THE KREMLIN

DAMASK, SILK, SERGE, GOLD THREAD,

PEARLS, PRECIOUS STONES

316 X 194 CM

INV. NO. TK-3129

This large memorial pall was prepared on the death of Grand Duke Sergei Alexandrovich, the Governor-General of Moscow who was assassinated in 1905 (see *phelon*, page 248). In 1908 a burial vault was built inside the Chudov Monastery of the Kremlin for the remains of Sergei Alexandrovich, and here the pall was laid.

The terrible death of the Grand Duke is reflected in the subject of the embroidery. The middle of the pall is occupied by an embroidered Cross of Golgotha with a crown of thorns in the center and an image of the Saviour not Made by Hands flanked by two cherubs. The embroidery is of colored silk of various hues, and gold thread encrusted with precious stones and pearls. The inscription,

woven into the reverse side of the pall, shows that it was commissioned by a group of Moscow cultural figures: V.M. Vasnetsov, a leading Russian artist, M.N. Ermolova, a great Russian actress, V.G. Sapozhnikov, the textile manufacturer, and N.M. Ivanenko, the brother of a civil servant with special responsibilities under the Moscow Governor-General. The inscription also suggests that the pall was woven by monks of various Moscow monasteries, including the Ascension Monastery of the Kremlin, from where, over the course of several centuries, some of the finest examples of Russian embroidery had emerged. The design of the embroidery shows it to be the work of Vasnetsov. Particularly characteristic of the work of this artist are the spiritual, subtle fea-

tures of the face of Christ, the floral motifs reminiscent of Southern Russian national embroidery, and the expressive turns of the wings of the angels.

The embroidery of the pall is on a ground of light tan figured damask, produced in Sapozhnikov's own factory. The foliate ornament on the material is clearly a stylized rendition of ornaments on heavy Italian damask of the seventeenth century, which was widely known in Russia. Such copying, characteristic of Russian weaving of the turn of the twentieth century, was encouraged by the Historical movement in Russian art at this time.

INDEX

✤

✤